WITHDRAWN

Signs. Legal Rights And Aesthetic Considerations

James Claus PhD
R. M. Oliphant
Karen Claus PhD

Published by
SIGNS OF THE TIMES PUBLISHING CO.
Cincinnati, Ohio, U.S.A.

FIRST EDITION

INTERNATIONAL STANDARD BOOK NUMBER 0-911380-26-4

II

ACKNOWLEDGEMENTS

There are a number of people to whom we are considerably indebted for their help in preparing this book.

We would also like to thank the members of the National Electric Sign Association Legislative Committee who made valuable materials available to us. Of that group, Merle Sepmeyer of Cummings & Company, and John Chamberlain of QRS Corp., deserve special mention. From the beginning, Mr. Sepmeyer and Mr. Chamberlain, as members of the Board of Directors of NESA, were very cooperative and demonstrated an understanding of the nature of our effort. Thanks should go to Hank Dye of Holder & Kennedy Co. in Nashville, Tennessee for his encouragement.

We would also like to thank Lawrence Corbett, Attorney at Law. We would like to make it very clear that any legal errors which might be found in the book are ours and we take full responsibility for them. John Ford and Dave Senescu of The Epcon Co., Seattle, and Luke and Chuck Williams of American Sign and Indicator Corp., Spokane, were most helpful in providing materials at various stages in the preparation of this manuscript. Robert Louden of this same company also deserves particular mention. Bob repeatedly found time in his busy work schedule to gather materials and information that were pertinent to our manuscript.

It is only fitting at this point that we mention Lionel Rice of Neon Products Ltd., Vancouver, B. C., Canada, who was of great assistance, and we would like to add a word of thanks to Jack Hartree of this firm who supplied some materials for us. Our special thanks goes to Karin Welch for her constant assistance in compiling and drafting materials for us.

One person who has indirectly helped to make this manuscript a reality is Frank Crist, Sr., Attorney at Law in Palo Alto. Of equal assistance has been Frank Blake, legal counsel in Washington, D.C. Finally, without the constant concern and aid of James Mueller, Executive Director of the National Electric Sign Association, this manuscript would have been much delayed.

7 M r '75 SS

TABLE OF CONTENTS

INTRODUCTION 1

CHAPTER 1. The Urban Landscape   5
Urban Structure   5
The Self-Fulfilling Hypothesis of Urban Evolution   12

CHAPTER 2. Landscape Formation as a
Decision-Making Act   17
1. Motivation: A "Felt Need"   20
2. The Goal or Purpose   20
3. Conceptual Strategy   21
4. Specification of Alternatives   22
5. Choice: Writing of the Ordinance   23
6. Effectuation   24
7/8. Evaluation and Correction/Supplementation   26
The Need for Understanding of the
Decision-Making Process   27

CHAPTER 3. The Actors in Landscape
Formation   31
The User   31
The Consumer   32
The Producer   32
The Public Decision Maker   43

CHAPTER 4. Rationales for Landscape Formation:
Site and the Question of Public Interest   47
Economics   47
Public Safety   48
Social Amenity and Aesthetics   49

CHAPTER 5. Conflicts Among Various Philosophical
Views of Landscape Formation   53
The Functioning of the Marketplace Economy   53
Regulation by Consensus   54
Regulation by "Experts"   54

CHAPTER 6. Conflicts of Interest   63
Producers of Conflicting Media   63
Opponents of the System   69
The Uninformed   70

CHAPTER 7. Legal Aspects of Sign Legislation 73

Police Powers vs. Eminent Domain 74
The Police Powers 76
Definition of Statute or Ordinance 76
Licensing and Permits 76
Zoning 77
Compensation 87
Summary 94

CHAPTER 8. Levels of Participation in the Legislative Process 97

The Role of the Sign Industry 97
Dangers of Poor Legislation 106

CHAPTER 9. Codification of the Decision-Making Act: By-Law Formation 111

Introduction 111
Proposed Standards 116
Types of Signs 118

CHAPTER 10. Annotated and Supplementary Bibliographies 119

ANNOTATED BIBLIOGRAPHY 119
  I General References on Visual Perception 119
  II Color Perception 124
  III Visual Perception and the Other Senses 129
  IV Visual Illusions 131
  V Factors Related to the Design
    Components of Signs 136
  VI Size and Shape Distance Perception 140
  VII Illuminated and Visual Perception 142
  VIII Speed and Accuracy of Perception 145
SUPPLEMENTARY BIBLIOGRAPHY 149

APPENDIX A.
  Guidelines for Ordinance Development 165

APPENDIX B.
  Maximum Projection Formula 213

APPENDIX C.
  Synopsized Ordinance Specification 216

APPENDIX D.
  "Clutter-Itis" 226

APPENDIX E
  Guidelines for Design Review 230

Introduction

The visual landscape has become a focal point of popular interest. More and more groups and individuals are manifesting a concern for how our cities should look, what type of housing is desirable, what kinds of industry should be allowed in urban areas, and what kinds of business should be allowed in certain zones. Seldom do concerned citizens realize, however, that the precise form of the visual landscape is dictated by the interaction of myriad explicit and implicit decision-making acts, their own included. Various sectors of the public speak of the landscape in widely divergent ways. Some use highly emotional terms; others, such as academics, may deal with it in a highly abstract and detached manner; and still others, such as businessmen, may deal with it in pragmatic but unconcerned terms. Each and every one of us has a part in the actual formation of that landscape.

Our entire urban landscape, and not merely the city, is an artifact of our culture. Strictly speaking, it is only to a very small degree controlled by physical limitations. Our ability to overcome physical limitations, coupled with the rapid growth in population and an increase in incomes, has given us a new control over our visual environment. As we assume more and more control over our physical environment, the public has become increasingly concerned with how the urban landscape is used—what areas of it will be used for particular purposes, and what rights individuals have over their own property.

There are essentially three sets of factors that determine our ability to control our landscape. The first and most limiting are the *psychophysical factors,* such as the distance and colors that the human can see because of the physical nature of the eye and the mechanics of vision. Secondly, there are the *environmental or natural constraints* which are ultimately limitations on the types of materials obtainable and the technology available at the time to use them. We have begun to free ourselves from such constraints. Thirdly, there are the *cultural constraints,* which are concerned with what the society as a whole will tolerate.

This cultural limitation is often a greater limitation than many of us realize. It can inhibit us from carrying out perfectly logical actions. The resistance in many communities to geodesic domes within particular areas is an interesting example of such a phenomenon. It is a perfectly adequate form of housing and generally meets most urban safety standards, but many communities simply are not culturally ready to allow this innovative use of the urban landscape.

Cultural constraints, the rules and regulations they foster, and the mechanisms of ultimate enforcement are the theme of this monograph. Special attention will be directed toward enforcement procedures. There are three general ways in which cultural constraints are enforced: through the use of *police powers, eminent domain,* and *taxation.* A thorough discussion of how these powers work to control the landscape would fill the pages of at least one large book. Therefore, the following discussion will outline some of the major aspects of enforcement procedures which affect the form of the visual environment, with specific reference to signs. For it is with signs that the public's desire to impose culturally-based constraints is perhaps most visibly manifested. And it is with sign regulation that everyone feels he is an expert; throughout his lifetime he has been reacting, sometimes positively, sometimes negatively, to this most overt of visual communications media. Thus, almost every sighted member of society senses himself capable of evaluating signs and establishing rules to control their use.

It is important for the businessman and the conscientious citizen to understand the areas of governmental control and its extent and orientation. Otherwise, he has little chance of influencing public policy.

This discussion will deal with how a conscious act of public decision-making is made manifest on the landscape, the various actors that participate in such decision-making, some of the philosophical points of view behind decisions and conflicts in interest, the legal aspects of sign regulation, and some of the common pitfalls in thinking about legislation. The final section will introduce a model sign ordinance, followed by an annotated bibliography for the reader who would like to pursue this topic further.

The sign industry is the focus of this discussion because signs are one of the most visible environmental manifestations of the decision-making which occurs within both the governmental and the private sectors. Signs range from mere building decoration to the most effective communications medium for a particular purpose. They create images by which specific customers can *identify and relate* to particular goods and services; they *provide information* and may be the only source of information about what is available at a particular site in the urban space system; and finally they *direct people* in our fast-moving society, both externally in the automobile-oriented retailing sector, and internally within a building itself. Thus, because the sign is perhaps the most visible result of all of the decision-making acts, the sign manufacturer will find himself in the forefront of landscape formation.

What is seen on the landscape is the visual manifestation of some person's or group's decisional act regarding land use. If this decision is irrational, societal and environmental pressure will eventually subject it to attack, ridicule and perhaps outright rejection by a majority of the public. North Americans have demonstrated a desire for rationality along with the right to control their environment. There is an inherent cultural desire to do what is fair and logical and to base decisions upon an objective assessment of the facts. Although there is an emotional tone to much recent public decision-making in the environmental pollution arena, the underlying cultural bias is still towards a rational considera- tion of the issues.

Manufacturers and users of signs must plug into this underlying current of rationality in North American public policymaking. The sign industry must demonstrate clearly the rationale behind society's need and desire for overt en- vironmental visual communication. The industry, in short, must allow the public to see the complexities of sign usage and use its expertise to defend the appropriate and proper use of this type of visual communication media. If a rational defense is presented, using a knowledgeable public-spirited approach, the need for signs in everyday life will be clearly understood and the public will insist upon rational control of this important communications media. It is important also that the information which is held by the industry be compiled and channeled into our educational system so that future control of signs will be based on facts rather than emotion and misinformation. Only when the public is in- formed of what constitutes a high quality sign will the consumer demand such signs. This can only come about through education by the industry and support of this effort by municipal, state or provincial, and federal governments. Such an approach would benefit both the community and industry.

It is recognized here that poor quality signs clutter our visual environment. This does not negate the fact that signs provide a necessary communications function which includes information, direction, image-building and advertising. Signs, indeed, can serve certain communication needs better than any other media. Poor quality signs can be eliminated through clear and well-enforced municipal controls. Rational controls can even foster more creative, aesthetic uses of visual space. It is the purpose of this book to point out how such controls can be encouraged and instituted.

Chapter 1/The Urban Landscape

The processes which create the urban landscape are complex and dynamic. In North America, we have seen the virtual disappearance of a dependence on low spendable incomes, relative immobility, and the confinement of the distance one could conveniently travel for work, shopping and leisure. In studying changes and developments in the urban environment, the authors have been impressed by the fact that, in the early part of this century, and even as late as 1950, retailing and commercial activities were found in relatively undifferentiated zones of land use surrounded by residential areas. All forms of commercial activity co-existed within a central cluster (usually the central business district) with no identifiable spatial specialization of site. However, beginning in the 1940s, planned and unplanned shopping centers, specialized ribbon developments, and specialty nodes began to emerge in many cities. These changes necessitated changes in land use planning.

The automobile is one of the primary forces in creating modern urban structure. The importance of the visual component of property for communication has been increasing with increased use of the automobile. The ability to use this visual component may mean the difference between success and failure for many businesses.

One of the themes of this book is that, unless we attempt to understand the urban landscape as it exists today, we cannot make any intelligent contributions toward regulation of that landscape. Signs, in particular, are closely related to the form and structure of the city and to the automobile because the automobile has vastly increased the need for readable signs in our urban environment.

This chapter will provide a brief introduction to the history of, and current trends in, urban form and structure and will discuss some of the more common theories of urban development that influence decisions made by planners and architects to regulate the landscape.

Urban Structure

Urban structure is the spatial pattern of zones of land use in our cities. The clustering of high rise apartment buildings around a central business district, outlying shopping centers, large areas of single-family dwellings, blocks of apartments, and linear developments of retail stores along major streets are all part of the urban structure. James Vance (1962) has emphasized that cities are continually experiencing periods of change and stress which show very clearly in the urban structure.

One of the most significant determinants of urban structure is the transportation infrastructure.[1] Urban areas generally reflect past and present dominant transportation modes and the changes which occur in these modes over time. Such successive forms of transportation are often referred to as "sequent" modes of transportation. As one type of transportation replaces another, new patterns of land use overlap old patterns causing the structure of the city to appear confusing and irrational. Nevertheless, the patterns on the urban landscape *are* rational, especially if seen in the light of changes in concepts of range, accessibility, and consumer profiles.

Vance (1962) has pointed out that there are sequent patterns of commercial structure in cities which mirror the dominant means of travel, and he illustrates a number of retailing patterns which reflect various transportation modes. These will be treated briefly here to provide a clear picture of the development of urban structure in response to various transportation modes.

Throughout the history of commerce and retailing in North America, the trapping point or the best location for these activities in the city has been recognized. However, the variables that determine the negative or positive effects of these trapping points with regard to the user, the consumer, and the dominant means of transportation have only begun to be studied. A detailed discussion of the traffic and site variables for automobile-oriented retail trapping points is beyond the scope of this book; but the following brief history of the shifts of commercial and retail meeting places in the urban environment and some residential adaptation is important to an understanding of current planning philosophies and present urban land use.

Zone Of Conflux Or Meeting Place

A zone of conflux is any point at which two dominant arteries of traffic meet. These meeting points function as commercial and retail trapping points. At a zone of conflux, there is a high probability of the development of an urban

---

1. For a more detailed treatment of the relationship between transportation and urban structure, see Mumford (1961). Also, many good articles on the subject can be found in planning and traffic engineering journals.

or rural settlement because the arteries are major generators of trade.

When North America was originally settled, river travel was an important means of transport and cities formed at the zones of conflux of two waterways. In the older farming sections of North America, a clear pattern can be seen of country stores located at zones of conflux (Figure 1). The range of the country store was limited to the distance a horse could travel in one-half day. When wealth and productivity of the area increased, the range often decreased because of the higher threshold available.

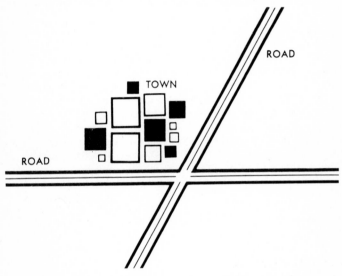

Fig. 1: Development of a town at the zone of conflux of two major roads.

As new and faster means of transportation were developed and possible travel ranges (distance to shop, etc.) increased, such trading centers either dissolved or grew in size to replace several small ones.

In today's large cities, occupation of a site is primarily a function of the ability to pay rent. Zones of conflux represent some of the most valuable areas in the city. These sites usually become the focus of retailing clusters because the business firm or the retailer is able to pay a much higher rent than an individual or an apartment block owner. In metropolitan areas, for example, a 50 x 100-foot residential lot is worth no more than from $5000 to $20,000. However, the average downtown or retail lot in a western California city will sell for approximately $10.00 per square foot. It is obvious, therefore, that where main arteries meet, the cost of the land can only be borne by a commercial or business firm.

It should be emphasized here that traffic trapping points must be carefully accessed. Often other factors, such as linkages to other activities or trade area influences can overshadow the street variables. Even the position on the street of a retail site will shift with the type of activity. For instance, for consumers that stop at a dry cleaning establishment on the way to work, a corner site may not be as convenient as the inside site where traffic is moving more freely.

Bulk-Breaking Point

When waterways were an important transportation mode in North America, the bulk-breaking point, or the point where a cargo was transferred or broken down, gave rise to many urban settlements. The fall line in the eastern United States presents an example of such a bulk-breaking point. Here, where the rivers flow from the hard crystalline rocks of the Appalachian area down to the sedimentary area of the Piedmont, extensive rapids and waterfalls exist. Boats had to be unloaded here in order to bypass the rapids. It was at these natural stops that settlements sprang up.

Vancouver, B. C., and San Francisco, Calif., provide good examples of cities built at a bulk-breaking point formed by the meeting of ocean shipping with overland transport. The central business districts of these two cities grew out of the retailing centers established at these points.

Bead Pattern

Rail, as well as water transport, demonstrates the same locational preferences. When there is a natural resting place on a long linear transportation route, retail outlets and other human activities will tend to cluster at that point. James Vance[2], dealing specifically with railroads, referred to this as a "bead position". Bead patterns of settlement come about because people can travel only a certain distance by any given means of transportation before they must stop for rest or refueling.

Early travel by horse was very limited in distance or range. Trewartha (1943) has pointed out that, although the location of country stores in the Midwest was conditioned by the density and kinds of farms in the area, they were

---

2. Information from lectures given by J.E. Vance Jr. at the University of California, Berkeley.

seldom farther apart than a horse could travel in one-half day.

The rail depot city structure dealt with by Vance is still recognizable in many parts of North America (Figure 2). Along a railroad track serving an urban population, stations are generally located 10 to 15 miles apart. A street feeds into the station from the hinterland, and around the station a settlement forms to serve the needs of the hinterland as well as the railroad.

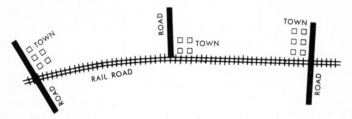

Fig. 2: Formation of a "bead pattern" of farm communities at regular intervals along a rail line.

Today the bead pattern is clearly manifested in long distance freeway travel. The traveler stops when he needs rest or refreshment or his car needs refueling. Clusters of retailing on the freeway consisting of such things as motels, restaurants, and gasoline outlets are located in a bead pattern at distances conditioned by the distance the average driver will travel without stopping. Obviously, other factors such as size of gas tank, fuel consumption rate, and road conditions will condition the intervals between these "natural stopping points."

The Emergence Of The Automobile

The automobile has brought about many changes in urban form and structure. We will deal here with three of them: (1) ribbon developments of commercial activities along major arteries; (2) sector development, and (3) multiple nuclei of commercial activity.

Ribbon Developments. One of the interesting land use changes resulting from the automobile, and one that is only beginning to be understood, is the linear or ribbon development of commercial and retail activities along a major artery. In the early 1900s, the mansions of the well-to-do were visible manifestations of wealth and these mansions generally fronted on a main street. With the advent of the automobile, with its dust and noise, however, the prestigious residences have moved away from major arteries and have been displaced by "buffer zones" of retailing activities. In fact, an additional row of apartment buildings is often used to increase the effectiveness of the buffer.

Recently, merchants and businessmen have begun to realize the potential of the visual exposure of such sites and are working out rules for the type of business which can best utilize the visual components of such property. Thus, *visibility* is the dominant factor in establishing the use of sites on such strips. The visual component once required for the town manor now serves the automobile-oriented retailer and his customers.

Sectors of Land Use. The concentric ring theory of urban development proposed by Burgess (1925, Figure 3), according to which rings of homogeneous land use develop around the central core of a city, was challenged by Homer Hoyt's sectory theory (1964). Hoyt proposed that "sectors" or wedges of residential land use would grow outward from the center of the city and that each sector would be pre-

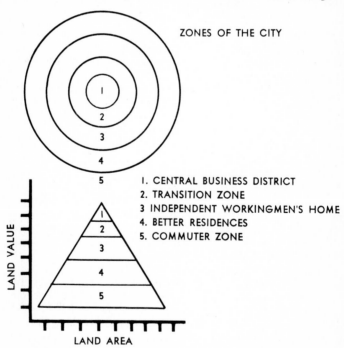

ZONES OF THE CITY

1. CENTRAL BUSINESS DISTRICT
2. TRANSITION ZONE
3 INDEPENDENT WORKINGMEN'S HOME
4. BETTER RESIDENCES
5. COMMUTER ZONE

Fig. 3: Burgess' model of concentric rings of urban structure.

vented from expanding laterally by sectors of other land use on each side.

Although it can be easily demonstrated that there have always been clusters of somewhat homogeneous land use in North American cities, with the advent of the automobile and the modern large-scale industrial/financial complex, these sectors of land use have expanded. Hoyt's theory provides a partial explanation, but a better rationalization of the process might simply be that, freed from time and distance constraints by our increased mobility (and with some governmental encouragement), our cultural preferences have apparently been toward the development of land use along main transportation arteries. It is not hard to see many economic and social advantages stemming from such development. There is some debate as to whether the segregation of residential tracts has led to segregation according to social and cultural groups, or whether the interjection of the automobile has created enough mobility to offset any potential isolation.

Multiple-Nuclei. The traditional model of concentric rings of land use around the main zone of conflux suggested by Burgess has remained popular among planners and architects who seek to regulate the landscape. However, this theory has apparently not reflected the natural growth patterns of modern cities. With the advent of the freeway, there has been a significant change in patterns of city structure. Undoubtedly the main zone of conflux is still the most valuable area but one can no longer accurately apply a concentric ring model, even with elongated rings, to the freeway city.

Rather, a linear succession of retail and service cores or multiple-nuclei as developed by Harris and Ullman (1945) will develop at secondary zones of conflux in the highway network (Figure 4). The automobile-oriented consumer can travel ten miles in ten minutes on a freeway and usually has within a ten-minute range all the zones of conflux of the city. Thus, concepts of time and accessibility overshadow traditional concepts of distance. These nuclei or dispersed cores are made up of groups of stores which are related by complementarity and linkages among goods, products, or services.

In the western United States there are many classic examples of the dispersed city. Because it is difficult to find a dominant core in such cities as Los Angeles, it has been suggested that they are actually only a series of small villages.

Berry (1967) has pointed out that within any one region, retailing is a function of population and income levels. In

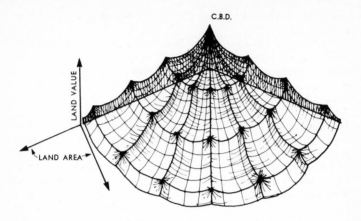

Fig. 4: Harris and Ullman's model for multi-nuclei theory of urban structure.

an automobile-oriented society in which both incomes and population are increasing, only tradition and existing zoning controls dictate that retailing should be clustered around the dominant bulk-breaking point or the central business district. Many policies are being set by municipal governments which confine retailing and related activities to particular zones which have traditionally been the core of merchant activity and often have little to do with consumer preference or the most attractive and efficient location for the facilities.

One of our contentions is that the majority of planners and academicians have not given sufficient thought to how increasing incomes, life-style changes and shifts in transportation have affected consumers' shopping preferences. If unimpeded by zoning controls, retail location might shift dramatically. Retailing has usually developed wherever it is most accessible to those it serves; the problem is how one defines accessibility. In a society in which the automobile is the dominant mode of transportation, the most accessible location may be an outlying shopping center or a ribbon of retailing along a major artery. Whenever retail or commercial activities are removed from the central business district, the importance of the visual aspects of property such as signs, building design, and layout are greatly increased.

The Self-Fulfilling Hypothesis Of Urban Evolution

Because the majority of planners have been schooled in a system where such untried models as the concentric ring theory of land use and the sector theory are accepted as truth, they have carried these conceptions of urban structure into their decision-making. Thus, they have often shaped the landscape to their ideas of what it should be, through zoning and building permits. As a result, they can point to the urban landscape as evidence that these theories represent the natural evolution of city structure.

Unfortunately, it never quite works out as ideally as it should, because reality must intrude on the model. The automobile has had a tremendous impact on the city structure and when a central core model is imposed on an automobile-oriented society, conflicts and inefficiency are the result. The tendency in these cases has been for the planner and the public to blame the automobile for the problems. Perhaps we would all be happier if we went back to the horse and carriage so that our models would continue to represent some part of reality.

Recently, the word "master plan" has fallen into disfavor in planning schools, because it presumes an expertise that is not possible in our dynamically changing society, and because past attempts to lay out long-term master plans have inevitably failed as the technological and economic changes in our society have demanded flexibility.

It is important to remember, however, when dealing with federal, state, or municipal planners, that there are two distinct schools of planning. The most recent is that group of planners whose decisions are based on empirical research and the needs of the public discovered through such research. The second and better established group is that of the "old school" planners who feel that part of their obligation is to condition the preferences of the public. They currently dominate many governmental bodies and will continue to do so for some time. The latter schools subscribe to the concept of a master plan and feel that they have the ability and the responsibility to master plan the urban landscape. The former school is made up of those who would not wish to be associated with the concept of a master plan because of the implications it carries.

The difference between the two planning philosophies is most clearly felt when some of the "intuitive" assumptions about how the city should be constructed become part of government policy. Because the government can bring to bear the weight of judicial authority to enforce its policies, the landscape will be formed the way they feel it should. When government officials felt that large tracts of single-family detached housing would naturally evolve from smaller ones in a progression away from the central core, this is what occurred. There was little, if any, proof that the city would evolve this way as if driven by some natural ecological force. But the power of government policy coupled with local ordinances brought this kind of residential land use into existence.

Because of this ability to control the formation of the landscape, research must be carefully conducted to establish whether the public wants such a phenomenon, or whether the public will live with the planners' ideal simply because the planner has created an environment in which the individual has no alternative.

Berry, B. J. L. *Geography of market centers and retail distribution.* Englewood Cliffs: Prentice Hall, 1967.

Burgess, E. W. The growth of the city: An introduction to a research project. In: Park, R.E., Burgess, E.W. and McKenzie, R.D. (Eds.) *The city.* Chicago: University of Chicago Press, 1925.

Claus, R. J. Geography of four corners. *Proceedings of the Canadian Association of Geographers,* Department of Geography, University of Manitoba, 1970.

Harris, C.P. & Ullman, E. L. The nature of cities. *Annals of the American Society of Politics and Social Science,* 1945, *242,* 7-17.

Hoyt, H. Recent distortions of the classical models of urban structure. *Land Economics,* 1964, *40,* 199-212.

Mumford, L. *The city in history: its origins, its transformations, and its prospects.* New York: Harcourt Brace & World, 1961.

Trewartha, G. T. The unincorporated hamlet: One element in the American settlement fabric. *Annals of the Association of American Geographers,* 1943, *33,* 32-81.

Vance, J. E. Jr. *Emerging patterns of commercial structure in American cities.* Proceedings of the IGU Symposium in Urban Geography, 1960. Lund Studies in Geography, Series B: Human Geography. Royal University of Lund, Sweden, 1962, 485-518.

Chapter 2/Landscape Formation As A Decision Making Act

Any man-made artifact on the landscape is the result of a particular decision-making act or set of acts. It can occur by default or it can be the result of a positive effort. There are certain components of a decision that should be clearly understood by anyone seeking to participate in the decision-making process.

Members of several academic disciplines have systematically studied the decision-making process, especially as it pertains to public policy formation and business administration. A wide variety of formulations have emerged from these studies; among the major approaches are systems analysis[1], managerial economics[2], social process evaluation[3], interaction pattern analysis[4], decision theory[5], and mathematical learning theory[6]. Although there are differences in the ways the decision-making process is divided, most approaches recognize that initially there must be sensitivity to a problem which is in need of solution, some consideration of alternatives, the actual selection or choice, and some type of action whereby the decision is implemented.

In a recent text concerned with the problems of business and government policy making, five stages of the deliberative process are distinguished: (1) problem recognition, (2) specification of alternatives, (3) choice, (4) effectuation, and (5) correction and supplementation (Mack, 1971). These general stages represent phases in a recursive or cyclical decision-making process whereby public policy is instituted. For the purpose of our discussion of municipal policy making as it refers to general plan and ordinance formation, it is necessary to further outline the process by which an ordinance is created and enforced. If we think of

---

1. For examples of systems analysis of policy decision making see Easton (1965) and Hall (1962).
2. Decision processes from the managerial economics point of view are discussed in Chamberlain (1962), Miller and Starr (1960), Spencer and Siegelman (1964) and Harlan, Christenson, and Vancil (1962).
3. Lindblom and Braybrooke (1963) discuss the nature of the day-to-day decisions made by politicians, executives and governmental administrators.
4. Gore (1964) focuses on legislative decision making and how the shared conceptions of individuals become the heuristic for making policy decision.
5. There are many excellent treatments of decision theory. Simon (1960) and Litchfield (1956) discuss the interaction of individuals, organizations and environment; Lee (1971) provides a readable review of behavioral decision theory.
6. Mathematical learning theory is best seen in Luce, Bush and Galanter (1963) or in Atkinson, Bower, and Crothers, (1965).

the municipal policy-making machinery as a cybernetic information-processing system having input, a transformation system, output, and a feedback loop, eight forms of output become apparent:

1. Motivation (felt need),
2. Goal or purpose,
3. Perceptual strategy,
4. Specification of alternatives,
5. Choice (writing of the bylaw),
6. Effectuation (enforcement),
7. Evaluation,
8. Correction and supplementation.

Figure 5 illustrates the sequence and activities of the system as policy decisions are made. At all stages accurate information is critical input to the system. Each output stage becomes input to the succeeding stage acting as a filtering mechanism for the information which is taken into the system from the environment.

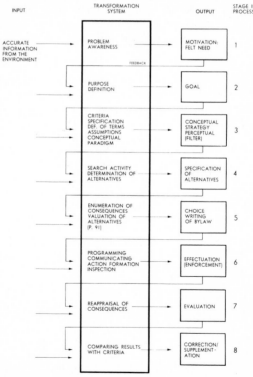

Fig. 5: Cybernetic model of deliberative decision-making process in public policy information.

The basic decision-making units involved in public decision-making at the municipal level are shown in Figure 6. These units form a hierarchical structure in which operational units are subsumed under management units, and management units determine the directive force of the stated social goals of the community. The social goals, which deal with the aesthetic and psycho-social qualities of the urban environment, are set by one or more segments of society and voiced through their elected officials.

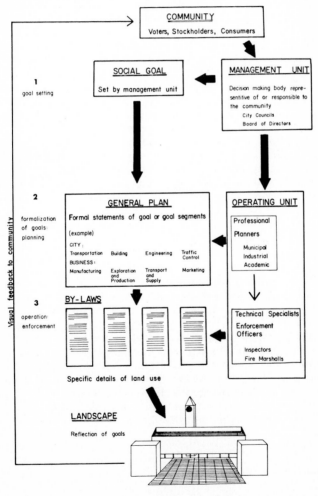

Fig. 6: Process of translating social goals into landscape uses.

By looking closely at the deliberative decision-making process (Figure 5), it is possible to isolate those areas where public officials may or may not be functioning according to the stated social goals.

1. Motivation: A "Felt Need"

Whenever a decision-making act is carried out, there must be some motivation or rationale to prompt it. This stimulus is a necessary antecedent to the act itself. For example, a group or individual may deem that what they think desirable has been encroached upon, or that what they would like to see is not being accomplished. Psychologists term this basic type of internal conflict between desired and actual circumstances "cognitive dissonance." Dissonance produces a tension which the organism (or organization) desires to alleviate. This desire is a "felt need."

This is particularly significant in understanding the current problems of industry with regard to municipal control. Too often, the representatives of industry simply wait on the sidelines until a decision has been made which affects them negatively before they will act. This is a negative motivation, having irrational undertones.[7] A positive and more healthy stimulus would be desire by the industry to present evidence of its own usefulness to the public. Active participation in the decision-making process implies a pride in self, an awareness of worth and contribution.

2. The Goal or Purpose

Once a stimulus for action is present, it is necessary to clarify the goals which will guide subsequent action. The goal or purpose of most municipal legislation in North American society is protection of a personal or a property right. An example of a common situation in which a decision-making act is initiated to protect a property right is found in zoning for exclusive residential areas. The goal of such legislation is to maintain the character of the area as a large single-family detached residential area with all of the amenities that would be expected in a neighborhood desired by upper income residents. Here the property right is the right to have a particular kind of home, surrounded by similar homes. On the other hand, in some cities we are

---

7. The classic dilemma of the schizophrenic is that the intention to not communicate, to withdraw from society, is in itself a communication with society. The paradox is that by denying communication, one must also deny that denial is communication. All behavior has message value, it is therefore impossible not to communicate. The question, then, becomes whether one's behavior has positive or negative (emotional) components.

now witnessing an attempt by minority groups to strike down such bylaws. Their goal is to have more small, easily purchased homes in accessible areas. Thus, in our pluralistic society, there are often conflicting goals involved in the same legislative issue.

If the goals of the municipal government are not made explicit by the elected municipal officials, the professional planner cannot create a plan which will give direction to legislation and serve as a guide in arbitration of land use conflicts. It is the responsibility of the elected officials to set clear and realistic goals.

3. Conceptual Strategy

Once a goal is defined, the conceptual framework will determine how one goes about obtaining the goal. The philosophical, theoretical stance of an individual or group will determine how information is perceived from the environment. The filtering mechanism of perception will color all subsequent acts and dictate selection of particular strategies or approaches. For instance, if a person's goal is to be educated in a particular way, his strategy may be attending a particular university because he perceives that specific form of education to be superior. When a particular type of landscape formation is the goal, the conceptual strategy controls the deliberative decision-making acts which are eventually manifested in the form of an ordinance or a bylaw.[8]

It is important at this stage in the process to expose the world view or conceptual paradigm of the decision makers. Underlying each decision-maker's approach to a problem is a metadomel or paradigm which describes the way that person thinks the phenomena in question function. Although this model may or may not coincide with reality, it will most certainly cause the decision maker to selectively attend to environmental cues. It will, in short, act as an effective filter, blocking out all those bits of information which are contrary or extraneous to the conceptual paradigm. This information-filtering process is commonly called "perception".

Perception processes are critical to decision-making because they provide the means by which information is gathered from the environment and determined to be rele-

---

8. The terms statute, ordinance, and bylaw are generally interchangeable. In western Canada, the most common designation is bylaw. In some parts of the U.S., the term bylaw is also in common use. In other areas, the word ordinance is used and it is not uncommon to find such legislation referred to as a statute.

vant to the problems. It has been said that:

Decisions . . . must flow from subjective estimates of factual situations. The perceiver's world of reality . . . must be the starting point for assessing the reliability of information. The effective administrator must learn quite early in his career that information cannot be interpreted indepedently of the perceiver (Alexis & Wilson, 1967, p. 69).

A decision-maker's paradigm will rest upon certain assumptions and it is important that these assumptions be aired during any deliberative decision-making process. Terms should be defined in operational format if some type of overt measured assessment is intended. Specific criteria should be established on the basis of the theoretical-conceptual stance of the decision-maker's basis for evaluation of the results of the decision-making acts.

Exposure of the conceptual strategies employed by the various participants in the decision-making process will often indicate that favorite theories may not be appropriate to given problems or may, indeed, not correspond to reality at all. For example, too often an ordinance is passed to control an industry without any real thought of the logical outcome when the industry attempts to adapt to that control. The planner seldom seems to realize that if a product is necessary in our society, there will always be a number of strategies available to sell that product. If one method is eliminated, the retailer will have to turn to another. The planner should consider then whether the alternatives might not be more unattractive than the current situation. In Canada, the National Housing Administration has come to favor one kind of design for housing. A house designed accordingly receives a favorable loan ratio and it is approved quickly. This particular kind of house is cropping up all over western Canada, yet the government does not seem to understand that it is responsible for creating this landscape form.

We would recommend, therefore, that whenever a city undertakes to meet a particular goal, it should take the time to analyze the values or conceptual framework of the decision and to think about the consequences of various strategies. Landscape phenomena are very complex and anyone who would present a simplistic solution has either not done adequate research, or is attempting to promote a particular point-of-view.

4. Specifications of Alternatives

The fourth stage in the deliberative decision process

concerns the collection of data and the listing of possible alternatives of action, given the data available. This stage is essentially one of search activities where data from many sources is presented. The critical role of the decision making unit at this stage is that of information receptor. A decision is only as good as the information upon which it is based. Faulty or inaccurate information will yield decisions which will not coincide with reality and will not stand with time. In fact, decisions made from a poor information base will often worsen the problem the decision maker is attempting to solve.

The professional planner also should keep abreast of technological and social developments, particularly in the industries with which he is dealing, because this sector will have the most direct and far-reaching consequences on the form and structure of the city. Such information is necessary to guide him in developing a plan that will function efficiently in the real world landscape.

5. Choice: Writing of the Ordinance

At the major decision point of the process, the subdecisions of earlier stages are crystallized in a definite selection, and in the case of ordinance, in the writing of the codes. From this point on the effects of the decision will be felt.

In decision theory, the choice process involves the valuation of the consequences of the various alternatives. The act of placing values implies selection of the alternative or alternatives which meet the criteria of utility (or values) established earlier. In making a selection among given alternative acts, Mack (1971, p. 91) indicates that the following steps should be performed:

1. Utility should be defined in terms of central values, secondary values, a weighting system, and constraints. Ideally, this definition should coincide with the goals designated earlier.

2. Determine level of expertise appropriate to decision situation.

3. The range of possible outcomes or consequences should be specified.

4. Possible outcomes or consequences should be given values and probabilities of occurrence.

5. Expected net utility for each alternative should be estimated.

6. Alternative which is best in terms of expected net

utility should be selected. The result of this process should yield a highly rational bylaw.

6. Effectuation

The sixth step is the enforcement of the decision-making act. This stage involves programming the system, communicating directives, formation of enforcement or action groups, and inspection procedures.

In the case of an oil company, the goal may be profit, and the decision choice may be marketing gasoline. The effectuation will be the particular way in which the retail outlets are operated. In the case of the bylaw, the effectuation is the method of enforcing the legislation.

Effectuation at the Municipal Level:
Mechanisms for Enforcement

The enforcement of a statute or ordinance is perhaps the least understood of all of the areas of legislative endeavor. There are three ways in which controls are enforced: (1) through the use of police powers, (2) through eminent domain proceedings, and (3) through taxation.

Police powers refer primarily to zoning codes, building codes, and fire codes. *Eminent domain* is the confiscation of property by the government for the general public good or public use. And finally, *taxation* can be a positive or negative influence on land use in a particular area. All of these are dealt with more extensively in Chapter 7 of this book.

Non-enforcement: Surprisingly often, existing controls are not enforced. In a recent case in Seattle, a detailed survey revealed that over 85 per cent of the signs that were the cause of objections raised in the newspapers and on radio and television were already nonconforming and should have been removed under existing regulations. A good proportion of them were put up without permits in the first place. Thus, the responsible sign companies were being condemned for the actions of particular individuals who were being allowed to use the landscape illegally. The irresponsibility of the particular sign companies involved is unquestionable, but the real problem stems from the fact that the bylaw, ordinance, or statute which had been constructed to deal with this was either unenforceable or was not being enforced.

There are four primary reasons for such non-enforcement, and any one of them will, in the long run, work to the detriment of the sign industry as well as the community.

The first of these reasons is simply too much latitude in

interpretation of the legislation by the enforcing officials. The terms used are often ambiguous or unfamiliar to those outside the industry. Lack of clear definitions can definitely work against industry when a city official overreaches the original intentions of the legislation. For instance, in one case, a planner refused to allow installation of a large legal floodlight pole in order to illuminate a new car lot because he felt that these poles would later be used by someone to display banners, which were not allowable.

The second reason for non-enforcement is fear on the part of the municipality of implementing a bylaw that is too strong. The public reaction against it often reaches such a proportion that they feel a need to tread softly.

A third reason for non-enforcement is simply the lack of personnel and resources to enforce the regulation. There are several ways that a municipality can solve this problem, and one of them we would particularly recommend. That is to place a user tax on signs that project over public space and to specifically mark the funds to be invested in enforcement. Although such a tax may appear to be an unattractive alternative to some people, we have found that it is a particularly beneficial one. Such a tax will ensure that only high quality signs are erected, that marginal signs are removed, and will provide revenue for removal of abandoned signs.

A fourth reason for non-enforcement is harassment by municipal officials who are overextending their powers under the bylaw or by the system itself which often presents so much red tape to the sign user that he cannot find his way through it. A number of signs are put up illegally because after repeated unsuccessful attempts to obtain a permit or a reason for refusal, the user has given up in disgust and installed a rough approximation of the proposed sign without a permit.

The cost in time and in human and capital resources necessary to deal with municipal governments is continually increasing. As society has become more complex, larger organizations have been necessary. In their development, industrial organizations have become increasingly sophisticated and have learned to deal with many factors that in the past they could not handle. But within municipal governments, the general trend has been in the opposite direction, with a lack of clear-cut operating units, management units, and goals as the norm. The diagram in Figure 7 illustrates a typical flow chart for obtaining a service station permit in Vancouver. Such a diagram of an organizational structure should reveal at what point a particular development was stopped and why. If the reason for the refusal can be eliminated, the proposal should then go to the next step in the decision-making tree. Many municipal governments are set up in such a way that a reasonable use of the land can be refused without any concrete reason and the decision cannot be pinpointed. In such a case, the party making application must take considerable time in an attempt to track down the reasons for a decision.

Companies who would improve the appearance of their sites often find it more expensive to obtain approval for a remodeling than to actually make the improvements.

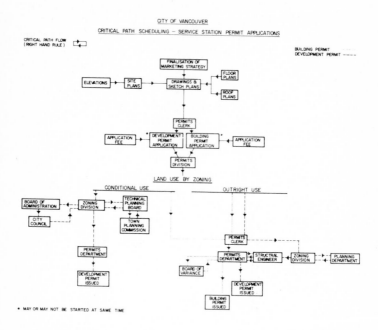

CITY OF VANCOUVER
CRITICAL PATH SCHEDULING – SERVICE STATION PERMIT APPLICATIONS

If a poor bylaw, which cannot be enforced, is allowed to stay on the books, poor landscape decisions are made by default. There is a reasonably high chance that this same bylaw will be used by other municipalities simply because the city planner, who is not an expert in law and does not understand the subtleties of signs, often adopts bylaws from other cities.

7. Evaluation and 8. Correction/Supplementation

Evaluation of the results of the decision-making act requires two steps: (1) Comparison of results with criteria established earlier, in stages 2 and 3; and (2) Determination of the degree of discrepancy from standards. The essential question involves the assessment of the degree to which the social goals, given the value orientation guiding the decision-makers, have been met. Are there fewer more attractive and effective signs, or have the regulations encouraged a new form of visual pollution in response to irrational constraints on appropriate use of visual space? If the latter situation has occurred, then stage 8 becomes important. Reappraisal of the consequences of alternatives should yield new estimates in light of the results of the evaluation. Corrective or supplementary legislation may be necessary.

The Need for Understanding
Of the Decision-Making Process

It is critical to the sign manufacturer to understand the decision-making process. His customer has a need and related goal which is to market a product. His perceptual strategy and choice revolves around use of the visual component of the particular sites to attract business. The decision is the actual installation of a sign on that property. At times the community's goals will come into conflict with the goals of the client. To the sign industry, the goal of an ordinance should be to protect a right to use the visual component of the property. When property rights come into conflict, the public good as determined by the public will always determine the outcome. The sign industry should be prepared to present its case in such a way that the public is aware of the benefits that accrue to it from the use of signs. The public should be apprised of the complexities of the issues surrounding the designing and selling of a sign and what factors determine its visual quality and its relationship to the environment.

Thus, whether the actor is a member of the community, an individual, or a government, the decision-making process should be the same. That it is not, however, is demonstrated by the lack of efficient goal-setting, clear definition of strategies, and efficient effectuation mechanisms manifested by most municipal governments.

Often the motivation behind a legislative decision-making sequence may be largely emotional and it is necessary to find an acceptable rationale to justify the subsequent action. This causes confusion and negativistic attitudes toward an industry. Much of this could be avoided if the decision-making process was clarified and the information was available to prevent emotional reaction to the problem. An important point to remember is that public policy making is *deliberative* decision making. Deliberation implies a forum for debate.

There is also the qualification that, in some cities, certain specific land uses are conditional. In Vancouver, British Columbia, a rather unique set of regulations provides that, even if a site is properly zoned and the user has met all of the requirements for such a site as specified in the bylaw, the use must be approved by city council. In most cities, when all the requirements set forth in the bylaw for use of a site are met, the user is granted permission automatically to use the site. However, even in such a case, municipal governments have found it possible to institute conditional uses by requiring a specific zone for a particular type of land use. Then no sites are zoned for this. The result is that anyone wishing to build such a structure must apply for re-zoning. Such conditional uses are becoming increasingly common as city officials seek more control over the landscape. The result is virtual discrimination against particular land uses.

Alexis, M. and Wilson, C.Z. *Organizational decision making.* Englewood Cliffs, N.J.: Prentice-Hall, 1967.

Atkinson, R.C., Bower, G.H. & Crothers, E.J. *An introduction to mathematical learning theory.* New York: Wiley, 1965.

Baybrooke, D. & Lindblom, C. E. *A strategy of decision: Policy evaluation as a social process.* London: Collier-Macmillan, 1963.

Chamberlain, N. *The firm, microeconomic planning and action.* New York: McGraw-Hill, 1962.

Claus, R. J. & Hardwick, W.G. *The mobile consumer: Automobile-oriented retailing and site selection.* Don Mills, Ontario: Collier-Macmillan, 1972.

Gore, W. *Administrative decision-making: A heuristic model.* New York: John Wiley & Sons, 1964.

Easton, D. *Systems analysis of political life.* New York: Wiley, 1965.

Hall, A. D. *A methodology for systems engineering.* Princeton, N. J.: D. Van Nostrand, 1962.

Harlan, N.E. Christenson, C. J. & Vancil, R. F. *Managerial economics.* Homewood, Ill.; Richard D. Irwin, 1962.

Lee, W. *Decision, theory and human behavior.* New York: Wiley, 1971.

Litchfield, E. Notes on a general theory of administration. *Administrative Science Quarterly,* 1956, *1,* 3-29.

Luce, R.D., Bush, R.R. & Galanter, E. (Eds.) *Handbook of mathematical psychology.* New York: Wiley, 1963.

Mack, R. P. *Planning on uncertainty: Decision making in business and government administration.* New York: Wiley, 1971.

Miller, D.W. & Starr, M.K. *Executive decision and operations research.* Englewood Cliffs: Prentice-Hall, 1960.

Simon, H.A. *The new science of management decision.* Ford Distinguished Lecture Series, Vol. 3, New York University. New York: Harper Bros., 1960.

Spencer, M. H. & Siegelman, L. *Managerial economics.* (Rev. ed.) Homewood, Ill.: Richard D. Irwin, 1964.

Chapter 3/The Actors In Landscape Formation

North American society is a very pluralistic one. This pluralism is manifested in segmentation of the population into more or less homogeneous groups with preference regarding any good or service, aesthetic taste, and kinds of social amenities sought. Anyone familiar with marketing has learned that some people prefer things that others find offensive. This simply means that the two come from different segments of the population.

Within this pluralistic framework, there are participant types of actors who will affect landscape formation, and each actor can represent anyone of the many segments of the population. These actors are: (1) the user, (2) the consumer, (3) the producer, and (4) the public or governmental decision-makers who supposedly represent the public as a whole. The following is a brief description of each of these actors and the role they play in landscape creation.

The User

The user of a portion of the urban landscape should not be confused with the consumer. The user of a site may be a merchant who wishes to sell a good or service to the consumer, or he may be a homeowner, or the owner or leasee of a particular commercial or industrial site. Generally, the type of use falls into one of three categories: (1) commercial, which includes retail and entertainment; (2) residential; and (3) industrial. There may be a fourth category which is recreational, such as parks, etc. In urban land use, the first three categories are usually dominant.

These land use types often come into conflict over land use rights. For instance, a person who lives near a commercial district, while he is in his home, might like to see the lights turned off. Yet when the same person goes shopping, particularly if he does so in an automobile, he may demand the same lights he would object to in or adjacent to his residential area. One may find conflicts even within the same family. A housewife may object to a particular use that a businessman finds particularly desirable, and vice versa. One case has been recorded in which a woman who led a community arts group and was very active in attempts to have signs abolished was married to a man who was responsible for much of the advertising for one of the major oil companies.

The Consumer

The consumer may use a particular site at a particular time, but he does not permanently occupy it. His interests may directly conflict with the interests of the user of other sites, but he provides the economic support for the user of the site which he frequents. It's very important to understand the difference between the person who will use the site and the consumer for whom he is using it. A businessman or merchant uses an on-premise sign to attract a second person to his property. The merchant is the user of the sign and the second party is the consumer.

When he purchases or leases his property, the user of a site acquires with it certain rights, depending on the land use zone in which the property lies. If it is commercial property, he has the right to use the visual component of the property to attract the consumer to the site in any way that he feels will succeed, as long as he does not interfere with the property rights of others. The consumer has certain preferences and needs and the user of a commercial site will try to meet the preferences of a certain segment of the consuming public.

The conflict that has developed in the past over this property right has resulted when a user takes advantage of this right to the extent that he infringes on the rights of another user to attract customers to his site or on the social amenity rights of the user of adjacent residential property. We are in favor of high standards enforced through positive legislation which would, through the use of formulas stipulated in Chapter 9, prevent a small, irresponsible user from encroaching on the rights of the conscientious user of his visual component of his property.

The Producer

The third actor who participates in landscape formation is the actual producer of a structure such as a building or a sign. In a cost-competitive society such as ours, merely because a producer of particular landscape elements exists, he becomes a major participator in landscape formation, usually to a much greater degree than he generally realizes. In producing a particular kind of building or a sign in making decisions about his product, he manipulates what is possible on the landscape. The user is the owner or leasee of the property; the producer is the builder or manufacturer of the structures on that property.

History of the Sign Industry

The first recorded use of signs as a means of communication for business occurred in Babylonia, where the merchant displayed a sign to draw attention to his wares. During the days of the Roman Empire, the sign became a widespread phenomenon employing pictures and symbols, rather than words, to inform an illiterate populace. Modern advertising is an extension of these early signs. Among the most obvious examples are the striped barber pole and the three gold spheres that indicate a pawn shop. It is interesting to note a modern-day return to the use of symbols in many areas of international traffic such as airports, as an alternative to the traditional use of words and phrases in several languages—a practice that was space-consuming and not nearly so attractive.

In thirteenth-century Europe, shopkeepers were required by law to hang signs on their establishments, and the sign soon became, in effect, a license to do business. By the eighteenth century, sign painting had become a profession, and signs became works of art as well as sources of information. This was the beginning of the sign industry as we know it.

With the advent of the incandescent lamp in 1879, illuminated signs began to grace North American streets and were greeted with enthusiasm as a source of beauty and excitement. The first electric signs were simple painted signs with gilded moldings, studded with bare bulbs. Soon opal glass letters and colored lamps softened the effect and provided greater variety.

One of the most significant developments of the early 1900s was the installation of the first neon sign in Paris, built by the French scientist, Georges Claude in 1921. The following year the first neon sign in the United States was erected by an automobile dealer.

Some years after the advent of neon, the introduction of molded plastic allowed the use of a wider variety of colors, and exact duplication of daytime effects at night through illumination of the plastic sign from behind. Electrical signs began to take on a new look, incorporating all the available methods with a greater degree of sophistication.

Meanwhile, with the perfection of large-scale silk screen and lithography techniques on paper, the 24-sheet poster or "billboard" became an increasingly popular means of third-party advertising.

While the original neon and plastic signs were largely produced at the local level for functional reasons, the more sophisticated contemporary companies have developed into various areas of specialization. Some national companies specialize in large quantity, scientifically engineered standard displays for national automobile manufacturers, oil companies, etc. A few sophisticated specialty companies have advanced into the field of digital data communication, on a national scale, much of it consisting of low maintenance solid state electrical controls, which are without a doubt representative of the highway sign of the future, which will be necessary to cope with increasing volumes of traffic at increasing speeds. Other companies are specalizing in the complete visual renovation of retail premises, incorporating the advertising displays into the design of the storefront in a way which symbolizes the character of the business concerned. There has been an increasing emphasis of environmental quality throughout the industry.

One of the problems of the sign industry is the disproportionate tendency among academics to relate to signs as to an age-old problem. The fact of the matter is that signs are primarily the function of some form of retailing and that retailing has recently undergone a rapid growth.

The major growth in the sign industry has occurred with technological innovations, increased incomes which have been reflected in the growth of the retailing sector, and finally the increase in use of the automobile, which makes the consumer much more mobile. In the 1940s most people reached retail shopping areas by public transit and on foot. Since then, however, almost 80 per cent of the retailing in most major cities has become automobile-oriented in some part of the journey to shop. For shops which rely on a high percentage of transient traffic, the sign and public exposure are a major component of economic success. The importance of signs has multiplied in direct proportion to the speed of traffic and the number of people who are single-stop or impulse shoppers at a site. Because of these shifts and the explosion in the use of plastics, much of the clutter which has resulted has been due to relatively untutored attempts to adjust to this high-speed, high-density retail environment. All of these things have combined to thrust the industry to the forefront in our visual environment. The sign industry has only recently begun to categorize its own knowledge of consumer needs into a format that can be taught. Thus, to our knowledge, there is no college curriculum in North America that treats retail signs, their effects, or how they should be used. There is only one work that deals with these subjects and the properties of a sign, and this book was only completed with considerable help from the industry (Claus & Claus, 1971). *City Signs and Lights* (Signs/Lights/Boston, 1971), which was a $400,000 project, shed surprisingly little light on this problem, although it was a start. Unfortunately, there was a great deal of bias in the study and argument toward assumed points rather than basic informational components and what makes them work.

The growth that has occurred in the last decade is demonstrated by the sales and distribution volume of the electric sign industry. In 1962, the sales amounted to approximately $300 million. By 1969, this total volume had increased to nearly $625 million.

Of this total, $50 million came from non-sign work, such as that in connection with storefront remodelling, interior signing, and so on, pointing out the increasing trend toward a total design package. Much more detailed information on the history and trends of the industry can be found in *The Visual Environment* (Claus & Claus, 1971).

Structure of the Industry

A clear schism has developed within the industry between quantity sign production and custom sign houses. This distinction is manifested in the amount of time and expertise that is invested in design at the local level. The fastest growing sector of the industry has been quantity production but custom design has also shown a substantial increase. Growth differences between the two sectors seems to be leveling off and there is no indication that quantity production will replace custom manufacture. The small independent retailer still makes up 50 per cent or more of our retail volume and he generally prefers a high degree of individuality in his visual communication. The standard sign is designed in one place and may be manufactured there or in several places throughout the country. It is then shipped to the outlets using the signs. It is not uncommon for the standard sign to be shipped across the continent from the point of manufacture.

Thus, the custom industry is based on the ability to tailor a sign to individual needs, while the standardized sign industry serves large companies who need a nationally recognizable image, such as fast food franchisers and oil companies.

There are five major operating units within the sign industry: (1) marketing, (2) design and layout, (3) manufacturing, (4) installation, and (5) maintenance. The maintenance division may come under installation or may stand on its own. As with other industries, the operating units do not have to be integrated into one corporation. All but marketing can be subcontracted to other companies. Some of the large sign companies are fully integrated. One of the primary reasons for this is that the standards and the skill in production that are required often cannot be met by small non-integrated companies and there may be lack of skilled labor available to carry out these functions. When there is a sparse geographic distribution of signs, the company also may find it advantageous to integrate in order to ensure that the various services will be available. Nevertheless, because of the industry's heavy commitment to marketing, it is common in some areas to find large sign companies which avoid maintenance, installation and even manufacturing. They have found that they can save costs by subcontracting these functions to others.

The nature of any industry can be appreciated through an understanding of the most important operating units within that industry. In the oil industry, for instance, among the fully integrated companies, the exploration/production and manufacturing units are usually the most important operating units. Marketing was primarily introduced to lower the risks by guaranteeing outlets for the exploration/production and manufacturing units. This partially explains why it is only recently that some serious marketing efforts have been begun within many of the major oil companies.

In the sign industry, on the other hand, the reverse is true. The most important operating unit in this industry is clearly the marketing division and the design and art departments which serve it. Although tremendous innovations have occurred in installation and maintenance of signs, and in the actual manufacturing of signs because of the tremendous growth in plastics and related materials, the heart of the industry has always been the marketing division. Any company which does not have a marketing unit is merely a supplier of services to the functioning sign companies.

The marketing function of sign companies varies considerably. Some sign companies try to sell their signs for cash, which is the predominant arrangement in eastern areas of the U.S., while some of the larger companies, particularly in the western United States and Canada, prefer to lease signs. One advantage of leasing is that a large proportion of those signs which are leased are renewed. While an original contract is always subject to miscalculation in estimating time and costs and may not be as profitable as anticipated, a renewal does not involve any other capital costs but is simply a commitment for maintenance on which a profit is made. The only risk is a rapid escalation in labor rates.

There are areas, such as the famous Ginza strip in Japan, where the people marketing signs perform no other function, but subcontract the whole process from design to maintenance to a miscellany of small entrepreneurs. Thus the overhead is minimal compared to that in North America.

The leasing strategy often turns the company into a primary leaser such as IBM. One of the advantages of leasing of signs is that the benefits are very evenly distributed. The sign company develops a continuing and dependable source of revenue; and the customer, or advertiser leasing a sign, can write off the total cost of that lease as an advertising expense, just as he does his newspaper advertising. On the other hand, he is limited in his ability to take tax deductions should he purchase the sign. Another advantage to the customer is that the sign contractor takes full responsibility for liability insurance over the public domain and takes care of many details, such as servicing the sign.

The third party that benefits from leasing is the community, because the leased sign will generally be better maintained than the owned sign. The leasing company has made a commitment to the user, who will demand that such commitments be carried out, whereas he might procrastinate about spending his own money. The maintenance division of the company is responsible for keeping the quality of a sign moderately high. Maintenance can be handled by the same people who install a sign, or it may be an entirely separate division of the company. When a sign is sold rather than leased, it is often not conscientiously maintained by the owner. Should the business of the owner fail, the sign quality will seriously decline. For this reason, some of the larger sign companies are insisting on maintenance agreements when they install signs. In addition, the leased sign is always removed when a tenant goes out of business or abandons the premises, while in many places in the U.S. there are literally hundreds of abandoned signs left on buildings. Furthermore, a sophisticated leasing company as a rule has a far more substantial design capability and turns out better quality products both from a physical and from a design standpoint.

The Vital Function of Communication

It is important to recognize that the sign industry is essential to the efficient functioning of our retail environment in our mobile age. Signs utilize the visual components of a property to communicate by advertising, directing people to goods and services, informing them of their existence, and creating images which appeal to various groups in our segmented society. The industry is marketing and communications oriented.

The importance of the visual component of retailing to society is only beginning to be recognized by much of the business community. Those entrepreneurs who intuited this and used signs to their advantage are often those who were extremely successful in their retail and commercial activities. That signs serve a significant function even for a pedestrian-oriented business is demonstrated by the case of Coney Island Park in Cincinnati where a refreshment stand was redesigned at a cost of $17,000 to add attractively to the visual quality of the area. Since the facility was on a main stream of traffic, it was decided that signs were unnecessary because activity at the stand would adequately indicate the nature of the business. However, business lagged significantly with regard to the previous year and in relationship to other refreshment stands. When proper identification signs were added, business increased by 35 per cent (*Signs of the Times,* August, 1964, p. 42).

Fig. 8: Addition of signs to this amusement refreshment center brought 35% sales increase.

As the automobile has become the primary means of transportation in our society, signs have taken on a greater importance than ever before. When the consumer is traveling at high speeds on major arteries, it is essential for public safety that he be able to quickly identify the retail outlet he seeks, whether a service station, a grocery store, or a restaurant. If the outlet is not easily identified, he must divert his attention from his driving to find it. The chances are, if he already knows the location of a particular outlet, this is because he has seen the sign on earlier trips to and from work or shopping.

Many retail outlets for goods and services are very dependent on quick recognition by the passer-by because a great deal of their business comes from the customer who stops on impulse on his way to another destination. Traffic participation formulas, which determine the percentage of passing traffic that will stop at a site, have become the primary means of predicting the economic success or customer acceptance of a new site. One graphic example of this is the experience of a California bank which located in a shopping center in the belief that a bank could be very successful if linked with a large department store and that the volume of business from the department store would provide half of the support it needed to survive. Much to the bank management's surprise, they learned that banking is a relatively specialized business and draws far more customers than they had expected from passing traffic. They learned that participation from passing traffic was actually more important than the multi-purpose shopping trip for generating business. By locating their banks among the stores in a shopping center where visual recognition from the street was difficult, they were losing the transient single-stop customer. Recently, the same bank bought a prime corner site, which offered a high degree of visibility. When a large oil company attempted to buy the site from the institution at a significant profit to the bank, they refused to sell it. The bank had come to realize through experience that a location with high visibility was more valuable than any retail linkages for the suburban branch.

On-premise signs represent a unique form of advertising and communication. They are efficient, and can relate specifically to the people who frequent a site or the segment of the market the advertiser wishes to serve. Because it is a permanent visual communication, more money may be spent on the sign initially than would be spent on other means of communication in the short run. But the sign relates to the shop itself and its only inefficiency is that it attempts to draw in new customers and therefore many people who may not stop at the establishment see it. Because it functions directly for the customers who stop at a site, it serves to reinforce what the site has to offer. It is the most effective means of communication in our society for this specific job. No other means of advertising will as effectively serve a retail site without a considerably higher cost per person reached. This is discussed in more detail in Chapter 6, but little in-depth work has been done on this subject that is not kept "in house". Because it is such an effective sales tool, those people who realize the value of on-premise advertising have not been eager to share this information with their competitors. The importance of the visual component of a retail site for its economic success has been touched on in *The Mobile Consumer* (Claus and Hardwick, 1971), but much more basic work needs to be done.

In an age of fantastic growth in the scale of enterprises, we have found that on-premise communication and advertising is probably the most efficient means that the small merchant has for advertising on a small budget. He must constantly compete against the scale economies of the larger firms who can utilize such strategies as magazine advertising

Fig. 9: A study of sign exposure by Alfred Politz Research, Inc. reveals that sign advertising is the lowest cost means of a businessman communicating with prospective customers—from 6 to 14.7 cents per thousand exposures, for signs costing from $175 to $10,000.

to reach various segments of the market and large-scale advertising campaigns. For this reason, we believe that custom sign divisions offer a unique and effective means of advertising to the small businessman.

The outdoor advertising industry, on the other hand, with its 100 per cent coverage, has the broadest, or most ubiquitous, coverage of any advertising medium for precisely the same reasons. It can be high quality; it is there all the time, not just during "prime time"; and it isn't restricted to one part of the market. People who would do away with billboards seldom understand how effective a form of communication such advertising can be.

We feel that well-done billboards are an asset to the urban environment. Unfortunately, too many of the billboards now in existence have not been allowed to shift to zones where they will have maximum circulation and value. Those that no longer are economically viable are often allowed to remain, rather than be replaced by newer more modern poster panels. When a company wishes to take them down and replace them with a better display in a more visible location, it is often prevented from doing so by the zoning laws.

One of the best testimonies to the effectiveness of outdoor advertising is the fact that, as pointed out by *Signs of the Times* (1966, 1967, 1970), many newspapers and television and radio stations use outdoor advertising to promote a particular program or writer, or simply to increase circulation. In the one case where records are available to us newspapers allocate as much as $50,000 a year in a city of half a million people to outdoor advertising to promote readership.

Because we live in a free enterprise system, those things that are vital to our economic functioning or to our normal social processes are most difficult to legislate out of existence. If a statute or ordinance is passed that is contrary to the public good, often the public or the electorate will demand its non-enforcement or repeal. Thus we know that the visual component of the property right, which is the right to communicate and advertise with landscape media, will always re-emerge. Cases can be cited in which municipalities have restricted or disallowed all on-premise signs and have found that the effect over time on the individual business, particularly the small entrepreneur, has been economically disastrous. They have had to reconsider and attempt to construct a more rational control of this type of advertising and communication.

The sign industry is now at a highly innovative stage. Several developments which have just emerged promise to add to the informational component and the general advertising or image-building functions of signs. One is the "face-lift". The other development is the emergence of sophisticated informational systems such as the time and temperature signs and message changers. Both of these promise a better visual environment for our cities as their use becomes more widespread. The industry is only beginning to realize its full potential and the advantages we can offer to the businessman by properly utilizing the visual component of his site.

The Function of Signs

Many planners, and even some people within the industry, seem to feel that signs should serve only an identification function. This is to overlook some of the most vital communications services that signs perform: advertising, information, and particularly image-building functions. We are a lettered people and a long history of writing has had an effect on our ability to recognize and understand symbols. For this reason, it is almost impossible to limit any sign to merely identification.

One of the most important aspects of signs is their ability to create images which appeal to certain groups in our society. Through the use of lettering or graphics, one can build an image that is particularly attractive to one segment of the population without abandoning the identification function of the sign. Often the image building or advertising function can be more important to a company than identification. This has certainly been the case for some of the more successful oil companies, for many successful clothing retailers, and for department stores, and there is no question that this function has been used successfully by prepared fast food merchants. The oval sign of one of the oil companies, Shell Oil's recent use of a solid background color, and some of the more sophisticated signs of the past all carry clear messages and images about the product they want to sell and to what group of people. Well over 50 per cent of the current retail market utilizes this image-building function. Thus the assumption that this kind of image-building through graphics, lettering, and coloring only occur within certain limited segments of the industry is naive and ignores the marketing and communication aspects inherent in signs. It is not purely by chance that such widely different stores as J.C. Penney's and I. Magnin's continue to survive. They serve different segments of the market while performing essentially similar functions.

For certain communication efforts there is nothing that can replace the on-premise sign in terms of advertising for many retailing and commercial functions. The image, information and direction functions of the on-premise sign make the visual component of his property one of the most valuable of the entrepreneur's property rights.

The Public Decision-Maker

Finally, the actor who may exert control over all the others is the public official, either as an elected representative or a hired municipal official. He decides what can be built on the landscape, where it can be built, and how it can be built. This fourth type of actor is usually manifested in the city council and the staff at city hall, or the equivalent officials at the state or provincial and federal levels.

By the very nature of their functions, such actors can have a profound effect on the landscape, often inadvertently. For instance, in one large city in western Canada, the fire marshall has taken it upon himself to interpret the fire code in a way that is unique in Canada. He has interpreted it to require that any gasoline facility in a parking garage must be open to the air from above. Thus, any parking garage built in this city either has a hole in the middle or a hole in the side where the pumps are installed. Quite unwittingly, this particular official is forming our urban landscape. There is some question whether he has this right and whether this requirement could legally be enforced, but it has not been questioned in a court of law and thus it continues to shape the urban environment.

Clearly land use can be dominated by the public decision-maker. The False Creek area of Vancouver, British Columbia, is long overdue for apartment developments. This would be the "highest and best use of the land", in appraisal language. Yet the city has refused to change the zoning from industrial to residential to allow this natural evolution to take place. The city is in the process of "master planning" the entire district and when the master plan is finished, redevelopment will begin in earnest.

The design of residential buildings is often greatly influenced by the loan specifications of the Housing Authority. This is particularly evident in Canada where a particular kind of house is favored by the NHA loan requirements.

The information which the public decision-maker acts upon, and the perceptual bias from which he acts are critical to the effectiveness of his decisions. It is generally not politics that motivate seemingly irresponsible or negative decisions. The politician, like anyone else, has a particular perspective on a situation.

One of the reasons for writing this book is that landscape formation, which should be a conscious process on the part of the public decision-maker, is often vicarious or accidental —a by-product of the decision-making act.

It is the responsibility of the elected public decision-maker to set goals for the community welfare. It is the task of the professional planner to implement the strategies which will bring about those goals. To do so, he must be aware of all of the ramifications of his legislation and he must ensure that the legislation is enforced.

Often municipal governments set out to create controls without realizing that as surely as these regulations will benefit one sector of the community, they will harm another. The classic case of this is the result of recent legislation to promote fewer and larger service stations. The prime sites for such service stations are falling to corporate actors who can afford them and can use them to the best economic advantage. The desirability of this is something which must be decided by the municipal council, but they should be aware that small unaffiliated dealers will be hurt by such a strategy. Many decisions have favored large corporations to the exclusion of small private entrepreneurs.

It is interesting to note that many large companies are encouraging legislation and the current push for pollution control as a method of eliminating their more cost-conscious competitors. It is very important that the planner realize some of the long-run effects of his decisions. The possibility of legislation which is not carefully thought-out being used by those whom it was intended to control to eliminate their competitors is dealt with extensively by Friedman in his book, *Capitalism and Freedom* (1962).

We feel that no legislation should favor one segment of an industry over another unless there is a clearly set rationale for doing so. In fact, society may suffer more at the hands of the "do-gooder" than from the cost-conscious individual who must meet the demands of the consuming public.

These four different types of actors make the decisions which form the urban landscape but, by the very nature of our society, it is not always very easy to categorize the decision-maker. A person who is a user of a site may also be a public official. The producer of signs, the public official, and the user are all consumers some of the time. A producer is also the user of a site on the landscape or the consumer of a particular landscape use. We all play at least two roles in landscape creation: that of the user and that of the consumer. It is primarily the role of the public decision-maker with which most of us are not very familiar, and it is there that the final authority to manipulate the landscape is manifested and the final functioning or logistics stage of decision-making—the enforcement stage—is carried out.

References for Chapter 3

Claus, R. J. & Claus, K.E. *The Visual environment: Site, sign and bylaw.* Don Mills, Ontario: Collier-Macmillan, 1971.

Claus, R. J. & Hardwick, W.G. *The mobile consumer: the Emergence of Automobile Dependent Retailing.* Don Mills, Ontario: Collier Macmillan, 1972.

Friedman, M. *Capitalism and freedom.* Chicago: University of Chicago Press, 1962.

Signs/Lights/Boston. *City signs and lights.* Boston: Author, 1971.

Signs of the Times. 78 Selling Appeals for Radio and TV Stations' Outdoor Advertising. October 1966.

Signs of the Times. Newspapers Utilize 32 Outdoor Appeals. July 1967.

Signs of the Times. Radio and TV Stations Present 91 Sales Appeals in Outdoor Advertising. August 1970.

Chapter 4/Rationales For Landscape Formation: Site And The Question Of Public Interest

The ultimate motivation for an act involving the use of a particular site on the urban landscape is usually that of public interest. The ideal of public interest or public welfare is basic to our society and goes back to our common law tradition. We have always felt that the public as a whole must benefit from the use of legislation, and any land use which benefits one group while infringing on the rights of another can usually be successfully challenged. Because of this belief, we have consciously attempted to discourage the public decision-maker power from openly discriminating against one user for the benefit of another.

Generally speaking, there are four reasons for control of the landscape in the public interest. These are (1) economics, (2) public safety, (3) aesthetics, and (4) social amenity. Social amenity and aesthetics will be considered as one category here, since in most cases, the courts have not allowed the public decision-maker to base land use decisions on aesthetic criteria alone. The courts have held that the rationales for the use of the power vested in the public official by tradition and law, must be clearly stated.

Economics

The first of these rationales has to do with extension of our private enterprise system. Our society has prided itself on being a marketplace economy. Thus, we have allowed the rules of the marketplace to determine most of our urban form and structure, as long as the public welfare is not endangered. If people are willing to pay for a particular use of a site or to support it, the courts have been inclined to assume that this is the will of the public and to allow it to continue. If it is not desired by a significant sector of the public, it is assumed that it will no longer be supported by them and will fail. Thus, if there is a conflict over the use of a particular site, the courts have usually been inclined to allow the economics of the marketplace to demonstrate which form the public will support. The user, the producer, and the consumer all participate in this. If a user wishes to put up a sign that attracts a particular segment of the market, or a producer proposes a particular sign to the user, as long as it is not in conflict with his right to use that property in a particular manner or with the property rights of others, he has generally been allowed to do so.

It is particularly important to understand this, because the right to rationally allocate a resource is very deeply ingrained in our society. By allowing the allocation of resources by the individual, we have discovered that, over time, the best or the most efficient allocation of our resources will usually survive. Thus, the public, who are in fact the ultimate decision-makers, can dictate how these resources will be used.

Public Safety

The first major area of encroachment by the public decision-maker into sign regulation is that of public safety. There are many municipalities which do not have zoning or sign codes but which have the usual fire and building codes to prevent hazards to public health and welfare. We have already discussed the unorthodox use of fire codes in one western Canadian city. This demonstrates how such public safety codes can in fact have the same effect as bylaws or ordinances to control the appearance of the landscape. Additionally the rationale given for the act, may not be the reason the code was enacted. In one of the western states, where there is a preference for wood construction, the public decision-makers have incorporated a height limitation on apartments into the building code. The result is that with the allowable heights and densities, wood has a cost advantage over any other material. This openly favors one of the local industries. Similarly, in Toronto and many other cities in Ontario, legislation has been in effect to enforce the use of brick as a building material. The rationale given is that it is for protection against fire, but many houses are built of brick with the second floor effectively part of the roof. It is obvious to even the casual observer that such a building would burn like a chimney. However, the real reason for the requirement is no doubt related to the fact that brick is a local product.

The sign producer should be aware that the fire and building specifications for his signs have many ramifications which in many ways will affect the appearances of signs. Unless such codes are very clearly worded and well thought out, they may very negatively affect the appearance of the landscape.

Signs are often limited by zoning codes or specific sign codes in certain areas where they might endanger the public by blocking traffic signals. This is certainly reasonable. But there are methods which can be used to determine the maximum size of on-premise projecting signs without allowing them to block traffic control devices or other signs. If the industry would make such formulations widely known, sensible and realistic bylaws could be drawn up to the benefit of the public and the industry.

One example of the lack of understanding of the technical components of communication and advertising on the part of public officials is the situation in which a planner or traffic engineer suggests that accidents may be caused because signs are a distraction. We have learned, on the contrary, that abrogation is not the most effective way to prevent such dangers in most cases. The most effective way is ensuring that the sign is designed to provide maximum recognition in a minimum of time. Furthermore, it has been found that on long journeys, signs contribute to safety by providing diversion and variety on an otherwise monotonous landscape. Thus, we can contribute to the effectiveness and legibility of signs by sharing what we have learned about color and lettering, and the effect that they have on the eye.

Social Amenity and Aesthetics

Social amenity and aesthetic considerations are often confused, but they can be very easily differentiated if defined properly. Social amenities actually deal with property rights of users of a particular land use area, and are manifested in zones of land use. It may be so profitable to carry on a particular activity in a particular area that the area will be zoned for that use, or a zone may be created for the social amenities which are to be expected by the user of residential property. Some planners and architects feel that there are areas—such as amusement, restaurant or nightclub sections—where signs are an excitement motif that is desirable and that signs should be allowed to develop there relatively unrestricted. The purpose of residential zoning is usually to enhance and protect the property rights of the homeowner or resident.

Aesthetics, on the other hand, deal with form or design of a particular building or structure. This kind of legislation is usually avoided by intelligent city governments and is frowned upon by the courts because such regulations are by necessity subjective and because aesthetic taste is neither static overtime nor consistent among various segments of the population. One need only consider the roccoco style on buildings that were typical of the 1930s to realize how tastes change.

Architects who would regulate public tastes should remember that not too long ago Frank Lloyd Wright had a great deal of difficulty in getting many of his design concepts accepted by the same architectural community which would now like to tell us what is good design.

The planner who would design the best possible sign for all of society is effectively saying that his tastes are the only ones which are acceptable. Many planners or architects assume that their own needs and tastes are, or perhaps *should be,* those of the whole of society. This form of cultural arrogance reflects a refusal to recognize that there are many different kinds of people in our society, and any building or sign which is successful must be pleasing to a significant segment of the market.

In one community in California, a design control board decided to exert control over the color houses can be painted and the types of shrubbery used. In such cases, the commonly-heard rationale is that signs, buildings, etc., because they are inescapable features of the landscape, constitute an "invasion of privacy". This has reached the point of the ridiculous. If one accepts this premise, he will soon be outlawing certain modes of dress, certain hair styles and perhaps even beards. And there is always the question of who decides what is an offensive use. If one can dictate the color one paints his house, it will not be long before he tells you or me that we cannot wear loud ties or mini skirts.

There is another reason such control should not be allowed. We often find what is called in legal jargon a "sweetheart" deal between the city and people seeking permits from the city, and this doesn't occur only in the sign industry. Recently a man in California applied for a permit for new modular component housing in the form of a semi-elliptical dome. The people on the architectural design committee which ruled on this supposedly only wanted to make sure that the building would not be totally offensive; that is, they did not wish to control the actual design, but just wanted to ensure that it wouldn't be a shack or something equally obviously undesirable. However, one of the men was basically opposed to this design, and he admitted that this was *"because he was a trained architect."* He went to great lengths to explain that he didn't feel *"it would fit in."* Therefore, it was refused a permit. The reason given was that it didn't fit aesthetically into the area. The municipality in which this occurred has a code very similar to one in Ohio which makes such a decision *ultra vires* or outside the powers of the municipality to enforce (see Chapter 7). They could not refuse a permit on those grounds. Such an attempt should have immediately occasioned a writ of mandamus against the city and the building permit should have been granted. Instead, the builder took a weak-kneed stance, saying in effect: "Let us try to talk to them, or educate them, or propagandize them, or drink them into allowing this thing; but don't force their hand." The basis of this reasoning was that if he resisted them at that time, the time would come when he would want to come back for another permit, and they would find some small point to prevent him from getting it.

There is no question in our minds that this is blackmail. Until a few people begin to go out of their way to explain to planners that they have no legal right to do such things and take them into court, we will continue to be faced with poor bylaws and this kind of blackmail. There is one analogy that seems to parallel the current drive to regulate aesthetics, and that is prohibition. The case that was made against prohibition undoubtedly could be applied here. The city planner speaks of stress and invasion of privacy in the same way that the prohibitionist spoke of sin. These are words that can be twisted to fit the cause of someone attempting to control others according to his own code. But prohibition wasn't worth the trouble it caused because it wasn't what the general public wanted. It is much the same with signs. People want signs; they are buying them and using them.

Chapter 5/Conflicts Among Various Philosophical Views Of Landscape Formation

The major area of conflict that generally arises among rationales for landscape regulation is between residential and commercial or industrial property rights. A homeowner may wish to eliminate any commercial or industrial activities in his neighborhood or he may wish to restrict certain uses of property in order to make them more compatible with his land use needs.

The Functioning of the Marketplace Economy

There are certain property rights that are inherent in each land use zone. In a residential area, one should expect a certain degree of safety for children and a certain degree of privacy and quiet at night. In commercial areas, exposure and high traffic densities are necessary for efficient functioning. At the heart of the arguments over use of land is a difference in philosophy as to who should control the use of the visual landscape. In most cases, our courts have ruled that the people should control the use of land whenever possible, and the best way they can do so is through the marketplace. By shopping at particular retail outlets, they will clearly manifest their preferences as to land use. If a sign is offensive, they won't shop at that outlet. Thus the final power to put a company out of business always rests with the people in our society, and if they don't like a particular sign or the way property is being used, they can manifest their discontent by refusing to support it.

One must keep in mind, though, when using this argument, that any marketplace economy is imperfect, and there will always be a need for checks to account for those cases in which a spatial monopoly exists and the consumer has no other choice.

However, there is little justification for criticizing devices such as the McDonald's sign, for instance, because it obviously has been accepted by a substantial segment of our economy, or it would not have been so successful. The appearance of the McDonald's Hamburger arches conveys to approaching prospective customers memories of the food, prices, and service that have been enjoyed at other units of the chain. Thus the approaching motorist knows exactly what to anticipate with confidence that he can get exactly what he wants. Thus the signs are all-important to such marketers in impulse shopping situations.

Regulation by Consensus

There is another point of view that the public decision-makers should take a consensus of public opinion and control the formation of the landscape accordingly. Although this is not very different from the marketplace method, the primary danger is that the government will overlook the pluralistic nature of our society and will force the viewpoints of one or two more vocal sectors onto the entire community.

Regulation by "Experts"

A third point of view is that the "experts" in our society should control all elements of it. Although when it is stated this bluntly, this appears to be very offensive, it was not an unpopular point-of-view a few years ago to suggest that the planning of the city should be turned over to planners. In fact, that was the origin of the term master plan. This viewpoint is still held by a good many intellectuals and is being espoused in many planning schools. There are many articles in which it is suggested that the manipulation of the landscape be turned over to planners and architects so that they, in their wisdom, can control what our landscape will look like and how it will be allowed to function.

This point-of-view is categorically in conflict with the opinion that the people should express what they want to see on the landscape through the marketplace mechanism. Inherent in this point-of-view is the use of the salaried city officials to interpret the regulations and participate in landscape formation. Recently one of the head planners of a Canadian city stated in an article that he felt that it was one of the obligations of the planner to manipulate public opinion and tastes. There is a current attitude among many architects and planners that it is a privilege and not a right to do business in a business district. One cannot help but feel that it is a right they would like often to eliminate.

One of the things that the industry does not seem to appreciate is that the measure of success of a municipal planner is the amount of successful legislation he has framed. And the term success has nothing to do with whether or not it works; it refers to whether or not it was passed. This undoubtedly has a great deal to do with explaining the amount of legislation being created. Many times the criterion for hiring a planner in another community is that he has framed legislation. Too often he has been trained to believe that he knows what is for the public good and that the mere creation of a bylaw will make a better city. Often, the planner has moved to better things before any effects, negative or positive, of the ordinance can be identified.

A very good argument against allowing any discretionary power to the professional planner, who is not a primary decision-maker, is that there is no legal recourse against a planner who misuses these powers. Criminal charges cannot be filed against him when he acts in bad faith, refuses to do his job, or makes completely subjective judgments against an individual or business. Much like university professors with tenure, the salaried municipal official occasionally seems to develop an antagonistic attitude towards the commercial sector of society or anyone who seems to be doing a constructive job. When such an individual becomes antagonistic to an individual or company, they can do nothing but go over his head with a writ of mandamus against the city.

A primary source of conflict between municipal decision-makers and the sign industry is based on a basic difference in philosophy. The planner generally feels that his ideals are, or should be, those of the rest of the community and he will attempt to impose his tastes on the landscape. The industry, on the other hand, is also composed of "experts", but these experts exist to fulfill a tangible need or desire of the public. If the public did not want signs, the industry would cease to exist. Therefore, the sign "expert" must be consumer-oriented.

Although the planner may not approve of the tastes of the majority, he has no right to impose a tyranny of an "informed" minority. Attempts at this have been made and have repeatedly failed. As Jacobs (1961) has pointed out, there is no indication that this kind of planning will make a city any more livable.

We do not feel that any discretionary power should be placed in the hands of the professional planner. Decisions should be made by the public official and instrumented by the professional. The result of placing powers in the hands of the professional planner can be tyranny of "professional" tastes over the desires and needs of the community.

The training of the municipal planner and the architect is very limited. Much of what is taught in their academic courses is untested theory and ideal, non-existent models of city structure. Unless a planner has had a varied background or considerable on-the-job training, his solutions to problems may be inapplicable or even aggravate the problem.

One of the reasons our universities are broken down into departments is that the amounts and kinds of research done by each department differs. The communications schools may deal with how communications reach the public without ever undertaking a detailed analysis of costs vs. the penetration rate of various methods. The social sciences generally have little, if any real-world application. The planners have been particularly reluctant to approach the sign industry for information. Even though the case study approach is used by clinical psychologists and is used extensively in the business schools, the planner seems to feel that he will become tainted if he accepts any of the testimony of businessmen as to the effectiveness of signs.

The educational and professional biases of these people can lead to particularly unfortunate results for the community. When social processes are codified in a statutory act, they have a high degree of permanence and are far-reaching in their effects on the community. Too often regulations are in reality a codification of specialized or incomplete viewpoints that do not accurately reflect the social needs of the community as a whole. Such acts may thwart the innovation that is necessary to maintain a dynamic society.

Thus the solutions proposed by the "expert" are often far worse than the problem and may have to be abandoned in favor of the workings of the marketplace. This lack of perspective is one of the prices one must pay for specialization. The educated guessing of the planner or architect will have very real and permanent effects on the landscape.

How little the average planner knows of current developments in the area of signs and their implications is evident from the attitude reflected in sign controls toward such developments as digital data displays and facelifts. These developments are indications of the dynamic nature of our society.

The digital data displays are highly sophisticated devices which have evolved from the mechanical time and temperature displays. With the introduction of electronics, these have become extremely effective communications devices (Figure 10). These are today used for identification, information, advertising, and prices, as well as for time and temperature which are public service messages. Surveys of users of such signs conducted by a sign company revealed that at least 50 per cent of these users contributed a significant portion of their display time to public service messages (Figures 11 and 12).

56

Fig. 10: Sophisticated electronics equipment permits dissemination of changing messages from remote position.

Fig. 11a: The jump clock is in essence an animated sign as it updates the time each minute.

Fig. 11b: On the opposite face of this same sign, the temperature is appropriately recorded as another public service.

Fig: 12: These same functions (Figure 11a & b) can be combined in one face in the "time and temp" unit.

However, many planners show a lack of understanding of the nature and value of these signs. Much confusion has developed over the regulation of signs containing flashing lights. Although these digital displays use light bulbs to comprise the message, they are not translated by the human eye as flashing lights. However, more than one planner has refused to permit such signs under an ordinance prohibiting flashing lights.

The facelift programs also are badly misinterpreted. Under such a program, the entire front or facade of the building is redesigned to harmonize with the architecture of the building and the sign (Figures 13A and 13B). This might better be called "remodeling and integration" to maximize communication. However, under a very literal interpretation of many sign codes, these facelifts have been interpreted as signs covering the entire face of the building. Many sign ordinances define the sign area as the entire face of a sign, including background, and then set a maximum size. This would eliminate most facelifts entirely.

Furthermore many planners have used the fact that such storefront remodeling must extend a few inches over the property line where the building covers the whole lot to prohibit such construction under old regulations intended to prevent living space from encroaching onto public space. Thus these facades are treated as architectural projections and are disallowed. The planner who interprets literally the existing regulations or lends his own interpretation to them, rather than considering the original intention of the regulations is thwarting innovation and creativity necessary to overcome our urban problems.

Certainly one of the more innovative techniques for on-premise signs is the utilization of polarized fluorescent light. The technique is capable of adaptation to outdoor advertising or even point-of-purchase displays. The system should make a significant impact on on-premise signs. "In the system, animation is produced by the working of two components in addition to the elements of a normal illuminated acrylic box. The first component is an animator which is a rotating disc containing a light wave filter placed between a light source and the translucent image it illuminates. The second component is an animation film which consists of a series of polarized screens adhering to a carrier placed against the inside face of the translucent image. The interaction of the treated light and the polarized screens can produce apparent motion in many forms." (Daniel Solomon, personal letter, 6 July 1971). This type of sign could reach a high degree of graphic design and have

Fig. 13a: A relatively new activity of many sign firms is rejuvenation of business street scenes such as this.

Fig. 13b: This is the same commercial block as proposed by a sign firm art department. Sign and architecture are integrated.

Signs. Legal Rights And Aesthetic Considerations/**59**

considerable flexibility for adaptation to different types of land use zones and types of traffic. Because of its recent advent and flexibility, the technique deserves special note under flashing or animation ordinance sections*.

This procedure may have considerable implications for safety as well as commercial signage. Simple readjustments to the speed of the polarized lenses in the back of these units can provide entirely new visual displays. Such adjustments, made periodically, could maintain the attractive power of a sign.

The psychological reasons for the attention-getting power of temporal or design changes in visual stimuli are founded on basic perceptual processes. Research on both humans and animals has indicated that near exposure to a stimulus is enough to build up some satiation for it. Not only does an individual respond less to the stimulus itself, but he is also less responsive to stimuli which are similar (Dember, 1960).

The attractive power of any stimulus stems from two major sources: novelty and complexity. Novelty involves temporal change. An individual is exposed to a stimulus which is then modified in some attribute at a subsequent exposure. Psychologically this creates an expectancy which is not confirmed. The worlds of advertising, fashion and entertainment have long known that novelty is crucial to attention-arousal and attention-maintenance. S c i e n ti f i c studies of both humans and animals have confirmed that the attractive power of novelty is a basic perceptual process. (Berlyne, 1951, 1957, 1958; Thompson & Solomon, 1954; Walker, 1956). Novelty not only induces an initial response, it also keeps an individual investigating or exploring the stimulus. The attractive power of complexity is based upon two design factors: spatial heterogeneity and incongruity. A complex stimulus psychologically conveys more information and consequently provides more potential opportunities for response than simpler stimuli. Successful advertisers have known that an effective message incorporates both aspects of complexity and change in order to heighten its appeal and effectiveness. Public safety signage can certainly do no less.

---

*SUGGESTED EXCEPTION FOR ANTI-ANIMATION SIGN ORDIN-ANCES: The polarization of fluorescent light by the placement of polarized light-wave filters, similar to the glare reducing light-wave filters utilized in sunglasses, shall be accepted within interior illuminated advertising displays, so long as the limits imposed by this department regarding the number of rotations per minute of such filters within each such display shall not be exceeded and the color sequencing effects that are produced upon the display faces are not alike, or directly similar to those employed by city, county or state traffic engineers in the utilization of polarization or other systems in traffic warning signals and signs. Light-wave filter rotation limits; message areas—limit to 9 rpm and pictorials—limit to 50 rpm.

Over-rigorous application of regulations also may favor one business type over another. Stringent control of signs in the older sections of a community where retail premises fill the entire lot may cause an area to stagnate and cause urban blight. The planner should devote more time to the business sector of our society, learning how businessmen see their signs, how they function, and how regulations can affect the economic viability of a site. Otherwise, the stagnation of the downtown core and the spread of businesses will cause the urban sprawl they profess to abhor.

References for Chapter 5

William N. Dember. *The Psychology of Perception.* New York: Holt, Rinehart and Winston, 1960.

D. E. Berlyne. Attention to change. *British Journal of Psychology,* 1951, *42,* 269-278.

D. E. Berlyne. Attention to change, conditioned inhibition (sIr) and stimulus satiation. *British Journal of Psychology,* 1957, *48,* 138-140.

D. E. Berlyne. The influence of complexity and change in visual figures on orienting responses. *Journal of Experimental Psychology,* 1958, *55,* 289-296.

Thompson, W.R. and Solomon, L.M. Spontaneous pattern discrimination in the rat. *Journal of Comparative Physiological Psychology,* 1954, *47,* 104-107.

Welker, W. I. Some determinants of play and exploration in chimpanzees. *Journal of Comparative Physiological Psychology,* 1956, *49.* 84-89.

Jacobs, J. *The Death and Life of Great American Cities.* New York: Modern Library, 1961.

Chapter 6/Conflicts Of Interest

There are certain groups of people who are opposed to signs as communication. We have categorized them into three interest groups: (1) the producers of conflicting advertising or communications media, (2) those who are opposed to advertising and the economic system in general, and (3) those who simply do not understand advertising and the components of quality.

Producers of Conflicting Media

The first group which comes into conflict with the sign industry is the procedures of other communications media, such as newspapers, magazines, television, and radio. Few of them could exist without their advertising budgets. It is ironic that these factions should suggest that the sign industry should only provide information and direction and should not be allowed to advertise, while newspapers, magazines, radio and television are so dependent on advertising.

This brings up an important point. Whenever there is an economic issue at stake and competing media argue for public intervention, the public decision-maker should become very suspicious. The use of the landscape for signs is a form of advertising. One of the primary sources of information about objections to signs recently has been the newspapers. Both magazines and newspapers may be more inclined to print articles and opinions which discriminate against outdoor advertising, because the limitation of such signs would increase their own sales potentials as the merchant attempts to communicate the information to the consumer that was originally provided by his sign. Often actions against signs are encouraged and magnified by these competing advertising media. Some of the methods used by those who are opposed to signs are completely unfair. Many of these groups use telephoto lenses and other techniques to distort and exaggerate the effect of signs on the landscape, and thus mislead legislators into over-reacting without truly realizing why they have been so motivated (Figures 14a and 14b).

Thus the more discriminating public legislators have sought to avoid abolition of signs because in doing so, they are giving preference to magazines, radio, television, and newspapers. They may in fact be inflicting an unnecessary cost burden on the merchant and thus ultimately on the

Fig. 14a: Sign clutter is often overstated by telephoto lens news media presentation.

Fig. 14b: Here is the same street scene as it actually appears.

consumer to find or convey the information normally contained in signs.

Competing advertising means often seek to sway public officials for their private economic advantage. How intentional or conscious such action is on the part of most advertisers is an open question. They may simply not be intelligent enough about their own visual environment and observation of it to attack only the elements of poor quality.

In light of their readiness to hop on the bandwagon of sign abolition we find it amusing that, as we have already mentioned, radio, newspapers, and television are advertising their own product through the medium of signs. This demonstrates that they are not effectively reaching all of the market through their own media. It is unusual to find them using other radio or television stations or newspapers to advertise, because they can get the best coverage for the dollar from outdoor advertising.

We have provided a brief introduction here to the advantages and disadvantages of the various advertising media in order to clarify the unique nature of signs.

Newspapers. One of the newspaper's primary advantages is the access to specific market areas. The advertiser can select a particular segment of the market through the use of local community papers of special neighborhood editions, or may reach all segments or the market through a widely circulated daily newspaper. It is also possible to be selective with regard to the editorial policy of the paper with which the advertiser will be associated.

Another advantage is timeliness, or the ability to present the ad to the public for a very specific period of time. This feature is particularly advantageous for special sales of a limited duration. The ability to limit the exposure time of an ad also presents a good opportunity to measure the effect of advertising on sales volume. Copy is easily changeable, and there is a wide variety of possible types of advertisements with which an advertiser can experiment.

Since the primary function of the newspaper is to present news, a message that is presented as a new idea or product is more likely to catch the attention of the reader than a message that is familiar or is presented frequently.

For messages such as food store ads, newspapers are the most suitable media, since long lists of specials cannot be effectively presented in the form of signs where space is limited, or on television, where the message is presented briefly and action is very important.

However, large, widely circulated newspapers may prove an inefficient means of advertising for the small businessman, because he is paying for the full circulation of the paper, while his potential customers may be drawn from a very limited area. He is paying for a great deal of waste circulation. It is for this reason that newspaper advertising is valuable to chain stores, which can serve all of the readers in a circulation area.

The success of a newspaper message is dependent upon "reader traffic." The reader traffic for any particular ad may vary from one per cent to one hundred per cent of the circulation of the paper, depending on such things as the size and extent of price-copy, the headline, the layout, and the ability to compete with other ads.

To compute the cost of an advertisement on the basis of reader traffic, one must consult local newspaper advertising men. A vertical half-page ad may attain one hundred per cent readership, while a two-inch ad in the same edition might attract as little as one per cent readership. To obtain the cost of an ad per one thousand readers, the cost of the ad is divided by the number of readers. Thus, for a paper whose circulation is 50,000, an ad which provides fifty per cent readership will be exposed to 25,000 readers. If the ad cost two hundred dollars, the cost per thousand readers is two hundred divided by twenty-five, or eight dollars per thousand.

The primary disadvantages of newspaper advertising are inefficiency for the small businessman, unless he is using a neighborhood paper; the high cost of obtaining national coverage for large companies and franchises, and the unreliable reproduction quality, particularly for color advertisements.

Magazines. Magazines share many of the characteristics of newspapers, including a range of editorial policies with which to associate one's message and the ability to reach particular market segments. Magazine advertisement provides many additional advantages however. National circulation is generally available in several types of magazine, and national campaigns can be carried out at very low costs; reproduction quality is very good, especially for color ads; and individual copies last much longer than newspaper copies, providing a pass-on readership above and beyond the actual circulation numbers.

The primary limitations of this kind of advertising are the expense involved in preparing layouts, the low readership among lower income groups, the lack of timeliness because of the long periods between issues, and the waste circulation for the local entrepreneur whose products are available within small trading radius.

Weekend magazines usually also offer national coverage and are read by a larger percentage of the public than most other magazines, although there is a low readership among the upper socio-economic groups. They provide low production costs and good four-color reproduction. The number of readers per copy is high. However, there are the same disadvantages as those encountered with other magazines, plus the relatively short life of the individual copy and a lack of prestige.

Television. Television is the most recent development in the field of visual communication and is the only medium available which allows "live" demonstration of the use of a product. This advantage does carry some potential disadvantages, however, since the sophistication of the medium demands considerable showmanship.

The complete sponsor of a half-hour program will have three minutes for commercials, which can be varied between long commercials, short reminders, demonstrations, and live sales messages, and which can be allotted among several different product promotions.

However, much of the value of a program with which a sponsor wishes to be associated is lost if he must share the advertising slots with other sponsors. Alternate week sponsorship can also diminish the value of program sponsorship.

In the selection of television advertising time, many factors must be taken into consideration—the variation in audience with time of day and type of program, the difference in cost between prime evening time and daytime spots, and the percentage of the circulation which can be tapped by a local establishment. If the full coverage can be used, a daytime spot need not cost a great deal, but it is advisable for the neophyte to experiment with times of day and methods of presentation to find one that is most successful.

Many of the advantages of advertising on network programs can be obtained through non-network programs, and the costs and length of commitment are more flexible. There is often a greater opportunity to tailor costs and market segment to meet the sponsor's needs. The use of non-network time allows a much more locally oriented advertisement, including dealer tie-ins. However, unavailabilities of time slots may handicap the market penetration, and the program climate may be of minimum prestige.

The Sign Industry. The most ubiquitous type of communication in our urban environment is the sign. Advertising signs can be designed to introduce a product or service to a consumer who is not familiar with it, to reinforce existing knowledge, and to convince the potential customer of the worth of a product or of his need for it. Advertising signs can be broken down into two major categories:

(1) the on-premise sign, which is a notice of business transacted at a site; and

(2) outdoor advertising, which advertises goods, products or services available elsewhere.

The importance of the on-premise sign to the consumer is seldom appreciated. Particularly in our automobile-oriented society, a sign which identifies the nature of an establishment at a glance has become necessary for the convenience and safety of the motorist who seeks specific goods or services.

To the entrepreneur, the on-premise sign can provide the primary competitive advantages and may determine the success or failure of his establishment. The importance of the high-rise-on-premise sign to motels, service stations, and other retail outlets located on highways has been demonstrated (Patty and Vredenburg, 1970). An on-premise sign carrying a national logo can account for a significant percentage of the volume pumped by a service station outlet.

In addition to their function of providing identification, on-premise signs can provide information and direction and project a particular image to reach a particular segment of the market. Among their advantages are (1) that they are relatively inexpensive for the length of time they are in use, and (2) they will reach the potential customer who frequents the area or is most likely to stop. With the addition of increasingly popular readographs, the message can be continually updated with changes in goods and prices.

Outdoor advertising includes posters and bulletins, commonly known as "billboards", and large, illuminated signs called "spectaculars". Outdoor advertising has the following characteristics:

(1) it does not circulate its message to a market: rather, the market circulates around the message.

(2) Promotions must reach an audience which is moving toward a destination.

(3) impressions must be made quickly, it is estimated that the average exposure time for a passing motorist is six seconds.

(4) the message must register at a distance.

The cost of outdoor advertising is generally lower than that of any other advertising medium in terms of the cost per one thousand people exposed to the message. Outdoor advertising offers an opportunity for an impressive and unlimited use of color, and the size allows monumental effects which will be visible from a considerable distance. The message can be displayed for as little as one month, or as long as several years, if copy is periodically repainted or reposted. Valuable repetition is achieved by the number of times any particular person passes and sees the same display or other displays of the same showing, i.e., identical displays in other locations.

The outdoor sign is the oldest advertising medium and the only one that presents its message twenty-four hours a day. In a dynamic society such as ours, there are multitudes of products to market and people to be reached. Since few people are exposed to advertising during their working hours, and none during their sleeping hours, advertising must reach them during their leisure hours or during the time spent traveling to place of work, to shop, and for recreation.

Outdoor advertising serves this function admirably, at a time when no other advertising reaches the potential consumer, outdoor advertising does. It is seen by the pedestrian on urban streets and by the driver of an automobile on his way to and from work, shopping, and recreation. It is particularly valuable as a base of and a reinforcement for, advertising seen or heard on radio or television or in the newspaper. It may also reach the customer who missed ads presented through the other communications media because of their time limitations.

One soft-drink manufacturer, when asked why he used outdoor advertising almost exclusively during the summer months, replied. "Man, you must be kidding! I use outdoor because some days are hotter than others. Those days the demand for cooling drinks peaks . . . I don't want our stuff to be forgotten then. And it won't be. On outdoor we're up there every day. You can't miss the hot days . . . (Outdoor Advertising Association of America, 1966, p. 33)."

Opponents of the System

The second source of conflict is that group of people who are primarily opposed to the current economic system. There are a large number of such people who are opposed in philosophy to the whole idea of advertising and the commercial system from which it springs. It is interesting that much of this philosophy stems from the university system where there is so much propaganda circulating regarding the value of an education to improve the individual. It is the products of this system who will attack commercial advertising as propaganda. The philosophical base from which they operate is that advertising conditions people to buy. In Erich Fromm's book, *The Sane Society* (1955), is one of the most articulate spokesman for the academic/noncommercial viewpoints. We would point out that if the public is being manipulated through the media is a chicken and egg question. Television violence is one case of this. When there was some concrete indication that television was encouraging violence, immediate limitations were put on it.

The point is that such people will take anything you say as positive proof that they are right. During the Morrow Commission hearings on pricing policies among British Columbia oil companies, the major companies all opened up their books to the commission for inspection. There was one particular expert who had been brought in to investigate the books, and after spending a great deal of time and public money, he fell back on a statement to the effect that he couldn't find anything wrong with the books, and that made him all the more suspicious. It was obvious to him that "they" were so clever that they were able to hide everything from the public. Although this may seem unlikely, the fact is that a great deal of the time such reasoning is used as proof positive of collusion to dupe the public into buying something. This is generally little more than an indication that the person doing the complaining does not like what other people are doing.

In the long run, this is probably the easiest faction to deal with, because where they have temporarily won the day, in time such a severe reaction occurs against them that they will usually lose entirely. But this group has been responsible for a great deal of anti-advertising legislation and misstatements about the industry.

The Uninformed

The third group of people who come into conflict with the sign industry are those who are misinformed or uninformed about the aspects of quality which can be built into signs to improve the visual environment. Often these people tend to oppose the medium itself, when their complaints actually have to do with correctable or illegal uses of the medium.

It is not unusual to find sign manufacturers debating among themselves regarding what segment of the sign industry has caused the most visual pollution. This is an example of two segments of the industry arguing about quality. They are not opposing the medium itself. This is obviously very different from being opposed to advertising or signs in general. Many of the sign companies can point out ways that the quality of signs can be improved. This is akin to an artist going to an art gallery and pointing out weak aspects in the work of other artists and suggesting improvements. It is based on information about what constitutes quality. Those who are uninformed or ignorant of these components of quality and yet advocate abolition are like the neophyte who objects to certain schools of art or certain artists and therefore demands that no art should be displayed because of its "low quality". As for the fact that signs infringe on the public space, we are sure that most of the people who complain about signs would not seek to prevent the sidewalk or park displays of artwork by individual artists which lend interest to our urban scene, although many artists would seriously question the right of many of these displays to claim the title "art." We believe that most people are intelligent enough to recognize the general trends of our society and to seek improvements in quality without limiting individual expression, communication, or advertising unless there are very good reasons for doing so. It is up to the industry to point out to the public that their complaints are based on particular aspects of signs and are not necessarily against signs themselves. This is an educational function that the industry should take seriously.

References for Chapter 6

Fromm, E. *The Sane Society*. New York: Holt, Rinehart and Winston, 1955.

Outdoor Advertising Association. *Outdoor Advertising in Canada: The modern marketing force*. Toronto: Author, 1966.

Patty, C.R. & Vredenburg, H. L. *Electric signs: Contribution to the Communications Spectrum*. Colorado: Rohm & Haas Company, 1970.

Chapter 7/Legal Aspects Of
Sign Legislation

In this chapter, we have selected examples of rulings which we feel reflect the current legislative atmosphere and trends in North America regarding signs. We have used examples from both Canadian and U.S. law because the two systems are closely enough related that the implications of many of their rulings are similar.

Many contradictory cases and rulings can be found throughout the literature. It is often felt that a legal decision in one court is thereafter the law. This is not necessarily so. The law is general, while court rulings are specific to one case. Thus cases can be found which contradict the majority of rulings on the same subject. There are actually cases on record where a billboard has been ordered removed by the court because immoral activities were taking place behind it.

In our court system there are basically three kinds of courts: the primary court, the appellate courts and the supreme courts, both at the state or provincial level and the federal level. One first seeks a decision from the primary court. Then either the plaintiff or the defendant can appeal that decision in an appellate court. It can then be appealed to the supreme court. Generally only when a decision is handed down by a supreme court have the legal remedies been exhausted.

In business schools and clinical psychology, as well as in the legal system, one case is often the basis for generalizations about a particular subject. However, their data is not systematically compiled from an aggregate of data sources and a ruling will apply only to those cases which have similar or nearly similar circumstances. Thus one must ask whether a decision applied to a case in which similar circumstances existed to those in question and secondly, whether the decision was upheld by appellate and/or supreme court rulings.

In the behavioral sciences two kinds of definition of words, concepts, or constructs are recognized: operational definitions and constitutive definitions. An operational definition is based on behavior. Thus intelligence can be defined according to performance on an intelligence test. Here it is an operational definition. A constitutive definition is based on other words, concepts, or constructs. A dictionary definition is a constitutive definition. One seeks to describe what *constitutes* a particular word, concept, or construct.

All legal definitions are basically constitutive. They are based on exhaustive combinations of words defining the situation, the rationale, etc. One must therefore be very careful not to get into semantic difficulties in applying court cases and generalizing from them. Furthermore words, concepts, and constructs change over time with the social climate.

Thus, one must ensure that any decision to be applicable to any situation (1) treats the same problem, (2) is the decision of a higher court, and (3) is a recent decision.

We will begin with a discussion of eminent domain and police powers, and the implications of their increasing interchangeability. We will then treat the subject of zoning as a manifestation of the police power, the rights of the municipal government when it comes to structural and design regulation, and the question of compensation.

Police Powers vs. Eminent Domain

Even as recently as five years ago, it was still possible to draw a clear distinction between eminent domain and the police powers. They are being used increasingly by municipal governments to supplement one another and the distinction between the two has become more and more difficult to define.

Under eminent domain proceedings, there must be compensation through due process of law. However, some time before expropriation under eminent domain, a municipality may hold the zoning (a police power) at a particular stage or even change the zoning so that the value of the property at the time of expropriation is minimal. As has been pointed out by Todd: "The courts have held that the exercise of police power by a governmental entity is a non-compensatable act (1970, p. 49)."

In order to clearly understand how these two legal functions are being used and even misused by many municipalites, it is necessary to distinguish between them. We will present here the views of several authors on this distinction.

According to Crouch ". . . there is a distinction between the power of eminent domain, which is assumed to be concurrent with an obligation to compensate, and the police power, which is assumed to represent (along with the power of taxation) the power of government to impose injury upon property without payment of compensation (1961, p. 4)."

However, Orgel rejects this definition on the grounds that "it fails to suggest what acts will be regarded as coming under the police power and what acts as coming under the power of eminent domain (1953, p. 8)."

A more useful distinction may be the following: "Under the police power of the state, the public welfare is enhanced by the regarding and restricting of the use of private property; whereas in eminent domain, the private property is taken or acquired by the state to promote the public welfare by putting the property to a particular use. (Jahr, 1953, p. 8)."

The same criterion is used by Palmer (1961, p. 27) and by Laurence (1967, pp. 20-24). But even this becomes confused when it is considered that a public utility may merely take the right to use an easement across property and restrictions will be imposed, but the property is not taken over.

This distinction depends on a definition of public use. First, expropriation of land for a private use, even with compensation, would not be allowed. Secondly, the ultimate decision as to whether a use is public or private is a judicial one, not a legislative one. Thirdly, no attempt has been made by the courts to define a public use permanently and finally because what is recognized as a legitimate public use is constantly changing. The uses which are generally deemed to be acceptable occasions for the use of eminent domain have been outlined by Jahr (1953, pp. 22-25).

In recent years some uses have come under eminent domain which a few years ago would have seemed an excessive use of that legal power. Many new uses may be expected to fall into this category in the future.

The selection of the property to fulfill this public use lies with the condemnor and, as Jahr has pointed out, "The only ground that may exist for court interference in the case of the selection of the site is where the condemnor, under the delegated power, does not act in good faith and his action is indicated to be capricious and injurious, or beyond the privilege conferred by the statute (1953, p. 51)."

The rationale behind the refusal of compensation under police powers is that, if a zoning change in a community benefits a property owner, he does not have to pay the city for this privilege. Likewise, if he loses value under such a change, the city does not have to pay him. However, the police powers can only be used to manipulate the land use or safety features of a site, and where the courts have found manipulation of land use by the municipality to be purely arbitrary, they have generally overturned the legislation.

Thus, eminent domain and the police power are different

in scope and intent. The police power must be based on the rule of reason for the public welfare and is applied over the long run, while eminent domain is the short term application of a legal power to acquire property for public use. The use of police power does not change the private nature of property, while the use of eminent domain converts it from private to public property. Recently it has not been uncommon to find that cities will use the police power to hold a sector of the city (particularly along highways) at a particular level, refusing to allow it to evolve to its highest and best use. They then can expropriate the property at its artificially low value.

The Police Powers

Control of the landscape can be achieved in many ways. It may come about by control by the financial intermediaries and the building codes. In small communities, it may come about by the tacit consent of the citizens and by the social ostracism of those who do not conform to accepted standards. Landscape formation was once controlled by deed restrictions. Deeds to property contained certain constraints, and such devices were once commonly used to keep certain areas of the city segregated from minority groups. This power of discrimination has been overturned by the Supreme Court in the U.S.

The most commonly used form of control today is the police powers of zoning, licensing and taxation. These all stem from governmental powers and are enforced through legislative acts. The extent of the police powers has been dealt with by the courts:

"The police power is a necessary one, inhering in every sovereignty for the preservation of the public safety, the public health, and the public morals. It is of vast and undefined extent, expanding and enlarging in the multiplicity of its activities as exigencies demanding its services arise in the development of our complex civilization. It is a function of the government solely within the domain of the legislature to declare when this power shall be brought into operation for the protection or advancement of the public welfare." (Motlow vs. State. 125 Tennessee 547: 145 S.W. 177.)

We will deal briefly here with licensing and extensively with zoning because zoning is the most used and misused of these police powers.

Definition of Statute or Ordinance

First, however, we would like to clarify what we mean

by an ordinance or bylaw. These terms are usually synonymous with statute when referring to municipal legislation. We have used these terms interchangeably throughout this presentation, but the term ordinance has the wider usage. An ordinance or bylaw is legislation by some authority using statutory powers ordering that an act be carried out, not be carried out, or be desisted from, subject to the penalty or penalties for non-observance of the directions of the legislation. The full force of the law can be brought to bear upon anyone who does not comply with the conditions set forth. The power that is brought to bear is entrusted to the municipality with its powers of legislation and constitutes a branch of the civil government of the state or province in which the municipality is located. The municipalities or cities have the power to write legislation in the areas that are covered by the legislative powers handed down to them by the superior state (U.S.) or federal government.

Licensing and Permits

Originally licensing was employed as a source of revenue for the city, but eventually it came to be used as a means of regulating business. "Attempts to prohibit business activities in the guise of regulation were struck down by the courts as being *ultra vires.* Today, however, in most jurisdictions the municipality is expressly authorized to prohibit as well as to regulate . . . (Todd, 1970, p. 23).

The emphasis in issuing permits for buildings should be purely structural. The criterion is generally one of public safety; in other words, the city seeks to ensure that a structure will be safe for the general public's use. It is interesting to note that in some cases the city has the power to refuse a permit to rebuild a previously existing facility in the interests of public safety. In one community, it was ruled that the municipal government could withhold permission to rebuild a structure that had been destroyed by dynamite for fear it might be dynamited again, endangering lives.

The primary distinction that should be made here is that licensing is concerned with the structural safety of a building. The form of land use is controlled by zoning ordinances and cannot come under this police power. Finally the structure or design of a building cannot be regulated purely for aesthetic purposes under this power.

Zoning

Zoning bylaws are a means of legal control of the use of urban land by the municipal government. Zoning control of land use is not ubiquitous across North America. Until recently, two large cities in the south were well-known for having no zoning control. The only control that was manifested was generally over type of building and was exercised by the financial intermediaries in the form of building codes. There was no control over type of land use or the area in which it was located. Interestingly the structure of these cities is not radically different from that found in cities where very rigorous planning is enforced through zoning. Without some kind of controlled experiment, the possibility cannot be discounted that this similarity occurred by chance. However, it does indicate that control by the municipal government is not necessary to prevent chaos. Effective control of structure and land use can be exercised by lending institutions and private developers.

Zoning was in effect as far back as the 1800s in Europe. Napolean III was a leader in the field of zoning, and the concept had become accepted in Germany in this same period. In the mid-1860s zoning was used in California to prevent indiscriminate location of slaughterhouses. However, in general it was slowly accepted in the United States because of the tendency of the courts to preserve and protect the individual rights in the use of property from arbitrary control there of municipalities (Yokley, 1965, p. 6). Even today this reluctance prevails. "To be a valid exercise of police powers, a regulation must be general in application and not a meddlesome interference with private affairs of an individual. It must have some real purpose and bear a direct relationship to enhancement of public welfare (Roby, 1967, p. 508)." The courts have been most amenable to the use of zoning powers to protect property rights of other members of the community.

The first comprehensive zoning ordinance was passed in the U.S. in New York in 1916. Within five years, 76 other communities were zoned. By 1930, the U.S. Department of Commerce reported that well over 700 communities were zoned. An early case was Village of Euclid, Ohio vs. Ambler Realty Company (272 U.S. 365. 1926), where the court ruled that the municipality had the right to channel encroaching industry from the nearby city of Cleveland to certain areas, even though by doing so, it was preventing expected increases in land value in the future.

The basis of most zoning legislation in the United States and certainly an influence in much of Canadian legislation is the 1924 Standard Zoning Enabling Act of the U.S. Department of Commerce. Zoning can be generally defined as the division of cities, towns, or municipalities into districts with respect to (1) the height and size or bulk of structures, (2) the area of the lot which can be occupied by permanent structures, including the setback requirements, (3) the density of human occupancy which will be tolerated, and (4) the type of trade industry or residence allowed.

Zoning powers are generally used for (1) economic reasons, (2) control of land use or social amenities in an area, or (3) protection of public safety. However, as pointed out in the case of the City of Chicago vs. Sachs et al. 115 N.E. 2d 762: "Cities have the power, through proper zoning ordinances, to impose reasonable restraints upon the use of private property, but in exercising such power, they must employ classifications which bear a substantial relationship to the public health, safety, or welfare." Whether all of the reasons given for granting police powers fall into this category of public health, safety or welfare is questionable. We will deal with each of these reasons briefly.

Economic Reasons

Often stagnant areas of a city are rezoned by the municipal government in order to promote the highest and best use of the land. In the past, attempts were made to seize such land under eminent domain for urban renewal proceedings. However, it is becoming more common now for cities to rezone such areas and to allow the normal functioning of the marketplace economy to establish their most desirable use.

Zoning has been said to play a part in stabilizing land values, and this is probably true to the extent that taxation of property is definitely affected by the permitted use.

Public Safety and Welfare

Although in the past public safety has been one area in which the need for police powers is not disputed, the courts hesitate to extend this area of control any farther into the realm of the planner because of the difficulty of establishing proof of danger to the public welfare. As was pointed out in the case of Hitchman et al. vs. Oakland TP et al. (45 N.W. 2d 306), "Whether provisions of zoning ordinances are reasonable must be determined from the facts of the particular case." Many of the recommendations made by planners have been based on little more than educated guessing or personal opinion, and one of the most noticeable changes in our society in the past few years has been the recognition that *a priori* reasoning and common knowledge cannot be relied upon as justifications for limiting private rights. Neither the planner nor the architect is trained in techniques of hypothesis testing or problem-solving, or even in decision-making, in his formal academic curriculum. Much as the lawyer, who is expected to understand existing case law, how the law has been justified, and the facts leading up to particular decisions, the planner is not expected to generate original research. The original research carried out in our universities has primarily come from the natural sciences, and increasingly from biology, psychology, and the recently emerging behavioral sciences. The courts have begun to recognize that common knowledge, or testimony by supposed experts who lack empirically based research, is not sufficient to justify the use of police powers in the name of public safety or welfare.

One can find throughout the case law minority cases that take positions alien to this. That is in the nature of the advocate system. But the use of police powers is increasingly being granted only where convincing evidence has been established by credible research studies.

Traffic Hazards: One of the charges that the planner and the architect have made in their efforts to extend design control or planning control has been that certain design or land use types cause accidents. In most cases, where such charges have been made and have been followed up by well-funded research studies, this argument has proven to be unfounded. It has been established, for instance, that signs are seldom, if ever, responsible for increases in traffic accident rates if properly placed in regard to traffic control devices. Some of the studies carried out have even suggested that there may be benefits to traffic safety from some signs. Proper research studies in this area have only begun to emerge within the last 15 years.

Spot Zoning. It has been fairly common among some municipalities in North America to require a special zoning for one particular commercial land use, so that a change in zoning is required for every site that is built for this purpose. How this can be done depends primarily on the charter under which the city is operating. In some provinces and states, the municipal charters specifically state the conditions under which a municiality can zone. It is common for charters to allow land use zones to be created, and to require that land use in those zones must be so provided for in the ordinance. Where one finds a particular retail use, such as fast food or gasoline retailing, coming under special restrictions or spot zoning, it is generally held by the courts that a clear-cut public nuisance must exist or that public safety must be endangered by such retailing. These have been the primary rationales used to counter the claim that such restrictions are discriminatory to one industry. Unless such arguments can be made, the actual right to restrict individual industries or retail uses would be denied. Such controls have usually been extended under the rationale of public safety, and many court rulings have gone so far as to require this.

Evidenciary Proof. If it can be demonstrated that a particular legislative act will favor one sector of the economy over another, such legislation has generally been avoided by municipal governments unless some evidence can be presented that a danger to public health, welfare, or morals exists. When such legislation is taken before the courts, proof of a hazard must be substantial before such discriminatory legislation is allowed.

Evidenciary proof for such claims, or research that can establish beyond a doubt that public safety has been endangered, is only now coming to light. As more research is being completed, it is becoming the basis for many rulings. When one is researching case law for examples of a particular ruling, he should not look solely for the nature of the decision, he should also consider the actual evidence on which the decision has been based. If public safety has been cited as the reason for a decision, and a later case presents well-founded evidence that public safety is not endangered, the courts will not hesitate to set aside an earlier decision which was based on subsequently refuted evidence. This is particularly critical, because much of the municipal law that is currently in existence has been established on flimsy evidenciary proof.

Thus even though an ordinance is passed on the basis of public safety, and is upheld by a court of law, this doesn't mean that the case will stand good if the case itself creates the evidence. The general rule is that a statement of evidence by a court doesn't make the evidence more credible.

Control of Design vs. Land Use Control

The control of the design or appearance of a structure and the control of land use within particular zones may not appear to be radically different forms of control. However, control of design has had a mixed reception in the courts because the fine points of design or structure inevitably come down to a question of taste.

The police power, however, is based upon public necessity. There must be an essential public need for the exercise of the power in order to justify its use. This is the reason why merely aesthetic considerations cannot justify the use of the police power . . . It is commendable and desirable, but not essential to the public need, that our aesthetic desires be gratified. Moreover, authorities in general agree as to the essentials of a public health program, while the public view as to what is necessary for aesthetic progress greatly varies. Certain legislatures might consider that it was more important to cultivate a taste for jazz than for Beethoven, for posters than for Rembrandt, and for limericks than for Keats. Successive city councils might never agree as to what the public needs from an aesthetic standpoint, and this fact makes the aesthetic standard impractical as a standard for use restriction upon property. The world would be a continual seesaw if aesthetic considerations were permitted to govern the use of a police power (Youngstown vs. Kahn Brothers Building Company, 112 O.S. 654).

In other words, aesthetics are (1) almost entirely dependent upon subjective viewpoints, and (2) almost totally ephemeral.

As pointed out in Hitchman et al. vs. Oakland TP et al., "Aesthetics may be an incident, but cannot be the moving factor in determining validity of zoning regulations (45 N.W. 2d 306)." Many courts have gone farther than merely limiting this and have disallowed any indiscreet use of the police power for aesthetics.

Two arguments which have been used by planners to justify aesthetic control are invasion of privacy and public nuisance. It is fairly clear that it is an overextension of these legal terms to apply them to signs. One must always be aware of what the law is and determine what cases have been used as a basis for such claims. Often these claims are groundless.

In the case of the Corporation of the City of Toronto and F.E. Wellwood vs. Outdoor Neon Displays Ltd., the court cites the reason why a high degree of discretionary power cannot be delegated to a municipal official. In the realm of aesthetics, decisions can only 'be based on individual judgment or the cultural standards of a particular time (146305 Series C—The Supreme Court of Canada). Because such discretionary power could easily lead to the corruption of a municipal official's power, the courts have been loathe to grant this discretionary power to the planner. The power to control the use of private property is seldom arbitrarily delegated to municipal officials.

Even those most antagonistic to signs admit that in order to introduce aesthetics as a basis of control, a reasonable use of the word "aesthetic" and its meaning to the entire community must be considered: "Ordinances based on police power . . . must be based on some reasonably supported objective if they are to win judicial approval (Ewald and Mandelker, 1971, p. 109)." With the large numbers of groups and individuals seeking to control the design elements of signs today, there is little reason to suppose that such control can be objective.

Regulation of historic sites in a city has been undertaken to maintain the quality of an area and this is certainly commendable if the majority of the community wishes to do so. This can be seen as a social amenity function to preserve the nature of the area, and there is no need to use the term aesthetics in this connection.

The control of land use within zones, however, is much more rigorously applied. People are entitled to expect certain reasonable uses within a property zone or land use area and not to have their own rights infringed upon. The courts have treated zoning as protection of a property right. The difference between this and arbitrarily controlling one site or type of site differently within a zone cannot be overstated. The latter has generally not been tolerated by the courts. They have taken the position that zoning must be uniformly applied to all sites within a zone. While it does not directly control the design of a building or the materials used except in the fire or building codes, where public safety is involved, zoning does limit the type of activity that can be carried out within the zone. Thus when one acquires property rights in a zone he can expect the zoning to be consistent.

Recently, however, such social amenity regulations have come under attack where they have been carried to extremes which amount to social or racial discrimination. It should be noted that this tendency toward sector zoning is not looked upon favorably in other countries. In France, for instance, industrial, commercial, and residential zones are often intermixed. In the United States throughout the 1950s the Housing and Urban Development Commission attempted to introject low income housing into higher income, single-family detached housing areas in the hope that the social contact would be beneficial to the low income groups.

The most rigorous control of structure or design is generally based on fire and safety considerations. When a building does not meet standards which will ensure the public safety, the courts have never hesitated to act immediately in enforcing the building codes, but this is very different from a zoning act and the two should not be confused.

The Right to Use Property in a Reasonable Manner

Certainly it is logical to allow control of advertising, information, or direction functions in a residential zone under the heading of social amenity factors. This is quite different from attempting to control normal and expected use of one's own property in a commercial zone for commercial activities. Under the general heading of zoning, the courts have recognized that there is a visual component of the property right in commercial and retail areas. In United Advertising Corp. vs. The Borough of Raritan (93 A. 2d 262), the courts held that: "The business sign is an actual part of the business itself, just as the structure housing the business is a part of it, and the authority to conduct the business in a district carries with it the right to maintain a business sign on the premises subject to reasonable regulations in that regard as in the case of this ordinance. Plaintiff's placements of its advertising signs, on the other hand, are made pursuant to the conduct of the business of outdoor advertising itself, and in effect what the ordinance provides is that this business shall not to that extent be allowed in the Borough. It has long been settled that the unique nature of outdoor advertising and the nuisances fostered by billboards and similar outdoor structures located by persons in the business of outdoor advertising, justify the separate classification of such structures for the purpose of governmental regulation and restriction." In this area, again, the courts have been slow to allow over-rigorous control by the planner. This quote also implies the necessity of providing concrete evidence of danger to public safety or welfare. In Kelbro, Inc. vs. Myrick (113 Vt. 64, 30A 2d 527) they went further in establishing the right of on-premise: "Plaintiff, an outdoor advertising company, filed its bill in equity to enjoin defendant Secretary of State from removing its signs which violated the statutory requirements. The Vermont statute prohibited non-point-of-sale signs within 300 feet of a highway intersection or within 240 feet from the center of the highway. The court stated that a public highway is a servient tenement while the adjacent private property is a dominant tenement. The dominant tenement has an easement of view over the servient tenement but like any easement of view must be connected with the enjoyment of the dominant tenement. It was then stated that point-of-sale signs are so connected but that non-point-of-sale signs are not. Since use of non-point-of-sale signs was not protected, the state could abolish the easement of view as to such signs. The court, in sustaining the validity of the statute, held that the distinction between point-of-sale and non-point-of-sale signs reflected a valid legislative classification." (See also Metromedia Inc. vs. City of Pasadena [216C. A. 270, 30 Cal. Rptr. 731])

When property use rights in commercial zones have been taken away or limited by the courts, compensation has been clearly established, not only for value of buildings and fixtures, but also for any costs of moving. Although the bulk of these cases to date in North America have dealt with outdoor advertising, it would seem that the same rationale should apply to the first party on-premise or free-standing sign that serves broad identification or advertising purposes for the owner of a site.

On the other hand, when one begins to seek detailed structural control in a zone largely because of cultural tastes, it will be difficult, if not impossible, to prove that one architectural form or design is preferred over another because of the intrinsic characteristics of the human eye. The courts will generally avoid any control which they see as an invasion of the right of self-expression through color or design on one's own property. Part of the reason is the difficulty of establishing concrete evidence for the desirability of a particular form.

We are now only beginning to fully realize the importance to our society of the use of colors, graphics, and form and design in conveying attitudes or images for a business venture or a commercial office building. Because the average planner has had little training in areas that deal with these factors—the behavioral sciences, particularly psychology or psychiatry, and neurology—the courts have been loathe to turn control over to the city for fear that the results will not be based on facts that have any statistical significance or could be replicated.

Functional Obsolescence. There are two types of deterioration of real property. One is physical deterioration; the other is obsolescence. The latter, in turn, can be broken down into social obsolescence and functional obsolescence. When one builds a home in a good residential neighborhood and the area surrounding the property changes in character due to zoning or normal social processes, the property has undergone social obsolescence. This involves changes outside of the property itself. Functional obsolescence, on the other hand, occurs because of the design of a structure. Anyone interested in the effects of longitudinal shifts in taste, or changes over time, should investigate the large amount of literature available on functional obsolescence. (See appraisal literature on functional obsolescence.)

Spatial Monopoly and Indirect Taxation Through the Use of Police Powers

Most urban residents do not realize that as municipal

control of retailing becomes more restrictive, and as densities increase, the cost to the consumer will go up. Thus, the city is often imposing indirect taxation on the consumer by making the land more expensive for the retailer and by creating a spatial monopoly so that the consumer is forced to pay the inflated prices or go far out of his way. The distance that a customer will travel to shop varies with the type of business, but trade areas can generally be clearly defined, and within a trade area, the customer will often find it expedient to pay a higher price rather than travel out of the trade areas to shop.

In a study of service stations in Vancouver, British Columbia (Claus & Hardwick, 1972), it was found that as the population densities increased and the oil companies were prevented by municipal legislation from building larger stations which would have helped to hold down their costs prices increased. If a municipal government freezes the number of service stations in an area, either directly through an ordinance or indirectly through spot zoning, a spatial monopoly results and the operators in the area may respond by raising prices. One oil company was forced to buy out a dealer in Vancouver in order to hold the price down because the dealer found that he could raise the price 2 to 4 cents a gallon and that any drop in gallonage would be more than compensated by the markup.

Any municipality has the right to pass such legislation. However, many councilmen will be defeated at the polls when the consumer becomes annoyed with the expense and inconvenience caused by these controls.

Municipal controls definitely affect the strategies that are used by retailers. For instance, in Halifax a city ordinance was passed which prevented any gasoline outlet, except parking garages, from remaining open 24 hours a day. The result, of course, was a proliferation of parking garages in particular locations where there was high demand for 24-hour service.

If a municipal council wishes to improve the quality of the visual environment, there are many ways to do so. For instance, if gasoline retailing is allowed to expand freely, the natural result will be a decrease in numbers of outlets in favor of a few large, high-quality stations. By imposing over-rigorous zoning controls, the city is forcing the fixed costs of the operation up and thus is forcing the price to the consumer to go up. If a city wishes to encourage rational land use, it must also allow a certain amount of flexibility in its controls. Often certain market strategies, such as car washes, can best serve the needs of both the city and the operator. The economics of automobile-oriented retailing are too complicated to be dealt with here, but they are treated extensively by Claus and Hardwick (1972).

Compensation

In some cases, the use of police powers curtail the right of an individual to use his property in the manner in which he intended when the property was purchased. In such cases, unless there is a very clear reason for limiting the private rights of the individual, compensation proceedings under eminent domain are preferable. As Senator Edmund Muskie stated concerning the 1965 attempt to control billboards and junkyards:

"Whenever an individual suffers loss because of some broad public benefit or broad public interest, . . . the public interest also requires that that loss be compensated . . . If we can't sustain that kind of concept in the public interest, then . . . the public interest ought to be reviewed (Todd, 1967, p. 130)."

The Fifth Amendment to the United States Constitution requires just compensation and the Fourteenth Amendment establishes due process of law to enforce this. The value used in compensation has been held to be the value as represented by the fair market price.

It has not been uncommon for the courts to rule that compensation is due when a municipality wishes to phase out a particular kind of business and bring in another, if there is a loss in value to the people who located in that particular land use zone in good faith and then have been forced to move or close down. The landowner files an action in inverse condemnation. Furthermore if the right to use property in a particular way is taken away from the owner or tenant, compensation must be made.

This has been most thoroughly established by the outdoor advertising cases following the 1965 Beautification Act, where compensation is actually part of the Act. That outdoor advertising attaches a real income value to the property is borne out by the law. Outdoor advertising differs from on-premise advertising in that it is usually third-party advertising, but it similarly carries a very high economic value to the user. Because of this, the courts have deemed that even the costs of moving a sign must be compensated by the legislative body sponsoring the act.

The question that then arises is one of value. The rulings in this area since the 1960s have generally not involved value to the user, but value in fair market sense.* Thus in some situations, the value to the user may be much greater than the value of the property on the open market to someone who is not similar to the user. The right to use one's property in a particular manner may be of more value than ownership of the property. In an urban environment, where zoning can contribute really to the income or value of a property, if the income functions are taken away, value is lost. In some cases, a drop in zoning may have the same effect as condemnation proceedings under eminent domain. Where this question can become particularly difficult is where there is a mixed residential area with apartments and single family dwellings, where the land value increases sufficiently because of the living densities to offset the decrease from commercial property.

The trend toward broadening the concept of compensation where property has been in use was most noticeable during the condemnation proceedings brought about by urban renewal. To begin with value was interpreted in a very narrow sense, but lately the courts have begun to recognize the true value to the user and have attempted to establish this value in a more rigorous way. A number of legal articles from Canadian and U.S. law demonstrate this change. Because of these changes and some of the subsequent alterations that have occurred within our society, it appears that the format for compensation will be seriously altered over the next two years.

Compensation for On-Premise Signs

The Federal Government has no legal right to regulate on-premise signs. But indirectly the Federal Government can control them by granting a bonus to cooperating cities or states by withholding Federal funds from those who refuse to follow the Federal Guidelines. The important question to be considered, if such a legislative situation occurs, is that of methods of determining compensation. There must be compensation in order that there be no discrimination from the control now exercised under the 1965 Federal Beautification Act: "However, once a compliance law is enacted in a given state, with a provision for compensation of sign owners and landowners upon removal of signs from the areas adjacent to the Interstate and Federal-aid highway systems, it will become almost impossible to justify future state police power legislation requiring removal without compensation of outdoor advertising signs along secondary and

---

*The Canadian courts have been more liberal and, in some cases, are considering value to the user.

other state and local highways. Indeed, it will become almost impossible to justify future municipal zoning regulations that require removal of signs along city streets without compensation, inasmuch as the compensation requirement in the state's compliance law will apply to all city streets that are Federal-aid primary highways. It is difficult to find any reasonable basis for unequal treatment of land that appears to be similarly situated." (Cunningham, p. 46-47, 1971).

But the question that must be considered if such a privilege is granted is that of methods of determining compensation. The value that is added to some sites in some zones by an on-premise sign goes considerably beyond the compensation allowed for billboards by the 1965 Beautification Act. Income to the user attributable to the sign often far exceeds the cost of replacement of the sign. The limitation of this right to use property can have a very negative effect on the viability of the enterprise. For many automobile-oriented retail sites, as much as 50 per cent or more of their retail business is dependent on the on-premise sign. This is particularly true for major companies, the majority of whose customers are single-stop customers with a high degree of brand loyalty.

The value of third party or non-accessory advertising is particularly difficult to determine because the consumer is once removed and the benefit of a sign to the advertiser may be very high or merely minimal. There is no method of relating value to a typology of sites. A clever advertiser may easily double his business by using billboards, but it is difficult to determine when this will be true. An averaging technique for determining the value of such signs can therefore be justified.

But for on-premise signs, typologies of sites can be used to determine the degree of dependence on the sign. Part of the legal problem here has been that most of the accurate information available about signs has been carefully guarded by consultants and retailing firms because of the marketing advantage of knowledge of the kinds of signs that are suitable for various types of site, depending on the character and speed of the traffic, the type of customer, and the nature of goods or service sold.

Sign Appraisal
There is currently a widespread movement on the part of municipal governments to use the police powers and, in some cases, eminent domain proceedings to reform the urban landscape. In conjunction with this movement, the role of

the professional appraiser has become increasingly important. He has been called upon by the courts to determine just compensation when the city has gone so far as to take a valuable property right from an individual or a group of individuals.

It is evident that the rulings of the courts concerning compensation are becoming increasingly liberal. The courts seem to have recognized that, although there are certain proceedings in our cities to take away individual rights for the general good, if an individual is hurt in the process, there must be an attempt to make him whole.

Along this line, signs present perhaps the most complicated field for the appraiser. In dealing here with appraisal of signs, we have taken the broadest possible position. Although it is possible to find references to many cases where decisions have been favorable for the broadest point of view with regard to compensation, we will not discuss specific legal precedents. In such cases, the tenant, the landlord, and the sign company may all be compensated for lost profit. What we wish to do here is to point out some of the ways that income is generated to the site or value is added through the existence of the sign.

Typology of Signs

In our discussion of signs, we will break down the various types of signs into three broad categories: outdoor, highway, and on-premise. A more complete typology of signs can be found in Claus and Claus (1971). The outdoor sign industry consists of owner-operators that lease poster panels and bulletins which are standardized throughout North America. This presents a complicated area for appraisal, because one must consider the land owner, the owner and the lessor of the sign, and the user of the sign.

The non-standardized highway signs are typified by those signs directing the traveler to motels and restaurants, which are not located on the premises of those outlets. While the outdoor advertising industry constitutes third party advertising, the highway sign may belong to the hotel, motel, or retail outlet to which it refers, or it may be rented by them, in which case it is third party advertising.

The on-premise sign is located on the premises of the site for which it is serving a communication function. This is a first party sign. However, it may also be leased or rented from a sign company and not owned by the merchant. Some sign companies, particularly on the West Coast, will lease at least 90 per cent of their signs.

This book is concerned primarily with on-premise signs.

In considering this aspect of the industry, the appraiser will have to consider both the communications device itself and the right to use the visual component of the property.

The Parties Involved

A sign is one of the most complex of all personal or real property devices to appraise or to legislate. It is often difficult to ascertain whether it is personal or real property. In our modern courts, signs have been treated both as appurtenances and as fixtures. Even in cases where it appears clear that they were appurtenances to the land, they have been treated merely as fixtures by some courts. We feel that a very good case can be made that signs are an appurtenant easement that runs with the land. There is an excellent discussion in Cunningham (1971) of some of these technicalities in which the author distinguishes between license easement in gross and the easement appurtenant.

We feel that there are three parties which should be considered as entitled to compensation when the right to use on-premise signs is taken away. These are (1) the sign company, (2) the merchant or user of the sign, and (3) the landlord or owner of the property.

The Sign Company

If a sign company is leasing the sign, it should be fairly easy to calculate the compensation due according to the amount of time left in the current contract and the probability of renewal, less the costs it would have had to expend in maintenance. The amount of money yet to be collected on the contract is clearly measurable. The renewal value may be a little more complicated, however. Patterns for renewal vary widely. In some cases, renewal will not show up as such in the company records because the user has opted for a new and improved sign rather than renew the old one. The manufacturers of the new digital data signs and the time and temperature displays have had almost a 100 per cent renewal rate on their contracts. This is not a question to be taken lightly, because the renewal value of a sign is often greater to the company than the rental for the remaining months of the current contract.

In some cases, the courts have treated signs as merchandise which can be resold so that some of the cost of production can be recovered. In the past, this may have been the case. Many of the old neon signs were saved and some of the materials recovered for new signs. However, the cost of materials has decreased and the cost of labor has risen so steeply that today, particularly with the new plastic signs, it is often more expensive to recover the materials from an old sign than to use new ones.

When the renewal value and the remaining contract rental are calculated, the costs of maintenance and repair that would be expended by the sign company over the calculated life of the contract and renewals can then be subtracted from the value to give a realistic picture of the value of the sign to the company. Perhaps the outdoor advertising industry has established some way of calculating true losses of revenue, since it has had some substantial payments of damages for billboards.[1]

The User

There are many factors to be considered when calculating value lost to the user of the sign or the merchant. First of all, the loss depends on whether or not he will be allowed to replace the sign with another which will serve his purposes as well. If this is the case, then the sign can be treated as a fixture and its value calculated fairly easily.

It is more often the case that the right to use the visual component of the property in a particular manner is taken away. If a merchant is forced to take down a projecting or a freestanding sign and replace it with a facia sign which cannot be seen as well from the street, his business may be substantially damaged, particularly if he depends on a high percentage of impulse or one-stop customers for his business support. The extent of the damage may be difficult to ascertain unless it is a business such as a motel, service station, or fast-food outlet, for which there is a history of the percentage of people who are attracted to a site by such advertising (Patty and Vredenburg, 1970; Claus & Claus, 1971).

---

1. The following payment schedule for painted multiple-panel displays, or "rotates", has been approved by the California Highway Department, subject to the indicated adjustments:

PAYMENT SCHEDULE

	Height to Base of Advertising Panel	
	Under 30 Feet	30 Feet and Over
Single Face	$ 9,350	$11,800
Double Face	$13,900	$17,550

ADJUSTMENTS

Wood Structure
If the sign is constructed of wood, 10% is deducted from the scheduled amount.
Poster Panel Back-ups
For each standard 12-foot by 25-foot poster panel reverse facing, $1,067 is added if unilluminated or $1,170 if illuminated.
Painted Bulletin Back-ups
For painted bulletin reverse facings less than the standard size of the front facing, $7.75 per square foot is added.
Embellishments
No adjustments are made for embellishing features, special lighting effects, freestanding letters, or space extensions.

Even though using a projecting sign or a freestanding sign which projects over public domain is a privilege, the fact is that the privilege was extended when the user entered into that lease or invested in a particular site. His business may depend on the continuance of that right, and such factors must be considered by the city when that right is taken away.

An ideal way to calculate the value of the visual component of property might be to calculate what it would cost the merchant to get the same effective coverage of a trade area through any other advertising means, such as radio, television, magazines or newspapers (Claus & Claus, 1971). When the right to use signs is curtailed, the merchant should be compensated for the loss of this valuable communications means, because he will have to invest considerably more in other means of advertising in order to remain in business.

The Landlord

Recently the courts have begun to recognize that there is unity in property. That is, you cannot take part of a piece of property or part of the rights running with that property without affecting the whole. Cunningham (1971) has discussed this with regard to standardized signs. When a sign or the right to use a sign is taken from a piece of property, not only may the tenant find himself faced with failure of business, but the landlord or owner of the site may not be able to lease it to other tenants for the same rent. In order to arrive at compensation for this, one would have to do a market study of the business type before and after removal of a sign. This could be done for several sites and used as a standard for evaluation. There is also the question of whether or not the landlord could lease the property to dissimilar tenants who did not require the visual component of the property.

Approaches to Appraisal

There are three methods of appraisal that can be used for signs. The first is the market data, or sales approach; the second is the income approach, which is particularly applicable to leasing, and the third is the cost approach.

The market data or sales approach is very difficult to apply here because signs are unique and are designed for a particular use and context. It is almost impossible to calculate how much a particular on-premise sign would be worth to someone else because of its individuality.

The income approach is the most valuable approach

when dealing with on-premise signs particularly with rentals or leases. Considerable thought must be given to renewal value on such signs.

The cost approach is probably the best approach to use if the sign is owned by the tenant or the landlord. The cost less the depreciation should not be very difficult to calculate, although it is often misinterpreted when applied to signs. The physical depreciation of a sign is small because most signs are sold with a maintenance agreement. What presents the most difficulty is functional obsolescence. Many signs will be in virtually new condition at the end of two or three years, but the design tastes of society may have changed so much in that time that the sign is no longer as culturally or socially valuable as it originally was. This is where the primary problem in calculating value of signs lies.

None of these approaches, however, really deals with the loss of the property right to communicate. Here, as in the taking of an affirmative easement, one must determine not what the easement is worth, but the damages or loss of value to the owner's remaining property or estate.

As our rules of compensation have been changing, we are seeking an increasing trend toward awarding the tenant and the landlord for loss of easement. The actual question is whether this constitutes a change in zoning or the actual taking of property, because there is increasing concern as to whether compensation should be due when the change is merely one of a change in zoning through the police powers.

Summary

When people begin to discuss the city at any level, the real motivation or purpose of an ordinance or bylaw becomes clouded and at some points difficult to follow. But we do feel that it can be said that an ordinance is intended to codify, not create, a social process. One must beware of misinterpreting the public will. Most of the models of city land use patterns discussed earlier in this book were thought merely to be codifications of natural social processes. In fact the term "ecological models" was used to describe these theories. Yet they did not represent the natural urban evolution.

In our society, municipal officials are elected to respond to the needs of the people and we do not turn over the actual creation of ordinances to a planning elite. Ideally the elected representatives react to what the people want when they create a bylaw or ordinance. When legislators react to pressure from political pressure groups, they are not creating but are reacting to a social process. When a legislator mis-reads the will of the people and over-reacts by creating overly stringent controls, the elected officials will be turned out of office and/or the proposed ordinance or use of the police powers will be rejected.

It should be understood that codification of a process is entirely different in the political sense from creation of a process. As an example, in the early 1960s, the implied assumption that better housing would make better people resulted in slum renewal. This seemed to be the general will of the people. However, when the rationale for improving slum housing was proven to not be as beneficial as people had originally thought it would be, either to the people enforcing it, or to the people affected by it, people began to react to this and such books as *The Federal Bulldozer* were published condemning such action. As soon as the rationale for action was found to be spurious, it was abandoned. This kind of thinking is characteristic of our society and is reflected in the courts' attitudes towards ordinances. If the majority of the people wish to take away property or property rights for some reason, they can do so within the due process of the law, and they must provide real value through compensation to the individuals from whom they are taking it. On the other hand, where public safety is involved, it is deemed to be the right and duty of the public official to act quickly in order to alleviate the potential danger. When those rationales are confused and the evidence will not bear out the need for public safety, then there must be a reassessment of the reasons for acting.

For those who are interested in pursuing this subject further, we would recommend Cunningham's report for control of highway advertising signs (1971), particularly Chapter 4, which deals with value under eminent domain.

Anderson, M. *The Federal Bulldozer: A Critical Analysis of Urban Renewal, 1949-69.* Cambridge: MIT Press, 1967.

Claus, R. J. & Claus, K.E. *The Visual environment: Site, sign and bylaw.* Don Mills, Ontario: Collier-Macmillan, 1971.

Claus, R. J. & Hardwick, W.G. *The Mobile Consumer: Automobile-oriented retailing and site selection.* Don Mills, Ontario: Collier-Macmillan, 1972.

Crouch, W. H. *The Meaning of Just Compensation: Condemnation Appraisal Practice.* Chicago: American Institute of Real Estate Appraisers, Special Technical Committee, 1961.

Cunningham, R.A. *Control of Highway Advertising Signs: Some Legal Problems.* Washington: Highway Research Board, National Academy of Sciences/National Research Council, 1971. (National Cooperative Highway Research Program Report 119).

Ewald, W.R. and Mandelker, D. R. *Street Graphics.* Washington: American Society of Landscape Architects Foundation, 1971.

Jahr, A.D. *Law of Eminent Domain: Valuation and Procedure.* New York: Clarke-Bordman Co., 1953.

Lawrence, G. *Condemnation: Your Rights When Government Acquires Your Property.* Dobbs Ferry, N.Y.: Oceana Publications, 1967.

Orgel, L. *Valuation Under the Law of Eminent Domain.* 2d ed. Vol. I. Charlottesville, Va.: Michie Co., 1953.

Palmer, B.W. *Palmer's Manual of Condemnation Law.* St. Paul, Minn.: Mason Publications, 1961.

Roby, R. *Police Power in Aid of Condemnation: Appraisal Journal.* October 1967.

Todd, E.C.E. *The Mystique of Injurious Affection in The Law of Expropriation.* Vancouver: *University of British Columbia Law Review,* 1967.

Todd, E.C.E. *The Federal Expropriation Act: A Commentary.* Toronto: Best Printer, 1970.

Yokley, E.C. *Zoning Law and Practice Vol. I.* Charlottesville: Mitchie Co., 1965.

Chapter 8/Levels Of Participation In The Legislative Process

The Role of the Sign Industry

There are two primary areas in which participation by the industry in the creation of sign legislation is badly needed. One is the need for information and the other is the provision of attainable and clearly set goals. Each of these will be discussed briefly to demonstrate how the industry can participate in the decision-making process to its own as well as the public's advantage.

Information

No act can be better than the information available to the actor. If the industry wishes to participate in or evaluate a legislative act, the first thing that must be done is to develop the information input.

There is an amazing lack of information available about signs, not only among planners, but within the industry itself. Those who participate in sign formation have seldom gathered the existing books and articles together for evaluation. The sign producer, particularly the on-premise sector, often does not understand his own industry and he has seldom attempted to supply such information to the public decision-maker. The simple act of supplying a large bulk of information often can ensure that a decision will be oriented toward and beneficial to the industry rather than against it.

For a number of years, one of the major oil companies in Canada compiled a booklet stating the number of service stations, average gallonages, and future trends, and also stating what it was planning to do with the stations that it had built with regard to appearance and general network or policy strategies. While the company was sending out this material to city governments, negative legislation dealing with its activities was minimal. Three years after this practice was discontinued, several bylaws were passed attempting to obtain precisely the results that the companies were seeking to achieve—that is, larger and fewer stations —yet the bylaws were structured in such a way as to almost thwart this common goal. They discovered that in each such case, there was a motivation, but no information to act upon and little if any knowledge of how to obtain such information that was available. If the sign industry does not prepare such information for inputs, it can not participate in the decision-making act.

Education. Education of the public to sign quality is critical to improvement of the visual environment. Legislation can only reflect the general community knowledge of sign quality and cannot create a standard which is not based on public consensus. As people understand and can afford a higher quality environment with an improvement in their standard of living, they will usually make the commitment necessary to obtain better quality. Although this may seem to be an overgeneralization, to us it points out the central problem in attempts at legislative control to improve our environment at various governmental levels. Any judicial or legislative act is based on words, concepts or constructs, and until most citizens understand the concepts and constructs involved, little improvement can be expected from government formalization of a decision through a legislative act. When the public has been trained and/or educated to understand what will improve the visual environment and why, a statute will be successful. Legislative or judicial acts can only codify social processes; they should not create a process of social/human improvement. Central to any code, then, is education.

Within our cultural framework we are essentially a rational people. We compare and weigh various inputs and outputs and arrive at what we feel is the most rational allocation of resources in a psychological, social, and economic sense. When people demand a different allocation of resources from the current one, it will be because they have begun to learn or understand new possibilities or components of a workable solution, and have changed their evaluation of the worth of various goals. Any governmental act that operates from a "superior" information base or a different goal from the rest of the public is doomed to failure.

If this were the best of all possible worlds, the locational variables that determine the functioning of signs would be clearly and carefully isolated and all our visual communication shaped accordingly. This would lead to a very rational use of our urban land. As James Vance of Berkeley has pointed out, people often embark on policies on the assumption that there is a paucity of space in the city. In fact, it is the lack of a consistent and rational approach that has led to the apparent overcrowding.

However, our city planners seldom consider what is the highest and best use of a particular site. This is so poorly understood that the rare developer who does know the best use of a site will have an astounding degree of success in allocating resources. Even for such activities as gasoline retailing, the rules of consumer behavior are only beginning to be understood. We do not yet know how to measure the value of a sign, although we do have some surrogate measures for the value of some kinds of signs.

The knowledge gained in this area has already led to a lower degree of attrition of sites and lessened proliferation of stations. However, the fact that our knowledge of locational variables is in its infancy does not excuse the planner from considering all the economic and social information available before creating an ordinance.

The educational component as a means of improving our visual environment is one thing that has been seriously lacking in most of the trade or professional organizations of the sign industry. The organizations in the industry have not yet begun to establish the amount of knowledge about the profession that should be required for professional membership. On its face, this may seem incidental to many of the problems currently facing the sign industry, particularly the current attempts at federal legislative control. Yet we believe that on closer examination the lack of professional requirements for entrance into the sign organizations will prove to be at the heart of many of the legislative problems facing the industry. Many of the companies in the sign industry have a considerable amount of information at their disposal as to the components of a high quality sign, but lack a means of expressing such information. This has allowed many legislators, planners, and architects to assume that the lowest common denominator in the sign industry, which is the new entrant to the field, is typical of the performance of any sign company. Thus the first step in critically improving the image of the sign industry and its products is to set out some general guidelines as to the use of lettering, color, graphics, and form or design in signs. When such information has been passed on to sign companies and to the users of signs, much of the current problems involved in poor-quality signs will be self-correcting.

The mere existence of common standards or an informational base could raise the standards of the profession across the board. If the sign industries take such a position, they will be well on their way to professionalizing the industry.

In this vein, we feel that the sign industry will have to spend a considerable amount of money structuring the taxonomy of educational objectives that are necessary to train an individual in the sign companies. This is going to involve use of some of the better educational psychological techniques that have been developed to build curriculums that can turn the knowledge that is currently held by some of the sign companies into publicly available information. Although on its face this may appear to be a herculean task, we feel that this structuring of curriculums will determine in the long run whether or not the sign industry will remain in business as we currently see it.

The quality of some of the papers presented at various industry conferences is very high, but it is appalling that they do not appear in print so that they can be purchased by university people or others who are generally interested in the subject. Years of empirically based knowledge which could have been published and become part of the common knowledge is not available. With such information, (1) those people observing signs could learn what to observe, (2) those people ordering signs would learn what to order, and (3) those marketing signs would have some kind of concrete format to work from.

In a study in Baltimore, it was found that throughout the entire Baltimore metropolitan area, there was only one course being taught that even vaguely related to sign design, and that was a course in calligraphics in Baltimore Institution. This knowledge exists in the design departments of the custom sign companies and of the manufacturers of quantity standardized signs, but it must be passed on to the public through the educational system if high quality signs are to be sought and permitted by the public.

Sources of Information. When compiling information, it is important to always check the accuracy or credibility of a source. Any court of law will certainly consider the credibility of sources to determine whether or not accurate empirical data has been gathered to substantiate the rationale for use of police power.

An example of how little is known of the field of perception by those who would regulate signs is one of the provisions of the 1965 Beautification Act in the United States. One of the stipulations of this act is that large billboards are to be set back 660 feet from the highway. Gibson (1950), who is considered one of the pioneers in the field of perception, established thirteen varieties of visual perspective. One of these categories is perspective of parallax, and the varieties of perspective in this category apply to perception of objects because of binocular vision. Even the most cursory reading of Gibson's work will reveal several reasons why a billboard placed back against the landscape will dominate the landscape and will seem more obtrusive than one close to the viewer. The result of this particular provision of the Beautification Act, therefore, could easily be the opposite of its intent. Similar examples are not difficult to find. We are only beginning to understand some of the fundamentals of human perception, and to act on "common sense" is dangerous.

Another common assumption is that the locational variables of a retail site are well-established and can be easily dealt with. Rothwell (1970) has pointed out that the typology of site and strategy of a company will vary radically with the location of the site and the segment of the market it will serve. There are some books that deal extensively with the subject, such as Nelson's book on retailing (1958) and *The Mobile Consumer* (Claus and Hardwick, 1972) present some models which can be applied to particular types of site. However, much more study is necessary before we can deal with such locational variables as simply as many planners are inclined to do.

There has been an emerging school of planners who hail Kevin Lynch (1960) as their mentor and who base their decisions on the assumption that the structure and form or design of the city will materially add to the happiness of its citizens. The simplification inherent in such a position is a form of academic autocracy. One should always question the empirical basis for such assumptions and their statistical validity.

In a Minnesota study, there was found to be a high correlation between traffic accidents and the presence of signs. This is similar to the claim that people drown because they eat ice cream. Most people who drown eat ice cream. Similarly most of our environment contains signs. In a subsequent analysis of the Minnesota study, no statistical significance could be found. Other factors, such as grade of the street, improper signaling, etc., were more significant in association with the automobile accident. A great deal of the literature cited by those who would regulate signs has been based on such "common sense" thinking.

Some excellent books on the sign industry have been federally funded, such as *Street Graphics* (Ewald & Mandelker, 1972) and *City Signs and Lights* (Signs/Lights/Boston, 1971). Both of these works apparently have been based on implicit assumptions and prejudices. Any book that is written by an architect or a planner with no help at all from the industry should be read cautiously. The current trends in the industry were overlooked in both of these books. Many of the improvements suggested by the authors, such as incorporation of the signs into the total building design, have already been initiated and promoted by the sign industry. Too often the conclusion of a book written by a planner is that the planner should control our visual environment, while that of a book written by an architect is that the architect should be allowed to design our visual environment. This control will no doubt be for our own good.

Both of these books suffer from very serious deficiencies in the credibility of research cited. In one book, the author makes several statements about perception and memory which the professional psychologist would shy away from. There has not yet been enough research to establish these claims. Statement that "the fundamental principles of how people see things from a moving car are already well-established (Ewald and Mandelker, 1971, p. 15)," is very misleading. This is not a simple subject and a very small amount of empirically based research directly related to signs has been done in this area. To our knowledge, there is no definitive work on how the automobile and human perception interact, either in a physical, psychological or cultural sense. The planner writes glibly of studies proving that signs cause traffic accidents, overload the information system, and cause psychological stress. Yet most of the studies cited have either been ambiguous or have been refuted by later evidence. The complexity of the subject of perception and signs is well-illustrated by Forbes (1939, p. 696) and Brainard, et al. (1961, p. 130).

Both authors seem to be opposed to advertising, which they seem to find separable from communication. They would deny that the image projected by a building designed to house a particular corporation is advertising. This shows a lack of understanding of communication and a lack of understanding or acceptance of our economic system. The importance of identification of a good or service with a particular segment of the market is only beginning to be appreciated. These books both imply that the North American economic system is out of line with people's needs and desires.

The continuous comparison of North American cities with European cities also is very spurious. To begin with the densities are not comparable. The entire population of the United States would have to be fit into an area roughly the size of New York State to even approximate the density of the Netherlands. Furthermore there is a real difference in income levels between the two countries. There also are large differences in legal tradition and cultural attitudes. In England, for instance, there have been laws severely restricting alienation of land, while in North America the alienation and free movement of land has been considered to be a right inherent in the property.

Our methods of transportation also have been very different because of the difference in population density. This difference is paralleled by the differences which exist between the east and west coasts of North America with regard to densities and transportation networks.

In Europe projecting signs may not be as important as they are in North America because retailing is primarily pedestrian-oriented. Because of this, a particular kind of facia sign intricate lettering is very common. It is used for facia or wall signs and can convey an image of prestige. Such delicate letters do not enjoy the same popularity on this continent because it is not designed to be seen from a moving vehicle.

Regional differences exist here also in attitudes toward signs. On the west coast, the sign industry is much more widely accepted than on the east coast, and innovations are more easily tolerated. To compare North American cities with northwestern European models is simply to admit a personal cultural bias.

A problem that has not been dealt with in either of these books is the fact that appraisers and realtors have done a great deal of work in the area of obsolescence because of poor design.

Recently there has been a tendency among architects towards grouping or categorization of land uses for regulation. However, if they had any knowledge of urban sociology, geography or commerce, they would realize that this is not a simple task. A few years ago, such classification was particularly in vogue in geography, but it has since been discovered that such categorization does not fit into any realistic typology of site. Within one trade classification types of site vary from purely automobile-oriented sites to purely pedestrian-oriented facilities. The importance of a sign varies with the type of site, not the type of business, and thus there is a great danger in applying such simplistic classifications to sign legislation. An example of the complexity of automobile-oriented retailing is provided by *The Mobile Consumer* (Claus and Hardwick, 1972).

Context and Orientation. One must also consider the context and orientation of information. It may be used out of context or it may not be meant to apply to signs at all. Such terms as invasion of privacy actually are meaningless in the context of signs.

The orientation of such information is also critical. The more buildings that must have an architectural seal, particularly if it is a local architectural seal, the more architects stand to benefit from the legislation. It is usually easy for people to understand a newspaper putting down signs, but it is often difficult for them to understand that an architect who receives fees for designing a building can be motivated to do the same thing. The suggestions of design control committees and architectural review boards may be more biased than is generally suspected because their orientation is to force design into the realm of the professional architect. It is money in his pocket and one has to always be realistic when it comes to a person protecting his own interests.

It is not uncommon to hear opinions that an advisory board should be composed of "one design-oriented lay citizen, one representative each of the architecture professions, the landscape architecture profession, the graphic design profession, and the sign industry, and the chairman of the planning commission serving *ex officio* (Ewald & Mandelker, 1971, p. 70)." It is not difficult to guess that the author of this statement is an architect, since the obvious vote on this commission is three architects, one sign man and one citizen.

Goals

The attitude of the planner toward control of signs has more than once been that of a knight in shining armor protecting the public from the crass profiteering of the merchant and the sign company. He is assuming that the public is somehow different from the merchant and separate from him and that the public state of ignorance will allow such encroachment on its sensitivity by the businessman. In actuality, the public is very good at protecting itself. Individuals can cause the total demise of a business by simply refusing to frequent it.

In our opinion, sign legislation should be designed to protect the interest of the merchant or the user of signs from encroachment by other merchants. The goal should be to allow the merchant to use the visual component of his urban property to the maximum effectiveness without infringing on another's rights to do the same, not to protect the public from the merchant. Poor signs, by any definition, will be rejected by the public.

It is extremely important to determine whether a goal is clearly stated, whether or not it is socially desirable, and whether it is obtainable, practically or legally.

Is the Goal Clearly Stated? In many cases, a goal is not clearly stated. Someone may become irritated at what seems to him to be an irresponsible act and will seek to control it without really understanding what the act was. A politician's rationale for action must be repeatedly attacked in the public forum. If this is done often enough, the politician will have to state the goal he sought in creating the legislation in the first place.

To the sign company, this is particularly critical because when the goal is clearly stated, you will often find that you are not in conflict with the interests of the planner, and that if he can understand the complexity of the sign industry—and it is your job to educate him—the legislation can be mutually beneficial.

Is the Goal Obtainable? This brings us to the second question: is the goal really obtainable? Often when it is put this way, people realize that many of their goals are not obtainable. If it is demonstrated clearly why this is so, much confused and damaging legislation can be avoided.

Is the Goal Socially Desirable? Whether or not a goal is socially desirable is often a question of what property rights should take priority in an area. This is not simply a case of the sign industry giving up the ghost. The whole area of our society cannot be made into one big bedroom community for a downtown commercial center. We live in a complex society in which automobile-oriented retailing zones make signs necessary from the viewpoint of the social welfare. They decrease accident rates by providing quick recognition and legibility, they can in many cases, prevent irrational use of the landscape, and they allow creativity of expression in our individualistic society.

As was pointed out conclusively in one study of the oil industry, certain automobile-oriented uses, such as freeway sites in tourist areas, or in a motel or hotel located next to an airport, where there is a high frequency of occupants who use that facility once, legible signs are necessary to the visibility of that business. The building of such things as airports, highways, or freeways, or changing areas to parks implies certain other logical land uses, and the simple restriction of these is not a socially desirable goal. We have built ribbon zones of retailing in our cities along highways and streets and these have become the focus of automobile-oriented retailing. The sign is the primary factor in visibility and thus in traffic safety as well as economic success. As the eye scans the street, which is basically the way the driver sees, it can pick up the information and the advertising of what is available in those land use zones. If one is truly opposed to urban sprawl as we have been led to believe, the restriction of signs in such zones is illogical because more sites may be necessary to serve the same population if the threshold of each site is reduced by inadequate signage.

The complexity of social desirability is illustrated by the story of a bank in California which sought to put up a highly attractive sign. The area around this particular site was not what could be called a particularly desirable social area in which to live. The bank applied for a sign permit and one planner, after a great deal of difficulty, allowed the institution to have its sign if it would be shut off at nine o'clock at night with a timing device. The manager of the bank wasn't particularly anxious to go along with this "sweetheart deal," which is a deal that is illegal but is being obeyed in fear of future negative action by a planner; but finally the bank installed a timing device and the sign was turned off every night. Immediately, from a different source in the city government, there was a protest. The chief of police claimed that the light from the sign was a factor in deterring crime and asked if the bank officials would leave the sign on as a favor to him. In such a case one wonders about the social desirability of allowing a planner to assume this kind of discretionary power.

Is the Goal Legally Obtainable? The city has certain legal rights, but it also can obtain acquiescence to demands that are not legal. This is usually referred to as a "sweetheart deal." One planner in Canada wrote a bylaw that without question was *ultra vires,* or beyond the powers of the municipality to enforce. In Canada, he was contravening the British North America Act by taking discretionary powers upon himself that were never deemed to be the realm of the planner. In the United States one would say that he was taking away property without due process of law. For several years, no one challenged this bylaw because they knew it wouldn't be enforced. This allows the landscape to be formed by default, legal precedent to be set by default, and it is a degradation of the industry's responsibility to defend the right to use one's property to a reasonable degree. If it can be demonstrated before a bylaw is passed that it is not legal, one will not be forced to take it to court later.

Dangers of Poor Legislation

We have arrived at a point at which we can accept our urban environment as our artifact. Because signs are such a visible part of this artifact, it is imperative that the industry participate in landscape formation and understand the viewpoints of the different parties involved. If not, they will find themselves continually caught up in the decision-making process as victims and scapegoats. Two of the most serious dangers in bylaw creation are time lag and emotional reaction.

Time Lag

First of all, in any decision-making act, there is a time lag between the start of a problem and action upon it. It takes time for the public to understand the problem. The first thing we would suggest to minimize this is to circulate information about your industry to all segments of the society and to keep this information up-to-date. Nothing is more tragic nor, surprisingly, more common than a bylaw that is written to counteract or prevent something that has already ceased to be a problem. Much of the Highway Beautification Act of 1965 and its orientation towards outdoor advertising and the subsequent treatment of it by many of the learned people in the field is in this category. Numbers of outdoor posters and bulletins have been declining in favor of quality and good location.

This is a problem of information. If the industry is going to structure good bylaws, it must take seriously the task of distribution of information to prevent the construction of bylaws reacting against problems it has already begun to deal with. This kind of bylaw provides the surest professional success for a planner and the worst problem for the sign industry.

Emotional Reaction

Emotional reactions, when codified into legislation, tend to intensify rather than lessen the problem they seek to solve. This can be seen in the farm policy that was instituted when we became emotionally concerned about saving the family farm. We created a farm subsidy program in the United States that guaranteed the market price to the large farmer and allowed him to buy large amounts of equipment, expand into capital intensive agriculture, and work on a marginal return. The result: the small farmer was forced out of business. He might have been doomed anyway, but governmental legislation to save him hastened the processes. One agricultural economist put it this way: "the right results for all the wrong reasons."

The same thing often happens with signs. In one Canadian city, a large sign was put up which was legal, but it was put up during a particularly reactive stage. The newspapers jumped on the bandwagon, fanned the flames, and spoke of desecration of the landscape. The reaction was that the zoning in the area was frozen and they allowed no more roof signs in any but a few specified zones, and for all practical purposes, no one would have normally put structures in those zones because they had very limited commercial use. However, the fact was that the industry in that particular city had been taking out over 5 per cent of their total number of signs each year and replacing them at a ratio of one to three or even one to five, using an imaginative and attractive application of triple message signs. They were using the most effective locations and were taking down the less attractive signs. Because the signs they were putting in were more expensive, they were largely high quality signs. When the zoning was frozen, the number of signs was frozen and it has remained so ever since. This is another instance of emotional reaction intensifying the problem.

Fig. 15: Trivision (rotating triangular louvers) display enables advertiser to feature three different selling points in the same space.

In one of the areas of San Francisco which had been declining, what many people considered the derelicts of society began to congregate there, and many X-rated movies were coming into the area. The municipal government moved to clean up this area, and one of their first moves was to materially limit signs. Now they really have a problem. The area has now totally deteriorated because this area was largely automobile-oriented and the signs were necessary to economic viability of any business. Now they have real urban blight on their hands in an area that could have been revived through some intelligent urban planning.

Some time ago, planners restricted oil company stations to strips or ribbon zones along main arteries and held them out of any of the better sites. This was a reaction against the proliferation of small stations that occurred following World War II. In those zones to which the planners limited these sites, the potential gallonage of any station was small and, since there is a relatively fixed demand for gasoline in an area, if one station can only pump a certain amount, you must put up another station a short distance away from it and add cross-merchandising in order to stay in business. The result was a proliferation of small cluttered stations. If they had been left alone, the oil companies would have located most of their new stations on prime sites where one station could take the place of several of the smaller ones; but once again, emotional reaction intensified the problem.

Brainard, W. Campbell, M. & Elkin, B. Design and Interpretability of Road Signs. *Journal of Applied Psychology,* 1961, *45,* 130.

Claus, R. J. & Hardwick, W.G. *The Mobile Consumer: Automobile-Oriented Retailing and Site Selection.* Don Mills, Ontario: Collier-Macmillan, 1972.

Ewald, W. R. & Mandelker, D.R. *Street Graphics.* Washington: American Society of Landscape Architects Foundation, 1971.

Forbes, T.W. A Method of Analysis of the Effectiveness of Highway Signs. *Journal of Applied Psychology,* 1939, *23,* 669.

Gibson, J. J. *The Perception of the Visual World.* Boston: Houghton-Mifflin, 1950.

Lynch, K. *The Image of the City.* Cambridge, Mass.: MIT Press and Harvard University Press, 1960.

Nelson, R. L. *The Selection of Retail Locations.* New York: F.W. Dodge Corp., 1958.

Rothwell, D.C. *Marketing Strategy and Its Effect on Retail Site: A Case Study of the Vancouver Gasoline Market.* Vancouver: University of British Columbia, unpublished masters thesis, 1970.

Signs/Lights/Boston. *City Signs and Lights.* Boston, Mass.: Ashley/Myer/Smith, architects and planners, 1971.

Chapter 9/Codification Of The Decision-Making Act: By-Law Formation

After the goal is set, and after the strategy has been selected for reaching that goal, the municipality must begin the task of actually constructing an ordinance. This represents the codification of the aims or goals of this community as manifested in the decisions of the council. It cannot be overemphasized that even if the motivations for the legislation are well-intentioned and will meet virtually no resistance from any sector of the community, and even if the goal is clearly and concisely stated, the writing of a statute can often thwart its entire purpose. During the codification of the decision, the mechanisms for enforcement and the meaning of the regulations must be clearly and precisely defined.

It is not uncommon to find enforcement of an ordinance far beyond the intent of the regulations. In many cases, the enforcement officer has formed an opinion of what should be done in an area and has interpreted the law accordingly. Only if the regulations are clearly and carefully worded can such individualistic and subjective interpretation be prevented. For instance, according to the American Society of Planning Officials, the word sign can refer to "an outdoor sign, light, display, device, figure, painting, drawing, message, placard, poster, billboard, or other things which are designed and intended to advertise or inform." Under this definition a sculpture could also be a sign, as could a car on a used car lot intended to attract customers. One must be careful to limit the control in the writing stage to prevent overapplication by administration in the future.

A very common example of the effect of ambiguous wording in ordinances is the frequent limitation of the "area" of a sign. What should be specified in any size limitation is the "copy area" of the sign or the area that contains the message. When copy area is not specified, enforcement officers often interpret the limitation as referring to the whole area of the sign. The result is that many large attractive sign backgrounds, as well as the desirable storefronts, are disallowed under such ordinances. The effectiveness of unrestricted background space for signs, as opposed to unrestricted copy area, in improving our visual environment is demonstrated in Figure 16-19.

Some steps can be taken to avoid the common areas of

Fig. 16: Copy area of sign is the actual area of the sign to which copy is applied. exclusive of background.

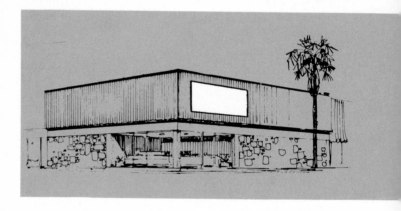

Fig. 18: The copy area of a sign on a building facade.

confusion in bylaw construction and the frequent need for reinterpretation. The first of these is a clear unambiguous definition of each term used. Legislation should be written so that even a person with no knowledge of the phenomenon being controlled can understand what is intended.

Furthermore we have found that it is extremely helpful for the industry to supply illustrations of the points being discussed, to be worked into the text of the legislation itself.

Any sign regulation should be divisible into two cate-

Fig. 17: Background area of sign is the entire background surface of the sign face or faces.

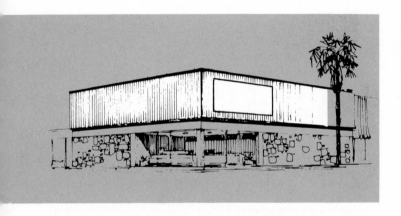

Fig. 19: In this same example (Figure 18), the sign area is the entire facade.

gories: (1) zoning schedules designating what signs and sign structures are allowable in any zoning district, and (2) material and construction specifications. Ideally, a sign code could be easily included in the building and zoning codes of the municipality. Any specifications which cannot be placed under either of these two forms of control would fall into the category of design or aesthetics controls, and, as we have demonstrated, there is no legally established provision for such controls in the legislative powers of the municipality.

Signs. Legal Rights And Aesthetic Considerations/113

However, there is one significant argument for codifying the regulations regarding signs into one separate sign code, and that is that the area of sign control and enforcement is so complex that it would be unfair and unadvisable to delegate it to the building inspector, as has been done in some municipalities. The enforcement of sign controls should be carried out by an administrator appointed for that purpose whose duties involve only the regulation of signs. Even in a small, relatively homogeneous municipality, signs form such a large part of the landscape that adequate enforcement, permit issuance, and inspection would require the full attention of at least one individual. Furthermore the administrator of the sign code should be well-acquainted with the goals of the community, the best methods of carrying out those goals, and current developments and trends in the sign industry.

We would like to make it very clear that we have not included this model ordinance as one to be adopted wholly by any municipality. We have tried to cover here many of the available methods of solving the sign problems of a community infringing on the merchant's right to use signs. But any sign control must be tailored to the needs of the particular community. These needs change with changes in land use, population density, and industrial base, etc.

As an example of the unique requirements of various kinds of cities, we have included a set of specifications, or a synopsis of ordinance control, for five municipalities in British Columbia (Appendix C). It is particularly interesting that these communities all border one another and are part of the Greater Vancouver area. Yet their requirements for a sign bylaw are very different. We strongly recommend that the reader compare these requirements to appreciate the varying needs of individual cities in the area of sign control.

We are very concerned that a municipality might attempt to adopt this ordinance without considering the goals they wish to achieve and the best ways of meeting them. Too often planners construct an ordinance out of large sections of other ordinances or simply adopt an already existing ordinance, regardless of its application to their own situation. This can prove disastrous if, for instance, one compares the needs of a small conservative community with those of a tourist-oriented city. The latter will often exert very little control over certain types of sign in some areas, particularly those associated with motels, drive-in restaurants, and other tourist industries.

The automobile has created certain trapping points in

the city where land values are extremely high. These are usually at the zone of conflux of freeways or major arteries. At these points, the probability of a customer stopping at a particular kind of outlet is maximized. Here retailing and commercial activities tend to cluster and land values are extremely high, as compared to other areas of the city (Figure 20). These are often treated by planners as standard commercial zones. The visual component of such property is extremely important and a highrise sign on such a

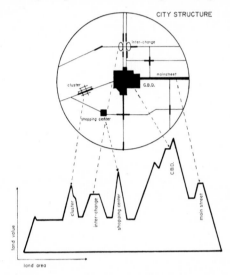

Fig. 20: The X and Y axes on the lower portion of the figure represent, respectively, land area and land value; the upper portion of the figure is a real representation of some patterns of urban land use.

Fig. 21: Extensive survey of the sign needs and how the signs proposed would fit into the scene, determined the size and height of professional developed signs. Each face of this effective museum sign is 288 sq. ft.

Signs. Legal Rights And Aesthetic Considerations/115

lot can double the volume of an outlet. For economic and public safety reasons, such areas should be recognized as unique and not subject to the same sign standards as the rest of the city.

Historical areas or even civic center districts of a city will also require special consideration to ensure that the character of the area is preserved. Such areas highlight the changes in cultural taste over time. It should be noted that in some cases, overly rigorous control in historical areas has led to a disregard for regulations and a proliferation of illegal signs. Sophisticated signing is required (Figure 21).

Once a municipality has clearly set out the goals of sign control for its own situation, parts of this ordinance can provide a general blueprint for constructing rational and effective legislation. Like a blueprint for a home, it will be modified as much as necessary to suit the individual needs of the municipality.

Proposed Standards

Signs were in existence long before the automobile. However, the automobile has made signs more important than ever before and has increased the necessity of regulations to protect the public from traffic hazards caused by distractions, and to protect the property owner from infringement upon his property rights by the users of signs. One of the necessary provisions of any sign regulation is that no sign shall obstruct the view of an intersection, railroad crossing, or any traffic control device, or otherwise provide a demonstratable traffic hazard.

Although some people contend that our society would be aesthetically more pleasing without signs, the role played by signs in our fast-moving automobile-oriented retailing environment is a very important one, and one without which our current economic system could not function as efficiently. Thus we have kept design control to a minimum in our ordinance, while dealing with those aspects of technical quality which contribute to the aesthetic appeal of a sign but can be judged objectively. This includes such factors as visible supports, type and durability of materials, and maintenance.

It is not felt that the solution to the problems of visual pollution in the urban environment lies in abolition. Because signs serve a vital function, such strict action generally results in non-enforcement or in eventual restructing of the legislation. In either case, the results on the landscape are not desirable ones. We do feel, however, that a well-written bylaw with a positive orientation can provide benefits for the community, for the user of signs, and for the sign industry by upgrading the quality standards of signs on the landscape.

Many of the unattractive displays of signs on our urban landscape are due to clutter caused by the overlapping of projecting signs along streets where buildings are built out to the property line and adjoining one another. Because such signs project over public space, there is no question that they are an extension beyond the property right. However, for many of these areas, there is no other way that the merchant can effectively reach the automobile-oriented consumer. These retail strips were originally designed for pedestrian traffic but today they often derive more than half of their business from automobile traffic. Only a projecting sign can provide quick and easy legibility in such an environment.

Thus rather than impose blanket limitations on signs, we feel that such a problem can be more effectively dealt with by application of a triangulation formula, such as that provided later in this text. (Appendix B), which stipulates the maximum projection of a sign on any building which will not obscure the sign on an adjacent building from passers-by. This will limit the necessity of bigger and more garish signs to compete with other signs, and the merchant will be more inclined to purchase a modestly proportioned sign at a lower price if he is guaranteed that it will not be obscured by other signs in the area. For retail sites built today, this is not a problem because the city usually provides a maximum percentage of lot coverage. This provides sufficient roof for projecting or freestanding signs which do not project over public property and generally eliminates the problem of overlapping signs on adjacent sites.

Because facia signs are to some extent architectural features of the building to which they are attached, as well as advertising devices, it is felt that some relationship should exist between the area of sign copy and building size. Maximum sign areas when stated as an absolute figure seem to imply that all buildings in a particular area are of equal dimensions. On the other hand, relating allowable sign copy to the street frontage of the building or to the area of wall surface seems both a fairer and a more desirable approach. It is important to note that the area of sign copy is used for these purposes, rather than the area of the sign itself. In some cases, a large format for the sign itself can serve to improve the appearance of an unsightly building.

Canopy signs are governed in the proposed ordinance by

a ratio which relates the allowable sign area to the canopy frontage or apron perimeter because this is also, to some degree, an architectural feature of the building itself.

In the case of freestanding signs, the relationship between signs and the buildings they represent is less marked. Rather the necessary size is dependent on the distance from the street or sidewalk. Thus height and area of freestanding signs is related to the distance from the center line of the highway, while an absolute maximum area standard is employed for all areas.

Roof signs are limited to one for each building in commercial zones, to be constructed either in the form of a penthouse or as double-faced blades with cantilevered legs and no visible bracing. Non-advertising faces are to be enclosed with suitable materials to conceal all structure and electric boxes. Suitable access for firemen, maintenance, etc. is provided.

Signs which would not be desirable in a residential neighborhood may be not only desirable, but necessary in a retailing or commercial area. A recreation, amusement, or tourist area might benefit from minimal controls. Thus we have given careful consideration to the sign schedules, which provide guidelines for the type and size of sign which can be constructed in a particular land use zone.

Types of Signs

Signs have been differentiated here on the basis of function and structure. Signs are categorized according to function as business and non-accessory signs. A business sign is a first-party sign which refers to the name of a business and may refer to goods, products, and services available at the site on which the sign is located. A non-accessory sign is a third-party sign which refers to goods, products, or services available at a location other than the site on which the sign is erected. This may be a directional and/or an advertising sign.

A classification of signs on the basis of structure refers to their location in relation to a building or to the site on which they are located. A clear definition of the various types of signs is provided in Part I of the ordinance.

Administration and Enforcement

The enforcement of the provisions of this ordinance is delegated to a sign code administrator familiar with signs and with the goals of the municipality and to those whom he appoints to carry out this function. A board of appeals is provided to hear questions of interpretation.

Chapter 10/Annotated And Supplementary Bibliographies

Annotated Bibliography
I. General References On Visual Perception
A. *Psychology of Perception*

Dember, William M. *Psychology of Perception*. New York: Holt, Rinehart & Winston, 1960, 1966. Hardback, approximately $9.

Purpose: This book was written as a text for a one-semester laboratory course in perceptual psychology. The book reviews the field of perceptual psychology from the viewpoint of one who is concerned with measurement, visual psycho-physics, and the effect of learning on perception.

Contents: The textbook covers topics such as the psychology rationale behind measurement techniques used to determine threshold levels of stimulation. Major visual psycho-physical relations and their interpretations are reviewed and discussed. The organization of visual perception is discussed in depth as well as the influence on perception of sensory, cognitive, and motivational factors. The text emphasizes the influence of learning on perceptual, motivational, and emotional processes.

Author's Bias or Position: Dr. Dember is Professor of Psychology at the University of Cincinnati. His emphasis in the textbook is on data acquisition and interpretation and the relation between theory and data. The emphasis of the text is psychological and does not go into the anatomical and neuro-physiological aspects of visual perception. Broad theories of visual perception are not treated in depth.

Applicability to Sign Industry: This text provides a general understanding of psychological research in visual perception.

Gibson, J. J. *The Senses Considered as Perceptual Systems*. Boston, Mass.: Houghton Mifflin Co., 1966.

Purpose: The author's theory is an attempt to answer the question: how do organisms secure the information from the world about them that is essential to their adaptation and survival?

Contents: The book discusses the senses and the fact that different forms of energy (such as intensity of light) vary from time to time so that we experience continuously changing sensations. Gibson is concerned with how an organism obtains constant perceptions in everyday life given continually changing sensations. He claims that the senses serve as channels of sensation or sensitivity to information concerning the permanent or stable properties of the environment. Although certain easily measured variables of stimulus energy do change, stimulus energy ratios (proportions do not change; they remain invariant with movements of the observer and with changes in the intensity of stimulation. He adds that these invariants of stimulus energy at the receptors of an organism correspond to the permanent properties of his environment. They constitute, therefore, information about one's permanent environment.

Perceptual systems are the ways in which organisms receive information. They reflect the five principal ways we have of orienting the perceptual apparatus of our body: by listening, touching, smelling, tasting, and looking. A perceptual system is a functional unit, not an anatomical unit. Perceptual systems are composed of other units, "organs," which are in turn composed of receptors. Each perceptual system orients itself in appropriate ways for seeking and extracting environmental information and depends on the general orienting system of the whole body; head movements, ear movements, hand movements, nose and mouth movements, and eye movements are all part of the perceptual systems they serve.

Author's Bias or Position: Gibson is a graduate of Yale University and Cornell University and is influenced by Hull. His philosophical stance is that a serious theory of perception should attempt to account for the fact that adaptive living is possible only if our senses provide us with continuous, stable information.

Applicability to Sign Industry: This work is a classic general text in perceptual psychology.

Rock, Irvin. *The Nature of Perceptual Adaptation.* New York: Basic Books, 1966.

Purpose: This text treats the question of whether memory can alter the appearance of objects.

Content: The author discusses perceptual phenomena through the study of prism adaptation. He first considers prism adaptation in the light of perceptual experiences under normal conditions. The text reports experiments with subjects who were asked to make perceptual judgments. Pre and post exposure tests, without the optical device, were conducted to prevent subjects correcting for error in making judgments. "Genuine perceptual adaptation should change the way the relevant stimulus is perceived, even in the absence of the optical device." The main structural component of the theory is a "memory trace," defined as "an aftereffect or residue of some kind in the brain, resulting from a previous experience which endures over time and 'represents' that previous experience." Rock's theory of adaptation assumes that these memory traces can affect subsequent perception: a particular memory trace is evoked, aroused when a familiar object is encountered. Configural adaptation is the main relational component of the theory and refers to normalization or displacement effects generated simply by continued exposure to certain patterns.

Author's Position or Bias: Dr. Rock is a professor in the Institute of Cognitive Studies, Rutgers University. His bias is Gestalt learning theory.

Applicability to Sign Industry: This work discusses some of the effects of memory and cultural conditioning on perception. This information has advertising applications, especially in situations where there is continued exposure to a certain display.

Taylor, J. G. *The Behavioral Basis of Perception.* New Haven: Yale University Press, 1962.

Purpose: The main point of this text is to explain perception as a function of behavior.

Content: Taylor's theoretical structure is based on Ashby's cybernetic theory of the relation of the organism to its environment—the two constitute a multistable system. Taylor describes a multistable system and describes two types of relationship between the subsystems: the *parallel and serial* arrangements. In the first the subsystems can adapt independently of one another and in any order, including simultaneity. In the second arrangement, adaptation of the first subsystem is a prerequisite for adaptation of the second one. Taylor's theory is illustrated through discussion of visual perception experiments (e.g., subjects participate in an experiment such as engaging in a number of activities while wearing prisms and report the resulting visual perceptions.) Set theory is used to manipulate stimulus and movement variables. Three components are isolated to describe theory: a) stimulation of the retina by features of the environment (afferent functions); b) activation of engrams (complex neural links); and c) response of relevant motor centers (efferent functions). An "engram" is a "network of neural connections such that if energy is fed into it, a specific response will be evoked." Engrams are formed through the mechanism of conditioning in union with Hull's principle of unlearned behavior. Major generalizations:

a) Development is adaptational rather than maturational.

b) Sense data are themselves knowledge.

c) Perception is a function of the behavioral history of the organism.

Author's Position or Bias: The author's behavioral orientation derives from Hullian learning theory. He uses a cybernetic approach which is compatible with information theory.

Applicability to Sign Industry: This text discusses visual perception in general and provides explanations of environmental effects of visual stimuli. Also discussed are the cumulative or historical effects of certain types of visual display.

Vernon, M.D. (ed.) *Experiments in Visual Perception: Selected Readings.* Baltimore, Md.: Penguin Books, Inc., 1966. Paperback/$1.95.

Purpose: This is a survey of experiments performed by psychologists in major problem areas in the psychology of vision. The book surveys approaches from demonstrations and observations to meticulously designed experiments and statistical analyses.

Content: The text reviews four central perceptual topics: the perception of form, space and distance, "constancy" phenomena, and movement. Variations in perception which occur within the individual and between individuals are also discussed. The book also contains excerpts from Piaget on perceptions in infancy. Effects of visual perception on mental set, attention, motivation, and personality are discussed. This edited volume contains approximately 40 of the more well-known articles in perceptual psychology.

Author's Position or Bias: M. D. Vernon is Professor of Psychology at Reading University, England. He has authored several books on visual perception: *Visual Perception, A Further Study of Visual Perception,* and *The Psycology of Perception.* The bias of this volume is toward experimental studies; little theoretical matter is included.

Applicability to Sign Industry: The book provides a review of some of the major studies in visual perception and is an inexpensive, ready reference for anyone in visual communications.

B. *Psycho-Physical Phenomena*

Childers, D. G. and Perry, N. W. "Alpha-like Activity in Vision," *Brain Research,* 1971, *25*(1):1-20.

Purpose: This article organizes empirical data and theoretical formulations for ready accessibility from the many diverse areas within vision and brain research.

Content: Alpha rhythm and alpha-like activity are discussed with regard to empirical findings in psychophysics, brightness, enhancement, flicker-fusion, electroencephalo-gram (EEG), electroretinogram (ERG), visual evoked response (VER), late receptor potential, ganglion cell responses, lateral ganiculate body, and cortical responses for phobic stimulation. Various models and theoretical considerations which are advanced in the literature to explain these findings are considered.

Author's Position or Bias: The author is from the Departments of Electrical Engineering and Psychology, Visual Sciences Laboratory, University of Florida, Gainesville, Florida. Bibliography consists mostly of studies published in the 1960s.

Applicability to Sign Industry: This article provides an excellent and readable review of the latest theory and research which touches upon the cognitive and emotional aspects of vision.

Heldon, H. "Adaptation Level Theory," In Koch, S. (Ed.), *Psychology: A Study of Science, Volume I.* New York: McGraw-Hill, 1959.

Purpose: To present the theory, extending it from psycho-physics to all aspects of behavior, including verbal, personal, social, and deviant.

Content: Adaptation level (AL) theory states that all experiences are ranged continuously and are bipolar (on a positive to negative scale). The position of the neutral region is the adaptation level at any particular time for the organism. This level is determined by the influence of three classes of stimuli or sources of variance: focal stimulus, background stimulus, and residual stimulus. Thus AL is an intervening variable which may be operationally defined in stimulus terms. Assumptions (7) stated e.g., "Quantitatively, adaptation level may be approximated as a weighted log mean of all stimuli affecting the organism." Adaptation level is within the range of present stimuli which means that constancy is relative to shifting adaptation levels.

AL theory and deviant behavior—There is a "psychological homeostasis": Normals adjust to extreme situations and stimuli as to ameliorate their severity. But if internal states, or past events, or imaginary events and objects are over-weighed, then the balance is lost, causing anxiety, neuroses, and psychoses. AL theory relates to other concepts of homeostasis (Cannon, Fletcher) but differs in the fact that AL is not necessarily normal."

Adaptation and negative aftereffects: Adaptation has both positive and negative effects simultaneously. A high AL sensitizes to negative qualities, a low AL to positive qualities. The neutral state depends upon all the properties of the stimulus (not only its frequency [Gibson]) as well as upon the effect of a residual stimuli. AL is a more dynamic theory than Gibson's.

In summary: Adaptation level theory provides an analytical approach to adjustment and organization by placing all responses in the quantitative framework of adaptation levels.

Author's Position or Bias: AL theory is firmly based on stimulus-response relationships but admits the uncontrolled variances of internal factors. Not being completely deterministic, it may be seen as a relaxed S-R approach.

Applicability to Sign Industry: General perception, particularly to signs after dark.

II. Color Perception
A. *General*

Ishak, I.G.H., Bouma, H. and van Bussel, H.J.J. "Subjective Estimates of Colour Attributes for Surface Colours," *Vision Research,* 1970, *10*(6):489-500.

Purpose: Investigation to test the adequacy of subjective estimates of color attributes as a method for studying color appearances of surface colors. Results are presented that show, (1) the standard deviations of single estimates and (2) some general trends in the assessments as they compare to data taken from the literature.

Content: A brief review of the work done in the last few years on subjective estimation is presented. Techniques discussed are (a) binocular matching; (b) memory matching; and (c) subjective estimation. In this study, subjective estimates of hue, saturation, and lightness are reported for 60 colored Munsell samples shown against seven backgrounds black, blue, grey, white, red, yellow, green) as judged by two observers. The results show the adequacy of this method for studies on color appearance. The standard deviations of single estimates were quite acceptable. It was found also that the estimates are not always lineraly related to the Munsell notations. The shifts due to chromatic surrounds are in accordance with results obtained by other investigators (from Journal Abstract).

Author's Position or Bias: Authors are from the Institute for Perception Research, Edindhoven, The Netherlands.

Applicability to Sign Industry: An excellent general work on color perception and the effects of background colors on perception of colors.

Kaiser, P. K., Herzberg, P. A. and Boynton, R. M.

"Chromatic border distinctness and its relation to saturation," *Visual Research,* 1971, *11*(9):953-961.

Purpose: This paper deals with one aspect of color contrast: "The fact that purely chromatic differences can sustain a visual border between two fields." This is called "Chromatic border distinctness." This aspect of color contrast differs from most studies of this nature. Authors such as LeGrand (1968) and Graham and Brown (1965) are concerned with the interactive effects between juxtaposed stimuli differing in hue (e.g.: a normally green field which appears blue-green in red surrounding).

Content: The distinctness of a border between precisely juxtaposed heterchromatic fields is evaluated by matching this border for distinctness with a comparison border produced by luminance differences in nearby achromatic fields. Two experiments are reported using this technique. The first shows that a chromatic difference usually adds very little to the distinctness produced by an achromatic difference, and can actually reduce it. The second demonstrates that distinctness of a border between white and various spectral stimuli, whose luminance are adjusted for a minimally distinct border with the white field, is related to the saturation of the colors produced by stimuli of these wave lengths. The results are discussed in terms of a quantitative theory of chromatic border distinctness.

Author's Position or Bias: Kaiser and Herzberg are from the Department of Psychology, York University, Downsview, Ontario, Canada, Boynton is from the Center for Visual Science, University of Rochester, Rochester, New York.

Applicability to Sign Industry: This article demonstrates the effects of color contrasts for perception of borders.

Luscher, Max. *The Luscher Color Test.* (Translated and edited by Ian A. Scott). New York: Pocketbooks, 1971. Also New York: Random House, 1969.

Purpose: This book presents a simplified version of the Luscher Color Test. The test is based upon the premise that a person will instinctively choose colors which represent his psychological or physical needs and that accurate diagnostic information can be gained about a person through analysis of his choices and rejections of colors.

Content: Chapter I gives a brief discussion of the origins of color significance and how color perception is related to physiology and psychology. Chapter I discusses the significance of the rank order of color preferences. Chapter III discusses the psychological characteristics of basic and auxiliary colors. Chapters IV and V discuss scoring of the test. Chapter VI reviews the meanings of the eight colors used in the short test presented in the book. Chapters VII and VIII deal with interpretation of the test. Color cards and interpretation tables are included within the text whereby the reader can analyze the psychological meaning of his own color preferences.

Author's Position or Bias: Dr. Max Luscher is a functional psychologist trained in Switzerland, who has been interested in color psychology since he was a young student. He has been a color consultant to a number of industries, including pharmaceutical firms and the Volkswagen Co. of West Germany. He is presently Professor of Psychology at the University of Basel, Switzerland.

Applicability to Sign Industry: Some insight can be provided into color perception and its relationship to particular segments of the market.

Sheppard, J. J., Jr. *Human Color Perception: A Critical Study of the Experimental Foundation.* New York: American Elsevier Publishing Co., 1968.

Purpose: This book is an attempt to provide an introduction to the critical study of the experimental foundation of human color perception in relation to three distinct fields of color vision: colorimetry, visual bio-physics, and visual psycho-physics. The book is primarily addressed to scientists who are interested in human color perception as an area for active research.

Content: The contents include an ordered discussion of experimental results selected from physics, physiology, and psychology, the process of color perception, involving the visual system and the domains of color vision, the standard observer and the technical aspects of colorimetry. All of the psycho-physical factors and physiological factors of retinal sensitivity are discussed as well as cerebral physiology and psycho-physiology with regard to color perception. Temporal phenomena, such as subjective color and various color effects, also are discussed. The book is a review of all the pertinent experimental literature. The author has attempted to organize the research according to areas of study.

Author's Position or Bias: The author writes from the viewpoint of a physical scientist. His intention is to point out the complexity of the field as well as the opportunities for inter-disciplinary research. The author is employed by the Rand Corporation in Santa Monica, California. The text is a very technical treatment of some of the basic experimental evidence in the field of color perception.

Applicability to Sign Industry: This is a general treatment of color perception.

Stromeyer III, C. F. "McCollough effect analogs of two-color projections," *Visual Research,* 2(9):969-978, 1971.

Purpose: This paper demonstrates that test patterns which modulate the lightness of red and green McCollough effects can produce many colors, based on the demonstration by McCullough (1965) which showed a color aftereffect specific to edge orientation which lasted for hours and even days.

Content: McCollough aftereffects were built up by viewing a black and green striped vertical grating alternating with a black and red striped horizontal grating. A black and white vertical test grating appeared red; a horizontal grating, green. Many hues of high chroma were, however, seen on a neutral test matrix of alternating vertical and horizontal gratings of various lightness and contrast when the matrix was viewed at the mesopic level or as a positive image.

Author's Position or Bias: Research was done at the Psychology Laboratory of Massachusetts Institute of Technology, the Laboratory of Psychophysics of Harvard University, and Bell Telephone Laboratories.

Applicability to Sign Industry: This paper provides insight into the aftereffects of color contrast.

B. *Illuminated Signs*

Flock, H. R. "Achromatic surface color and the direction of illumination," *Perception and Psychophysics,* 1971, 9 (2A):187-192.

Purpose: Three experiments were performed to replicate Hochberg and Beck's finding of optical-shift effect.

Content: Hochberg and Beck (1954) found that an objectively upright trapezoid, when illuminated from above, appeared darker if viewed monocularly and lighter if viewed binocularly. Illuminated from the front, the same trapezoid appeared lighter under monocular and darker under binocular vision. Since the target appeared slanted under monocular but upright under binocular viewing, these changes in apparent lightness could be attributed wholly or in part to the apparent angle of incidence of the illumination on the surface. In two experiments, when eight-minute periods of dark adaptation were introduced between monocular and binocular viewing, with conditions approximately the same as those of Hochberg and Beck, their results could not be observed. A third experiment demonstrated that the monocularly observed trapezoids did appear slanted (journal summary).

Author's Position or Bias: The author supports the proposition that "perception of illumination functions as a cue to apparent achromatic surface color (lightness)." The author is from York University, Downsview, Ontario, Canada.

Applicability to Sign Industry: Demonstrates how the direction of illumination affects perception of color.

Remole, A. "Luminance thresholds for subjective patterns in a flickering field: effect of wavelength," *Journal of the Optical Society of America, 61*(9):1164-1169, 1971.

Purpose: The author attempts to show that it is possible to obtain quantitative data with regard to the minimum luminance necessary for the appearance of patterns.

Content: When a uniform field is intermittently illuminated, it will often appear to contain various geometric patterns. This study deals with the threshold luminance at which such spurious patterns appear and with the dependence of this threshold upon the frequency of intermittency and upon the wave length of the stimulus. The log threshold luminance increases roughly lineary with the frequency of intermittency over the major part of the frequency range tests. The threshold is affected by stimulus wave length; blue and green require higher luminances than yellow or red. However, these differences of threshold vary with frequency of intermittency and reach maxima at approximately 14 cps. The wave length effects are modified by chromatic preadaptation.

Author's Position or Bias: The author is from the School of Optometry, University of Waterloo, Waterloo, Ontario, Canada. This research report is an abridgement of a doctoral dissertation done at Indiana University, Department of Physiological Optics.

Applicability to Sign Industry: The effect of color—flicker in illuminated signs, especially on plastic backgrounds is indicated.

Siegel, M. H. and Siegel, A. B. "Color name as a function of surround luminance and stimulus duration," *Perception and Psychophysics, 9*(2A)):140-144, 1971.

Purpose: To attempt a systematic investigation of the effects of both exposure duration and surround luminance upon color naming. A Bezold-Brucke effect and tritanopia, when brightness, rather than stimulus intensity varied.

Content: A color-naming experiment was performed in which both surround luminance and exposure duration varied. The data showed substantial effects from these changes, but none could be interpreted to indicate the presence of a Bezold-Brucke shift or tritanopia. The author concludes that both variables, surround luminance and duration interact. Variety of responses due to color shift when luminance and duration changed is discussed.

Author's Position or Bias: The authors are part of the research group studying color naming under various conditions (Kaiser, 1968, Luria, 1967, Boyton, et al, 1964.) They are working at Albion College, Albion, Michigan.

Applicability to Sign Industry: This paper provides some information applicable to color perception of illuminated signs.

Sokol, S. and Riggs, L. A. "Electrical and Psychophysical responses of the human visual system to periodic variation of luminance," *Investigative Ophthalmology, 10* (3):171-180, 1971.

Journal Abstract: The temporal resolution of the human visual system has been determined at photopic and scotopic levels of luminance by measuring responses to periodic variations of luminance. At any given level of luminance, the contrast level of the light is varied over a range of frequencies in order to determine the minimal contrast of each frequency for eliciting a response. Three different modes of response have been explored: (1) psychophysical judgments of flicker or fusion, (2) electrical responses of the eye (electroretinogram), and (3) potentials evoked in the occipital region of the cortex (visually evoked cortical potentials). A periodic variation (contrast) of 5 per cent is typically sufficient for detection by photopic vision at low frequencies, whereas detection by scotopic vision requires significantly higher contrast. Even with 100 per cent contrast (i.e., with flashes of light separated by dark intervals of equal duration) scotopic resolution is limited to frequencies below 18 H_2, while at photopic levels the frequency range extends typically above 50 H_2. Significantly higher resolution (above 60 H_2) is shown by the electroretinogram responses than by the psychophysical or cortical responses.

Author's Position or Bias: The authors performed these experiments at Hunter Laboratory, Brown University, Providence, Rhode Island, under the U. S. Public Health Service Grant. Dr. Sokol is now at Tufts University, School of Medicine, Boston.

Applicability to Sign Industry: This provides some indication of the effects of flicker and fusion in illuminated signs, particularly those using fluorescent tubing.

III. Visual Perception and the Other Senses
A. Vision and Sound

Anderson, R. H. and Deffenbacher, K. A. "Effect of Sound Stimulations on Visual After Images," *Perceptual and Motor Skills*, 1971, *32*:343-346.

Purpose: This study seeks to confirm and extend the Soviet findings concerning the effects of sound frequency and intensity on reported size and brightness of Purkinje after images.

Content: (From Journal summary) The report describes the structure and operation of a device which provides reliable measurement of changes in the apparent size and brightness of achromatic negative afterimages. Utilizing this device, two experiments were conducted to assess the effects of pure tone intensity and frequency on reported size and brightness of afterimages. Intense sound stimulation produced very pronounced increases in afterimage size and brightness. These results are discussed in light of previous Soviet findings. They confirm Zagorulko's (1964) finding that intense auditory stimulation increases the apparent size of Purkinje afterimages.

Author's Position or Bias: The author is from the University of Nebraska at Omaha.

Applicability to Sign Industry: There may be some applicability to the effect of traffic and industrial noises on the effect and effectiveness of signs.

B. *Vision and Tactile Sense*

Walker, J. T. "Visual Capture in Visual Illusions," *Perception and Psychophysics*, 1971, *10*(2):71-74.

Purpose: This report deals with experiments to demonstrate visual capture in the Muller-Lyer and Ponzo illusions in the absence of any distortions of the optic array.

Content: "Visual capture is the resolution of visual-tactual conflicts in favor of vision. In each previous demonstration of this phenomenon, a distorted optic array, or some mechanical analog for a distorted optic array, has produced a conflict between erroneous visual information and presumably veridical tactual information." Experiments reported in this study used adjustment methods to measure the magnitude of these illusions and the amount of visual capture produced by each.

The two reported experiments show that visual capture can be produced by visual illusions, as well as the visual distortions that have previously been shown to produce this phenomenon (from Journal abstract).

Findings of some importance: The absence of statistically significant effects of instruction conditions shows that visual, tactual, and objective judgments are not differently influenced by the visual illusion. One interaction was found statistically significant—the triple interaction between temporal order of judgment, sex, and illusion vs. control group. $(F = 5.16, df = 2/24, p .05.)$ The author states that "this interaction implies that the pattern of illusion magnitude as a function of judgment order differs slightly across male and female illusion and control groups."

Author's Position or Bias: In the tradition of Gibson (1966) and Rock (1966). The author is from the University of Missouri, St. Louis, Missouri. Definition: Visual capture: The resolution of visual-tactual conflicts in favor of the sense of vision.

Applicability to Sign Industry: This indicates methods of enhancing visual perception dominance over other sense perceptions and provides some insight into perceptual differences between males and females in this area.

IV. Visual Illusions

A. Cultural Influences On Illusion

Restle, F. "Instructions and the Magnitude of an Illusion: Cognitive Factors in the frame of reference," *Perception and Psychophysics* 1971, 9(1A):31-32.

Purpose: To test experimentally the Helson AL equations (1964), wherein a mathematical model of the frame of reference is used to explain contrast illusion and the moon illusion.

Content: Definition: "An *illusion* arises when a given stimulus is observed in two different frames of reference differing with respect to some stimulus (S_1)." "The *magnitude* of the illusion depends upon the weight (w.) given S_1, the illusion-inducing stimulus."

Hypothesis tested in this experiment: "If the weights of the elements of the frame of reference are determined by the·visual array interacting with receptors, then instructions should not affect them, and the effect of instructions must be through response compensation. If, on the contrary, the weights are partly under control of the S, then it should be possible to influence them through instructions. Therefore if the weights are under voluntary control, these two groups should show different illusions, each placing more weight on the stimulus to which attention was directed."

Experiment: Two groups of subjects judged the length of a horizontal line having vertical lines at the ends and a vertical line crossing at the middle. As has been shown in previous studies, judgments of the horizontal line varied inversely with the length of the vertical segments. One group of subjects was told to use the end lines as frame of reference and ignore the center line, and the estimated weights of end and center line were .22 and .02. The other group was told to ignore the end lines and use the center line as a frame of reference. The weights of end and center line for this group were .06 and .22. It was concluded that the Helson AL equations are valid, but that the weights of parts of the field are partly under voluntary control and are not simply a function of the visual field (from journal summary).

Author's Position or Bias: Results support author's (1970) position with respect to individual differences in the magnitude of the moon illusion, that "various Ss might use different frames of reference (e.g., magnitude of objects on the horizon), employing different strategies, and for that reason make consistently different judgments." Author is from Indiana University, Bloomington, Indiana.

Applicability to Sign Industry: This paper deals with the effect of cultural influences in perception of illusions.

B. *Size-Shape Illusions*

Cooper, M. R. and Runyon, R. P. "Error Increase and Decrease in Minimal Form of Mueller-Lyer Illusion," *Perceptual and Motor Skills*, 1970, *31*:535-538.

Summary: Based upon prior research showing that the error associated with the Sanoer parallelogram is maximal when the diagonal lines are physically omitted rather than physically present, an attempt was made to determine whether a similar finding might result from eliminating the shaft in the Mueller-Lyer illusion. An interaction was found between shaft vs. non-shaft condition and fins-in vs. fins-out. Eliminating the shaft significantly increased the error in the fins-in condition and significantly decreased error in the fins-out condition. The results were judged consonant with the previous study (by the same authors) involving the Sander parallelogram (journal summary).

Authors' Position or Bias: The authors are working from C. W. Post College, Department of Psychology, Greenvale, New York.

Applicability to Sign Industry: The article can shed some light on the relationship of design components to perception of illusions.

Fisher, G. H. "Geometrical Illusions and Figural Aftereffects: The Mechanism and its Location," *Vision Research*, 1971, *11*(3):289-309.

Purpose: The essential point of departure of the experiments reported is a direct comparison between illusion and aftereffects employing composite and component versions of the same figures in an appropriate experimental situation.

Content: Previous experimental studies of figural after-effect phenomena are discussed. Particular reference is made to the general question of establishing the locations of perceptual mechanisms, to the possibility of the same mechanism being responsible for both aftereffects and illusions, and to difficulties arising for evaluation of research in this field. The "distorting" and "distorted" components of Ponzo's illusion are distinguished and prepared as I and T figures. An apparatus is described with which any after-effect due to the former (I) can be determined accurately by adjustments made in the latter (T). Analysis of data strongly suggests that the same mechanism underlies both forms of perceptual distortion. A schematic analysis of projections of I and T figures reveals that they are represented topographically upon the cortex in essentially similar ways. It is concluded that the mechanism concerned is located in sub-cortial regions, probably within the retina itself.

Author's Position or Bias: The author is from the Department of Psychology, University of Newcastle, England and is supported by a Medical Research Council Grant (England). In the tradition of Gibson (1933), Kohler (1940), Kohler and Wallach (1944), and Ganz (1966).

Applicability to Sign Industry: This article illustrates the perception of illusions and aftereffects.

Humphrey, N. K. "Contrast Illusions in Perspective," *Nature,* 1971, *232*:91-94, July 9.

Purpose: The author discusses depth-size illusion, size-weight illusion, and contrast illusion as similar phenomena originating in the contrast between the actual and the expected values.

Content: The author uses numerous examples to illustrate for the reader his answers to the question "Why should apparent depth have such an influence on perception of size." He formulates his value theory thus: "If the stimulus has an actual value of "x" and an expected value of "E," the subjective estimate is out by an amount proportional to x-E." Some examples used are: in visual form, the influence of contrast on the size of a circle and the orientation of the line with regard to a circle is judged to be smaller when surrounded by larger circles than by small circles; a line is judged to slope away from another line which crosses it. Author refers to Chinese, Italian, and French paintings for instances of perspective and illusion. A physiological explanation is given proposing a common mechanism for illusions. Evidence of electrophysiology suggests that for many stimulus dimensions, there are nerve units which respond preferentially to stimuli of certain values. An explanation for illusion is that those units which respond preferentially to the "expected value" are selectively depressed. Depth-size illusion is discussed with reference to graphic artists.

Author's Position or Bias: The author is from the Sub-Department of Animal Behavior, Madengley, Cambridge. His general theme is that "the same sort of phenomenon that makes a large object seem lighter than a small object can be linked with the evolution of perspective in painting."

Applicability to Sign Industry: Size and shape perception, particularly with regard to combinations and shapes.

C. *Illusory Motion*

Biederman-Thorson, M., Thorson, J. and Lange, G. D. "Apparent Movement due to Closely Spaced Sequentially Flashed Dots in the Human Peripheral Field of Vision," *Vision Research*, Sept. 1971, *11*(9):889-903.

Purpose: This paper describes some properties of a phenomenon called "a fine-grain movement illusion." The authors report experiments which clarify this movement illusion by examining its relation to involuntary eye movement, limits of perceived temporal order, the perception of real movement, and the phenomemon of metacontrast.

Content: Two dots in the peripheral field of vision, so close to one another that they are not resolved spatially when flashed together, induce a strong illusion of movement when they are flashed sequentially. Light adaptation changes the range of adequate interflash intervals. Stabilized vision and a number of variants of the two-flash program do not abolish the illusion whereas putative dichogeniculate presentation does. The authors state that they have not been able to rule out the view that the illusion shares a common basis with the phenomena of metacontrast and real-movement perception (from journal abstract).

Author's Position or Bias: Thorson and Biederman-Thorson are at the Max Planck Institute in Germany. Lange is from the Department of Neurosciences, School of Medicine, University of California, San Diego.

Applicability to Sign Industry: Particularly applicable to digital data displays and animated signs.

Blakemore, C. "A New Kind of Stereoscopic Vision," *Vision Research*, Nov., 1970, *10*(11):1181-1199.

Purpose: To demonstrate that the binocular grating phenomenon depends on the interpretation of spatial periodicity rather than on positional disparity.

Content: A vertical grating of different spatial frequency in the two eyes mimics the views gained of a real grating rotated about its vertical axis. This is exactly the sensation that such a binocular stimulus produces. The impression of rotation is complete and global: The whole grating seems fused until the difference in spatial period exceeds about 30 per cent. At low (below 0.6c/deg.) and high (above 15c/deg.) spatial frequencies the phenomenon does not occur. The break in fusion comes at the same ratio of periods whatever the angular width of the grating. The sensation is not affected by movement or a slight reduction in contrast of the grating in one eye. This kind of stereopsis may be dependent upon a comparison of the spatial periodicity of the patterns in the two eyes, rather than a point-by-point analysis of positional disparity. The author suggests that there may be binocular neuroses with different optimal spatial frequencies in the two eyes (from journal summary).

Author's Position or Bias: The author is from the Physiological Laboratory, University of Cambridge, England.

Applicability to Sign Industry: Relates to rotating and revolving patterns, particularly the speed of rotating necessary for illusion to occur.

Day, R. H. and Strelow, E. "Reduction or disappearance of visual aftereffect of movement in the absence of patterned surround," *Nature,* March 5, 1971, *230*:55-56.

Purpose: To investigate a previously demonstrated phenomenon that "The apparent movement of stationary patterns goes in the opposite direction to their immediately preceding real movement."

Content: The authors have shown, experimentally, that the visual movement aftereffect is reduced or eliminated in the absence of a patterned surround and that the presence of a surround is a stimulus condition necessary for its occurrence. They suggest that surround variables must, in the future, be taken into account in explaining the movement aftereffect phenomenon. The findings indicate that the movement aftereffect is essentially a relative movement phenomenon. These findings are similar to the observation by Wohlgemuth "that the aftereffect occurs only feebly after movement of the total visual field." The authors extrapolate that the presence of a patterned surround may be a significant determinant of other aftereffects such as those associated with tilted contours, (Gibson) and orientation-specific afterimages obtained with stationary and moving patterns (McCollough, Hepler, Stromeyer).

Author's Position or Bias: The authors are from the Department of Psychology, Monash University, Melbourne, Australia.

Applicability to Sign Industry: Relates to the illusion of motion and design of background.

Kinchla, R. A. "Visual movement perception: A comparison of absolute and relative movement discrimination," *Perception and Psychophysics,* 1971, 9(2A):165-171.

Purpose: Visual movement perception, its terminology, and some theoretical models are discussed. An experiment is reported for which the models seem appropriate.

Content: It is proposed that there are two types of visual movement perception: absolute and relative. The former occurs when an object is seen to move in an otherwise homogeneous field. Relative judgments occur when one object is seen to move with respect to another, i.e., the separation between them is seen to change. The results of the experiment appear relevant to a theory of size or length perception as well as to the general perceptual issue of absolute and relative judgments. The models developed attempt to show the differentiation between the two types of judgments.

V. Factors Related to the Design Components of Signs

A. Light and Dark Patterns

Davidson, M. and Whiteside, J.A. "Human brightness perception near sharp contours," *Journal of the Optical Society of America,* 61(4):530-536.

Purpose: (From journal abstract). The appearances of fields that contain luminance discontinuities (e.g., the contour between a bright and a dark region) do not conform satisfactorily to predictions from models of spatial brightness interaction. Yet when the luminance distribution is systematically varied in regions separated by sharp contours, mach-band-like gradients near the contours vary as predicted. A mechanism acting after spatial interaction may be important when fields contain contours.

Content: The authors review models of spatial brightness interaction and show their deficiencies. Two experiments are described: a contrast-matching and a cusped-rounded experiment. Brightness mechanism is discussed as well as a brightness-integrating mechanism. Findings from the contrast-matching experiment suggest a series of interlaced spatial-interaction systems with various spatial frequency characteristics. This type of highly tuned spatial filter could not be used to account for the results of the cusp-rounded experiment, nor to explain Cornsweet's illusion *(Visual Perception,* Academic, New York, 1970).

Author's Position or Bias: Author's are from the Department of Psychology, University of Rochester, New York.

Applicability to Sign Industry: Relates to the perception of light and dark patterns in signs.

Stanley, G., Finlay, D.C. and Bartlett, W.K. "Regions of brightness and darkness in the sequential presentation of partially overlapping straight lines," *Journal of Experimental Psychology,* 1971, *88*(3):314-318.

Journal Abstract: "Four subjects made estimates of the location of regions of brightness and darkness with respect to a reference code when two partially overlapping illuminated rectangles of 80 x 6mm. were presented sequentially at 0 or 50-msec. interstimulus interval. The stimuli were presented in a left to right order for a duration of either 25 or 50 msec. under conditions of 20-, 30-, or 40-mm. overlap. The results indicated that with increasing stimulus-onset-asynchrony (SOA), there was a shift of greatest brightness from the overlapped region toward the' leading edge of the rectanled presented second. Darkness judgment also shifted from two banks flanking the overlapped region at 25-msec. SOA toward a single region in the area of overlap at greater SOAs. The results are discussed in terms of Beksey's (1967) concept of brightness funneling.

Bekesy (1967) reports a funneling phenomenon whereby regions of lesser excitation pool or summate with regions of greater excitation. Findings also consistent with Stanley (1967) and Stanley & Jackson (1969) "that brightness summation processes are associated with the leading edge of a continuously moving arc-line" and supports their conclusion "that excitation and inhibition processes are important considerations in the sequential presentation of stimulation."

Author's Position or Bias: The author is from the University of Melbourne.

Applicability to Sign Industry: Direct application to perception of digital data signs and design components of illumination signs.

B. *Special Materials and Techniques*

Benson, W. and Whitcomb, M.A. (Editors) *Current Developments in Optics and Vision,* (1967).

Contents: Part II *Holography,* Stanley Ballard, Chairman:

a) Upatnicks, J.—describes development, basic principles and properties of Hologram Photography.

b) Goodman, J.W. and Brooks, R.E.—In separate review applications of holography in areas of "wavefront reconstruction imaging" and some aspects of optical data processing usually included in holography (microscopy, interferometry, vibration analysis, contour generation on 3-D objects, imaging through aberrating media). Authors point at the development of sensor technologies as promising factor in the development of holography.

Applicability to sign industry: Possible application to plastics and sign manufacture.

Benson, W. and Whitcomb, M.A. (Editors) *Current Developments in Optics and Vision* (1967).

Content: Part III—Image Restoration and Enhancement, Brown, J.L., Chairman.

(a) Hall, R.J. and Dossett, W.F.—"The Elastic Surface Transformation." EST is an attempt to develop a display processing technique that will permit the observer to manipulate and enhance marginal signals. The concept of display processing is seen as an entity operation instead of "processing and display" as separate functions. The process is described; EST maintains element and size constancy. It integrates and conveys more than conventional recording and display techniques. Photographic and sonar-gram examples are given as suitable areas of implementation.

Position: The authors foresee "Element Modulation" coupled with direct recording on a prestretched surface as a powerful signal processing and display technique.

(b) Harris, Sr., J.L.—"Image Processing as it relates to the human System"—Image processing exists as an attempt to increase the information efficiency of the display system. Examples from present optics and computer technology generalize that it is now possible to display information in any fashion.

Position: Image processing is seen as a tool for research in the human visual system.

(c) Lohmann, A.W., Experiments in spacial filtering definition includes algebraic formulations. The author and his optics group have developed a new approach for making spacial filters, as an outgrowth of their work on computer-generated holograms. Three areas of application are given: (1) repetition of classical methods with computer-generalized spacial filters; (2) differential operations for enhancing certain features such as edges and corners; (3) pattern recognition with matched filters and other types of filters.

Position: The author states that spacial filter produced

by digital computer can be used in a relatively simple optical data processor, since it has the capability to handle many input data simultaneously.

Applicability to sign industry: Relates to digital data systems, automated displays and computer graphics.

(d) Blackwell, H.R.—"Visual Factors Related to the Design and the Use of Direct-View Electro-Optical Devices," Images produced by these devices are reasonably literal displays of natural objects with enhanced luminance and amplified noise properties. Approach to research: to optimize the design of electro-optical device with the eye of the user. The visual system is seen as capable of isomorphic mapping. Describes an analytic computer program to compute "the element contribution function" (ECF). Comments on quantum noise.

Position: Limitation of this theory due to restrictions of the real world (e.g., search and scanning as opposed to magnification and field view of the telescopes). Notes on physiology: Different portions of the visual field possess up to four separate classes of receptor processes, differing intrinsically in spectral response, spacial frequency response and integrating time. It appears that neural networks from some receptor population may differ in their spacial frequency and temporal characteristics.

(e) Morgan, R.H. "The influence of spacial and temporal band width on the threshold contrast sensitivity of the eye." This paper presents a method for calculating the noise levels of visual signals which differs from work by Rose and deVries. The method is based upon statistical principles used to calculate noise in physical systems.

Position: This method appears to have value in the development of models of visual perception in which predicted and measured data are closely similar.

(f) Tanner, Jr., W.D., Main, D.B., and Cohn, T.E. "Visual Detection of Oscilloscopic Tracings." The problem in reading physiological records is explored. The approach suggested would use computer and human observers. The programming of a "template" by the experimenter for the physiological response is proposed.

Position: The authors are critical of the averaging computer and suggest that assumptions behind averaging be examined. They propose that working within the framework of theory of signal detectability would be more beneficial.

VI. Size and Shape Distance Perception

Benson, W. and Whitcomb, M.A. (Editors) *Current Developments in Optics and Vision: Meeting of Committee on Vision, 1967.* Armed Forces National Research Council Committee on Vision. Washington, D.C.: National Academy of Sciences, N.R.C., 128 pp. Inquiries to be addressed to above at 2101 Constitution Avenue, N.W., Washington, D.C. 20418.

Content: (a) Hyman, A. and Gold, T.—"Dynamic Visual Cues in Flying." Reported experimental studies in which dynamic visual cues are presented to subjects. Carried out for Navy by Sperry Gyroscope Division of Rand Corporation. (1) Presents characteristic findings of the study of visual perception in carrier landing and quantitative data covering the visual judgments of position and aim point. (2) Describes a program planned in a study of visual requirements for optical projection displays sponsored by JANAIR Committee specifically to aid in developing optimal designs for virtual image optical projection systems in the following areas: Binocular disparity, tolerance for differing convergence requirements (i.e., focusing), permissible disparity at boundaries of viewing region, alleviation of retinal rivalry, minimum desired exit pupil size, axial head position. (b) Burg, A.—"Vision and Driving." The role of vision in driving. Critical review of present research shortcomings. Report on research at UCLA on Dynamic Visual Activity (DVA), 17,500 subjects tested. Inconclusive results but the author strongly suggests the adoption of a test by the Department of Motor Vehicles and continued research to provide more information on the relationship.

Applicability to the sign industry: Relates to distance perception, driving, optical display, and digital data.

Frost, N. "Clustering by Visual Shape in the Free Recall of Pictorial Stimuli," *Journal of Experimental Psychology,* 1971, *88*(3):409-413.

Purpose: This article reports on an experiment to test the hypothesis that visual memory organization can be reflected in a verbal memory task.

It was hypothesized that if visual memory (for pictures) is searched during recall of picture names, then recall should be organized according to visual similarities. Stimuli were 32 drawings of common objects, drawn so that they clearly fell into four shape categories. These stimuli were randomly presented to subjects who then gave free recall of the objects' names. Recall was scored for clustering according to the shape categories. Additional subjects were presented the written names of the objects, and their free recall, scored according to the shape categories, was used as a control. It was found that subjects who had seen pictorial stimuli clustered by shape during free recall, while control subjects did not. Furthermore no evidence was found to differentiate the performance of subjects who were led to expect a verbal task (recognition of names) from that of subjects who expected a visual task (recognition of drawings).

Position: The author is from the University of Oregon. The project was supported by the Advanced Research Projects Agency of the Department of Defense.

Applicability to sign industry: Pictures are easier to recall than words and shapes help recall. Relates to advertising coverage.

Landers, W.F. and Cognan, D.C. and Hart, R.R. "Development Changes in the Perception of Inverted Triangular Forms: Closure and Order Effects," *Perceptual and Motor Skills,* 1971, *32*:587-592.

Purpose: This study approaches the problem that "some relatively basic questions concerning the effects of age, closure, and order of presentation on the accurate perception of inverted geometric forms remain unanswered." Authors are attempting to provide some evidence concerning the possible interaction of these variables.

Content: (From Journal summary). Ninety pre-school and school age children were required to judge the orientation of simple triangular forms of varying completeness presented in one of three orders: increasing completeness, decreasing completeness, and randomly. Results indicated that the number of correct responses varied as a function of age, degree of closure, and presentation order. A reliable interaction between age and presentation order indicated that the random presentation order was more difficult for the younger children. These results were taken as substantial support for the perceptual development viewpoint typified by Gibson, Hebb, and Piaget.

Position: The author is from Texas Tech University.

Applicability to sign industry: Design of signs for children, and shape perceptions.

Content: Investigates the influence of texture density gradients on bisection judgments. Artificially deformed texture density gradients were used in the design of the experiments in order to discover whether relative distance judgments are influenced by texture density gradients of stimulation. The author states that "the apparent mid-point specified in the texture density gradient will then be different from the objective mid-point determined by the physical characteristics of the apparatus." Subjects made monocular relative distance judgments by moving a marker to the apparent physical mid-point between two other fixed markers which were placed on a surface along the subjects' line of sight. Judgments were significantly influenced by the texture density gradients of stimulation derived from the surface over which they are made. The author suggests that certain surfaces may provide more "adequate" gradients of texture density than others; that accurate perception may be possible only when certain well-defined textured surfaces are present. This differs from Gibson's suggestion that all surfaces will provide subjects with sufficiently well-defined texture density gradients to permit veridical judgments of distance.

Position: The author is from the University of Birmingham, and a follower of J.J. Gibson.

Applicability to sign industry: Relates to texture and distance judgments.

VII. Illumination and Visual Perception

Heywood, S. and Churcher, J. "Eye movement and the afterimage. I: Tracking the Afterimage," *Vision Research,* 1971, *11*(101:1163-1168.

Purpose: The suggestion made by Mack and Bachant, 1969, that "slow pursuit-like movements may occur when a subject experiences an afterimage" is experimentally examined.

Content: Methodology: Horizontal eye movements were measured by binocular recording of the electro-oculogram (EOG). The eye movements, after amplification, were written out on Kodak Linagraph Photosensitive paper at a speed of 10 in./minute. Findings: Although subjects failed to make smooth eye movements when tracking an imaginary pendulum in the dark, when given an afterimage to track they exhibited sustained smooth eye movements despite the absence of a moving visual stimulus. These results suggest that smooth eye movements may be a product of two processes, one which stabilizes images on the retina, and one which inhibits saccadic behavior. (Saccadic movements occur 1-3 times each second.)

Position: Authors are from the Institute of Experimental Psychology, Oxford.

Applicability to sign industry: Relates to perception of signs after dark, from a moving vehicle, digital data, flashing, and computer graphics.

Kulikowski, J.J. "Some stimulus parameters affecting spacial and temporal resolution of human vision," *Vision Research,* 1971, *11*(1)83-93.

Purpose: The experiment explores the relationship between the two mechanisms of spacial and temporal contrast thresholds, which are determined by the same analyser, especially at higher frequencies.

Content: Contrast threshold was measured psychophysically for a sinuosoidal grating presented periodically with a variable temporal frequency for various parameters of patterns. Special attention was paid to the range of high spacial frequencies as defining the resolving power of the eye. Within this range, the contrast thresholds were found to be almost independent of many parameters of patterns. It was found also that the sum of certain spacial and temporal resolution indices was proportional to the logarithm of the contrast; this sum was also a logarithmic function of the average luminance in the mesopic range of luminance (Journal abstract).

Position: The author is a follower of psychologists in the field summarized by Westheimer (1965) in "Visual Acuity," *Annual Review of Psychology, 16*:359-380.

Applicability to sign industry: Relates to flashing signs and illumination.

Pantle, A. "Flicker adaptation—I. Effect on visual sensitivity to temporal fluctuations of light intensity," *Vision Research,* 1971, *11*(9):943-952.

Purposes: Experiment is reported which was conducted to (1) determine what changes, if any, of the temporal frequency-response curve of the eye would result from flicker adaptation and (2) to test the validity of single-and multiple-channel models.

Content: Human sensitivity to temporal fluctuations of light intensity was found to be lower after adaptation to a flickering light than it was after adaptation to a steady light of the same time-average retinal illuminance. Such a difference of sensitivity defines a flicker adaptation phenomenon. The magnitude of the flicker adaptation effect was used as an index of strength of visual interactions that occur between stimuli of different temporal frequencies. On the basis of the results obtained it was tentatively concluded that the temporal aspects of visual signals are processed by more than visual channel or filter, each with its own frequency-response characteristic (From journal abstract).

Position: The author is from the Department of Psychology, University of California, Los Angeles. The basic premise of this field of study is that "human visual sensitivity to periodic, temporal fluctuations of light intensity depends upon the rate at which the changes occur."

Applicability to sign industry: Relates especially to illuminated and flashing signs.

Prestrude, A.M. and Baker, H.D. "Light adaptation and visual latency," *Vision Research,* 1971, *11*(4):363-369.

Purpose: After a brief review of findings from research in the field, the authors conclude that adaptation should perhaps be the major factor in determining the effects of illuminance upon latency of the visual response. Experiments were set up to assess the relative contributions of adaptation and target-background contrast to visual latency.

Content: Two procedures based on binocular latency difference measures were used. The temporal resolving properties of the eye are considered in terms of binocular latncy differences. Experiments demonstrate that temporal resolution is a function of visual adaptation. The effects of target-background contrast on visual latencies appear to be consistent with the effects of field adaptation. Thus the authors suggest that the mechanism of visual adaptation is sufficient to account for the relation between intensity and latency. (From journal abstract).

Position: Other investigators of related problems were Dodwell (1968) and Rushton (1962, 1965). Prestrude is from the Department of Psychology, Virginia Polytechnic Institute, Blacksburg, Va. Baker is from the Department of Psychology, Florida State University, Tallahassee, Florida.

Applicability to sign industry: Time factors in the visual perception of illuminated signs at night.

Thijssen, J.M. and Vendrik, A.J.H. "Differential luminance sensitivity of the human visual system," *Perception and Psychophysics,* 1971 *10*(1):58-64.

Purpose: This paper concerns an investigation of the applicability of Weber's law to the differential sensitivity of the visual system under various conditions of the adaptation level.

Content: The differential sensitivity of the visual system is investigated by means of two simultaneously presented stimuli in a yes-no procedure. The sensitivity measure 6I appears to be proportional to stimulus intensity (i.e., Weber's law). The curve displaying Weber's law is little affected by variation of the background intensity or of the adaptation level. An increment threshold experiment using only one stimulus yields a proportionality of 6I with the square root of the background intensity. An additional experiment shows that the sensitivity measure 6I for two flashes decreases first, from dark up to a particular background intensity, and increases when the background tends to mask the flashes. So, in general, two background levels exist with the same differential sensitivity. The results cannot be easily explained by the simple quantum fluctuation concept. A model based partially on electrophysiological data from the literature is proposed which involves a particular adaptation mechanism, a transducer with a limited lynamical range, and a range setting mechanism (Journal abstract.)

Position: The authors are from Jijmegen University, Nijmegan, The Netherlands.

Applicability to sign industry: Deals with flashing lights and background interaction.

Thornton, W.A. "Luminosity and color-rendering capability of white light," *Journal of the Optical Society of America,* 1971, *61*(9):1155-63.

Purpose: This article examines the question: what is the optimum spectral power distribution (SPD) of artificial light? The optimized SPDS found are close to the ultimate for the combination of high luminous efficiency with high color-rendering index (CRI).

Content: The spectral power distribution of white light required to maximize luminous efficiency and the color-rendering index is approximately by an additive combination of three spectral lines near 450, 540, 610 mm. The two wave length regions near 500 and 580 mm. are disadvantageous. These results are related to the color-mixture functions of human color vision. Three functions that indicate the effectiveness of red, green, and blue light for composing high-performance white light are shown (Journal summary).

Position: The author states that the proper objective for research programs on the designs of lamp emission is for white light composed of three spectral colors near 450, 540, and 610 mm. Also he projects for next century as follows: "(a) luminosity of white light will still be important and the SPD of all artificial light will have approached the optimum three-line distribution asymptotically, or (b) luminosity will be unimportant because of greater availability of power and ease of dissipation, and the composition of artificial light will have moved down the curves to broad, structureless distributions with low luminosity but superb color rendition." The author is from Westinghouse Fluorescent and Vapor Lamp Divisions, Bloomfield, New Jersey.

VIII. Speed and Accuracy of Perception

Goodglass, H. "Stimulus duration and visual processing time," *Perceptual and Motor Skills,* 1971, *33*(1):179-182.

Purpose: This paper describes findings in a study in which the technique of backward masking is used to determine the time for the recognition of a verbal image in iconic storage. The particular question asked is whether varying the duration of a supra-threshold tachistoscopic stimulus influences the values of the critical inter-stimulus intervals (ISI).

Content: The ISI is regarded as the perceptual processing time for the target. The results of the experiment shows that at target exposures near the 90 per cent recognition threshold, each requires 2m.sec. These results suggest that during the process of recognition, the progressively fading iconic image is scanned continuously until enough information is extracted from it for encoding to take place. Increasing the duration of the "on" phase beyond the recognition threshold level may be presumed to provide greater detail or greater intensity in the iconic image. As a result the scanning process more quickly accumulates the information needed for identifying the stimulus.

Position: The author follows earlier studies by Kinsbourne and Warrington (1962). Other investigators who have studied these problems are Haber (1970) and Haber and Nathanson (1969). The author is from the Boston Veterans Administration Hospital, supported by NINDS grants to Clark and Boston University.

Applicability to sign industry: Relates to digital data display, flashing lights, and computer graphics.

Gummerman, Kent. "Selective perception and the number of alternatives," *The American Journal of Psychology,* 1971, *84*(2):173-179.

Purpose: To examine the concept of selective perception by using a before-after experimental design different in number of stimuli (16 instead of 4) from the original experiment (1970, same author). A tachistoscope is used.

Content: The subject saw one of four of one of 16 letterlike stimuli, with the choices reduced to two before and after (for two groups of subjects) or after (for two other groups) the stimulus, which was followed by a masking figure. The outcome suggests that selective perception occurs with prior knowledge of alternatives—but only if that knowledge simplified the task. Selective perception appears to consist of "instructions" as to which of the stimulus attributes are task-relevant and should be processed.

Position: The first studies in this area were done in 1954 by Lawrence and Coles. Selective perception was then called "perceptual tuning". Other researchers who used similar techniques are Long, Reid and Henneman (1960), Egeth and Smith (1967), Sperling (1960), Neisser (1967), and

Friksen and Collins (1969). The author is from the University of Texas at Austin, Texas.

Applicability to sign industry: Pertains to the number of stimuli which can be perceived in short time; particularly relevant to perception of signs when driving.

Holding, D.H. "The amount seen in brief exposures," *Quarterly Journal of Experimental Psychology,* 1971, *23*(1): 72-81.

Purpose: The author seeks further experimental support for a conclusion reached earlier by Holding (1970), which was "that letters not selected for attention appear to be not recoverable or not 'seen' " The author investigates partial reporting behavior in an attempt to meet possible objections (e.g., eliciting verbal guesses tends to impose a strategy of guessing).

Content: The experiments reported are a series of attempts to test consequences of assuming that a subject exposed to briefly presented tachistoscopic information does not have access to a visual image. The partial report procedure is examined under several conditions with the letter row cues immediately following stimulus exposure, and at different levels of cue delay. The results of eye movement monitoring and of instructing subjects where to look, agree with the guessing data of a previous experiment in showing a sharp decline in the number of letters correctly reported when the subject is looking at the wrong row, in conformity with the anticipative selection hypothesis. The result of varying the subject's uncertainty about what is to be reported is to vary the slope of the delay curve; with the implication that inefficient strategies of rehearsal, rather than visual image decay, are responsible for the reported delay effects (Journal summary).

Position: The author is a follower of Sperling (1960) and Neisser (1967) and the selective attention hypothesis from the Department of Psychology, University of Louisville, Louisville, Kentucky.

Applicability to sign industry: Relates to driving and signs; importance of cuing content is most important. A person may read the wrong line unless cued.

Holt-Hansen, Kristian. "Perception of a straight line briefly exposed," *Perceptual and Motor Skills,* 1970, *31*:59-69.

Summary: The stimulus used in this experiment was a verticle, straight red line, 17 cm. long and about 2 mm. wide, which for 60m/sec. was projected onto a medium gray screen 2 m. from the subject. Fixating then ethermost point of the line the subject experienced the sensation that the line grew from the point of fixation to full length in order and then decreased in length to the point of fixation. The experienced time of lengthening-shortening was on an average about 570 m. sec. for 37 subjects and was measured by means of a special methodology. Subjects experienced a regular oscillating phenomenon of perception. The author has sought a functional relationship between this oscillating phenomenon of perception and the oscillating processes of the brain.

Position: The author is from the Psychological Laboratory at Copenhagen University.

Applicability to sign industry: Relates to perception of signs from a point of fixation.

Link, S.W. and Tindall, A.D. "Speed and accuracy in comparative judgments of line length," *Perception and Psychophysics,* 1971, 9(3A):284-288.

Purpose: This experiment is the last of a series of five experiments designed to investigate theoretical issues concerning the relationship between speed and accuracy.

Contents: The paper presents an extension of Henmon's (1906) finding that reaction time (RT) decreases as the difficulty of discriminating a difference between two line segments decreases. It is shown that when a critical time deadline is imposed on the experimental task, RT remains constant with respect to changes in discrimination difficulty, but that correct response probability increases with increasing difference between two line segments. The data is examined in terms of current theories for the speed-accuracy trade-off (Journal abstract).

The authors conclude that the "subject must be controlling the length of his response time." The authors also presume that "the temporal process (or processor) controlling RT imposes limitations on the amount of information fed to the decision process. In a sense, then, the temporal process dominates the decision process.

Position: The authors are followers of Henmon (1906), who argued that "differences in sensation should be equal if it takes equal time to perceive them." Henmon supported his argument with results showing that RT did become shorter as the difference between two line segments increased. Authors are from McMaster University, Hamilton, Ontario, Canada.

Applicability to sign industry: Relates to perception of signs from a moving vehicle.

SUPPLEMENTARY BIBLIOGRAPHY

Abramson, Paul. "Blockage of Signs by Trucks." *Traffic Engineering.* 1965, Vol. 14.

Abramson, Paul. "Blockage of Signs by Trucks." *Traffic Engineering.* 1971, Vol. 41.

Abse, Wilfred. "Some Psychologic and Psychoanalytic Aspects of Perception." *Perception and Environment: Foundations of Urban Design.* (Ed.) R. Stryse, U. of N.C.: Chapel Hill, 1966.

"Accident Rates as Related to Design Elements of Rural Highways." *National Cooperative Highway Research Program Report.* 1969, No. 47.

Accident Experience in Relation to Road and Roadside Features. Michigan State Highway Department, Planning and Traffic Division, 1952.

Adams, James W.R. "A Town Planner Looks at Outdoor Advertising." *Building.* August 19, 1966.

Ady, Ronald W. *An Investigation of the Relationship between Illuminated Advertising Signs and Expressway Accidents.* Traffic Safety Research Review, 1967, Vol. 11 (1).

Allen, T.M. & Straub, A.L. "Sign Brightness and Legibility." *Highway Research Board Bulletin 127,* 1955.

Allen, T.M. "Night Legibility Distances of Highway Signs", *Highway Research Board Bulletin 191,* Night Visibility, 1958.

American Association of State Highway Officials Committee on Planning and Design Policies *Design Controls and Criteria* Washington, 1954.

American Society of Planning Officials, Planning, Advisory Service, "The Elimination of Non-Conforming Signs" *Information Report* No. 209. Chicago, April, 1969.

Architectural Psychology. Salt Lake City, University of Utah, 1967-68, Vols. 1-5.

Arctander, Eric H., "Signs You'll See Appearing Out of Thin Air." *Popular Science,* 1969, Vol. 47, No. 8.

Ashley, F., Myers, J.R. & Smith, D.C. *City Signs and Lights, A Policy Study.* The Boston Redevelopment Authority, The U.S. Department of Housing and Urban Development. January, 1971.

Appleyard, Donald and Lynch, Kevin. *Signs in the City.* Cambridge: The Massachusetts Institute of Technology Press, 1963.

Appleyard, Donald. *The View from the Road.* Cambridge, Massachusetts, The Massachusetts Institute of Technology Press, 1964.

"A Review of Transportation Aspects of Land-Use Controls". *National Cooperative Highway Research Program Report*. 1966, No. 31, Chapter 3.

Association of National Advertisers Inc., *Essentials of Outdoor Advertising*. New York, 1958.

Automobile Safety Foundation. *Traffic Control and Roadside Elements: Their Relationship to Highway Safety*, 1963.

Baker, W.T. The New Jersey Milepost System. *Traffic Engineering*, 1967. 37 (9) 28-30.

Banford, J.C. *Environmental Traffic Standard*. Unpublished M.A. Thesis, U.B.C., 1963.

Bezkorovainy, G. Optimum hazard index formula for railroad crossing protection for Lincoln, Nebraska. *Traffic Engineering*, 1967, 38 (3) 14-21.

Bezkorovainy, G. & Ku, C. The Influence of Horizontal Curve Advisory Speed Limits on Spot-Speeds. *Traffic Engineering*, 1966, 36 (12) 24-28.

Bezkorovainy, G. & Holsinger, R. G. The use of stop signs at Railroad Crossings. *Traffic Engineering*, 1966 37 (2) 54-59.

Blake, Peter. *God's Own Junkyard*. New York, Holt, Rinehart and Winston, 1963.

Bogart, Leo. *Strategy in Advertising*. Harcourt Brace & World, New York, 1967.

Brower, Sidney, *Signs in the City*. Cambridge, Massachusetts. Institute of Technology, Department of City and Regional Planning, June, 1963.

Brainard, W., Campbell, M., Elkin, B. "Design and Interpretability of Road Signs." *Journal of Applied Psychology*, 1961, 45, 130.

Bronn, I.D. "Measurement of Control Skills, Vigilance, and Performance on a Subsidiary Task During 12 Hours of Car Driving". *Ergonomics*, 1967, 10, 665.

Bryant, J.F. Research notes—Research on Traffic Signals. *Australian Road Research*, 1968.

Buchanan, Colin D. "Standards and Values in Motor-Age Towns". *Journal of the Town Planning Institute,* XLVII, 10, 321-328.

Buck, L. "Errors in the Perception of Railway Signals". *Ergonomics* 1963, 6, 181.

Burg, A., and Hulbert S. "Predicting the Effectiveness of Highway Signs". *Highway Research Board Bulletin 324,* 1962, 1.

Benepe, Barry. "Pedestrian in the City" *Traffic Quarterly*. New York. Columbia University Press, Vol. XIV, No. 1, 1965.

Blatnik, J.A. "The Need for Highway Safety" *Traffic*

Quarterly. New York. Columbia University Press, Vol. XXII, 1968.

Bankley, S. "Charming But Impossible", *Boston Globe,* August 10, 1967.

Birren, Faber. "Safety on Highways: A Problem of Vision, Visibility, and Color". *American Journal of Ophthalmology*, 1957, 43, 265-270.

Buzzie, Giancarlo. *Advertising, Its Cultural and Political Effects.* Minneapolis, University of Minnesota Press, 1968.

British Columbia Lower Mainland Regional Planning Board, "Suggested Standard Sign By-Law", 1967.

Brown, A.T. and Sherrard, H.M. *Town and Country Planning.* Melbourne University Press, 1951.

Biggs, N.L. Directional Guidance of Motor Vehicles: A Preliminary Survey and Analysis. *Ergonomics*, 1962, 9 (3), 193-202.

Barrett, R., and Hetherton, Ross. "Issues and Problems of Proof in the Judicial Review of Roadside Advertising Controls", *H.R.B. Bulletin 337*, 1962, 24-40.

Bloomer, Richard H. Perceptual Defense and Vigilance and Driving Safety. *Traffic Quarterly*, 1962.

Brattinga, P. "Signs of Life: Street Signs", 1964, March, *Print 18*, 32-37.

Cameron, C. A Comparative Evaluation of Speed Control Signs. *Australian Road Research,* 1968, December.

Conner, R.E. The Revised U.S. Manual on Uniform Traffic Control Devices. *Traffic Engineering and Control,* 1971, 13, No. 5.

City Club of Portland. "Recommended Revision of Portland Outdoor Advertising Sign Regulations". *Report on Sign Code Revision.* Portland, Parkland City Club Bulletin, 1971, 11, No. 3.

Claus, R.J. and Claus, K.E. *The Visual Environment.* Toronto: Collier-Macmillan, 1971.

Cloud, S. and March R. "The Great Billboard Sellout" *Cry* California. California, California Tomorrow, 1967, 11, No. 3.

Dodge, Cyrille, E. Traffic Signal System Capacity. *Traffic Engineering.* 1970, 40, No. 8.

Davis, Russell. "Railway Signals Passed At Danger: The Drivers, Circumstances, and Psychological Processes." *Ergonomics*, 1966, 9, 211.

Dempsey, M. *Pattern & Complexity: Psychophysical Needs as Determinants in the Visual Environment.* U.B.C., 1968, August.

Dirksen, Charles J. Advertising Principles and Problems. Homewood, Ill., R.O. Irwin, 1968.

Ewald, William R. *Street Graphics,* Washington, D.C. American Society of Landscape Architects Foundation, 1971, June.

Daber, Richard P. *Environment Design.* Toront, Van Nostrand, 1969.

Elwood, P.H. "Highway Accidents in Relation to Roadside Business and Advertising". *Highway Research Board: Roadside Development Report,* 1961, 40, p. 54.

Enfield, C.W. "Control of Outdoor Advertising: Federal Laws and Standards". *Highway Research Board: Roadside Development Report,* 1949, 29, p. 105.

Forbes, T.W. et al., "A Comparison of Lower Case and Capital Letters for Highway Signs". *Highway Research Board Proceedings,* 1951, 30, pp. 355-371.

Forbes, T.W. Factors in highway sign visibility. *Traffic Engineering,* 1969, 39 (12), 20-27.

Forbes, T.W. "A Method for Analysis of the Effectiveness of Highway Signs". *Journal of Applied Psychology,* 1939, 23, p. 669.

French, A. "Capacities of One-Way and Two-Way Streets with Signals and with Stop-Signs." *Highway Research Board Bulletin 112,* 1955, p. 16.

Fischer, John. "How to Look at a Billboard". *Harper's Magazine.* New York: Harper & Brothers, 1955, 220, No. 1316.

French, R.A. "Coordinated Traffic Signalling System" Sydney, Australia *Traffic Quarterly,* New York: Columbia University Press, 1965.

Forbes, T.W., Pain, R.F., Fry, J.P. (Jr.) and Joyce, R.P., "Effect of sign position and brightness on seeing simulated highway signs", *Highway Research Record,* 1967, No. 164, 29-37.

Fatigue, (Ed.) W.F. Floyd, A.W. Wilford. London: H.K. Lewis & Co. Ltd., 1953.

Forbes, F.W. et al. "Effectiveness of Symbols for Lane Control Signals" *Highway Research Board Bulletin* 244 (1960).

Gibson, J.C. "Perception as a Function of Stimulation". *Psychology: A Study of Science.* (Ed.) Sigmund Kach. New York, 1959.

Granger, J. and Quang Quy, N. "Safer Left Turn Signing". *Traffic Engineering,* 1971, 41, No. 12.

"Garden State Asks Removal of Signs Diverting Drivers," *New York Times,* December 22, 1968.

Gaines, G. "Environmental Stress and the Urban Dweller" *Michigan Mental Health Research Bulletin.* Winter, 1969.

Gaines, G. "Men Under Stress" *Science and Technology,* January, 1968.

Gaines, G. "Man, City, Auto" *Ekistics,* January, 1968.

Goldensen, R. "Stress" *Encyclopedia of Human Behaviour.* 1st Edition, Vol. 2, 1263-1264.

Glancy, D.M. "A Study of Highway Characteristics at Locations of Traffic Accident Occurrence", *Thesis.* Ohio State University, Columbus, December, 1956.

Gerlough, D.L. and F.A. Wagner, "Improved Criteria for Traffic Signals at Individual Intersections" *National Cooperative Highway Research Program Report No. 32.* Planning Research Corporation. Highway Research Board.

Gnan, Mrs. Paul. "Ohio Roadside Council Research in Highway Safety" *Twenty-first Short Course on Roadside Development.* Ohio Dept. of Highways, 1962, 5-21.

Greenshields, B.D. Attitudes, Emotions and Accidents, *Traffic Quarterly New York:* Columbia University Press, April, 1959.

Gossage, H. "How to Look at Billboards" *Harper's Magazine 220.* 1960, 21, 12-16.

Haber, Ralph Norman. "How We Remember What We See". *Scientific American.* New York, Scientific American Inc., 1970, May, 104-112.

Hoftiezer, Gaylord J. "Combating the Crime of the Streets". *Industrial Design.* New York, Whitney Publications, January, 1969, Vol. 16, 44-47.

Hooper, David L. "Trees or Billboards?" New Moves Against Visual Pollution. *Washington Highways.* Olympic. September, 1971 p. 10-11.

Hsuck, John W. *Outdoor Advertising, History and Regulation.* Notre Dame, Indiana, University of Notre Dame Press, 1969.

Haddon, Wm. Jr., Suchman, E.A., and Klein, D. (Eds.) *Accidents Research, Methods and Approaches.* New York, Harper & Row, 1964.

Hammer, C.G. "Evaluation of Minor Improvements". *Highway Research Record 286,* 1969, p. 33.

Hummel, C. and Schneidler, G. "Driver Behavior at Dangerous Intersections Marked by Stop Signs or by Red Blinker Lights". *Journal of Applied Psychology,* 1955, 39, p. 17.

Hanson, D.R. and Woltman, H.L. and 3M Company. "Sign Background and Angular Position" Highway Research Record. Washington, D.C.: *Highway Research Board* No. 169, 1967.

Hanron, Robert B. "Billboard Curbs Urged", *Boston Globe,* April 4, 1969.

Highway Research Board. "Traffic Control Devices", Three Reports, *Highway Research Record No. 151*. Washington, D.C., 1966.

Head, J.A. "Predicting Traffic Accidents from Roadway Elements on Urban Extensions of State Highways" *Highway Research Board* Bulletin 208, 1959, p. 45-63.

Highway Research Board, Bureau of Public Roads. *Scenic Easements*. Washington, 1968.

Highway Research Board Regulation of Outdoor Advertising Under the Police Power. *Highway Research Board Special Report No. 41*, 1958, p. 38-49.

Hall, Edward T. *The Hidden Dimensions*. Doubleday & Co. Inc., Garden City, New York, 1966.

Harris, Peter. *Puzzle: Find the Traffic Lights*. Vancouver Sun Weekend Magazine, 1960.

Head, J.A., "Predicting Traffic Accidents From Roadway Elements on Urban Extensions of State Highways". *Highway Research Board Bulletin No. 208:* Traffic Accident Studies, 1958.

Hypothesis

Accidents on urban extensions of highways can be predicted from a number of elements such as average daily traffic, commercial and residential units, intersections, signalized intersections, indicated speed, pavement width, effective lane width, and the number of lanes.

Data Gathering

Head uses a survey approach: (1) field observation and notation of the above elements, and (2) documentary analysis of accident data.

Sample: 466 urban sections of highways were studied. These ranged from 0.1 miles to 2.1 miles in length; the average length of those analyzed was 0.4 miles. In order to compare sections of varying lengths, accidents per million vehicle-miles were considered. All data concerned Oregon in 1954 and 1955.

Findings

(1) Accident rates on low volume roads have no significant relationship with any roadway features.

(2) In higher A.D.T. areas, accidents increase when:

    (a) the number of commercial units increases

    (b) the number of traffic signals increases

    (c) the number of intersections increases

    (d) indicated speed decreases

    (e) pavement width increases

Rival Plausible Hypotheses

(1) Since signals were introduced to reduce congestion and accidents it is probable that traffic signals reduce acci-

dents (rather than increase them, as implied in the conclusions).

(2) Since accidents increase with the number of commercial units, and since signs increase with the number of commercial units (because businesses invariably have signs), it could be hypothesized that signs cause accidents. However, a rival hypothesis is that congestion caused by commercial units, and not signs, causes accidents.

Ing, Albert. *An investigation of sign regulation and its effect on the Urban Environment.* Unpublished M.A. Thesis, U.B.C., 1968.

If Highway Signs Confuse You There Could Be An Answer. *Commercial Car Journal,* 1970, 120, No. 4.

Improved Criteria for Traffic Signals at Individual Intersections. *N.C.H.R.P.R.,* 1967, No. 32.

"Improved Criteria for Traffic Signal Systems on Urban Arterials" *N.C.H.R.P.R.,* 1969, No. 73.

International Union of Local Authorities, Survey Concerning the Control and Supervision of the Exertion and Placement of Advertisements in Ancient Towns and Rural Areas in Various Countries. The Hague, May, 1950.

Jackman, W.T. Driver obedience to stop and slow signs. Investigating and forecasting traffic accidents, *Highway Research Board. Bulletin, 1957,* 167, 9-17.

Jellicoe, G.A. *Utopia.* London, Studio Books, 1961.

Johanson, G. and Kare, Rumar. "Drivers and Road Signs". *Ergonomics* 1966, 9, p. 57.

Johnson, D. "Structure and Content of State Control of Roadside Advertising Along the Interstate System." *Highway Research Board Bulletin No. 337,* 1962.

Kalbeek, J.W.H. "On the Measurement of Deterioration in Performance Caused by Distraction Stress". *Ergonomics,* 1964, 7, p. 187.

Kepes, G. *What Signs Can Be.*

Kerian, J.R. "Valuation of Advertising Rights" *Highway Research Record* Washington, D.C.: *Highway Research Board No. 166,* 1967.

King, L.E., "A Laboratory Comparison of Symbol and Word Roadway Signs" *Traffic Engineering and Control.* 1971, 12, No. 10.

Keeble, Lewis. *Principles and Practice of Town and Country Planning.* The Estates Gazette Ltd., London, 1952.

Kipp, O.L. Final Report on the Minnesota Roadside Study. Highway Research Board Land acquisition and control of adjacent areas, 1951 Bulletin No. 55.

Kipp, O.L. Minnesota Roadside Survey. Progress Report on Accident, Access Point and Advertising Sign Study in Minnesota. Highway Research Board Land acquisition and Control of Adjacent Areas, 1951, Bulletin No. 38.

Kelly, S. "Expo 67, Message from the Sponsor" *Industrial Design 13* 1966, September, p. 66-73.

Lauer, A.R., & McMonagle, J.C. "Do Road Signs Affect Accidents?" *Traffic Quarterly*, 1955 9 (3), 332-329.

Lusch, Pfefer, Moran. Effect of Control Devices on Traffic Operations. *Highway Research Board,* 1967.

Lawshe, C.H. "Studies in Automobile Speed on the Highway". *Journal of Applied Psychology,* 1940, 24, 318.

Lynch, K. and Students. *Signs in the City.* Department of City and Regional Planning. Institute of Technology, Massachusetts, June, 1963.

Lucas, D.B., and Britt, S.H. *Advertising Psychology and Research,* New York: McGraw-Hill, 1950.

Laner, S. and Sell, R.G. An Experiment on the Effect of Specially Designed Safety Posters. *Occupational Psychology,* 1960, 34, 153-169.

Kuprijanow, B. "Motorists Needs and Services on the Interstate Highway" *H.R.B. Report 64,* 1969.

McMonagle, J. Carl, "The Effect of Roadside Features on Traffic Accidents". *Traffic Quarterly.* New York, 1952, April, 228-243.

Data Source of McMonagle's Study—100 mile stretch of highway in Ohio. From here data gathered on (1) "rate of accident occurrence per large and prominent advertising sign, at each of the 100-foot increments of distance of the accident from advertising signs" (2) accident and sign density. Data Source on this stretch was the 3025 accidents that occurred in 1947, 1948, 1949.

Data Gathering Technique used by McMonagle: Documentary—accident reports: Field Study—to establish where the large and prominent signs were situated, and sign density.

McMonagle's study concluded that advertising signs make no significant contribution to accidents along the highway used. The study stated its own rival plausible hypothesis that accidents could be related to roadside friction from uncontrolled access and egress to certain business establishments, private drives, and traffic volume. Considering that primarily documentary data was used, and the source was from 1947 the conclusions appear relatively reliable considering the plausible rival hypothesis.

Myer, J.R. and F. Ashley. *City Signs and Lights*—A Policy Study. Boston, Signs/Lights/Boston, January, 1971.

May, A.D., the Effectiveness of Motorway Control Signals. *Traffic Engineering,* 1970, 40, No. 8.

Millard, R.S. Roundabouts and Signs. *Traffic Engineering and Control* 1969, 11, No. 8.

Meadows, R. "Road Advertising and Identification" *Traffic Quarterly* 1968, 22, p. 609.

Marsh, Susan. "Interstate Sign Malls Rout Billboard Clutter", *New York Times,* December 22, 1968, p. 17.

MacBryde, Cyril Mitchell. *Signs and Symptoms.* Philadelphia, Lippincot, 1964.

Marks, H. and Spitz, S., "A Review of Transportation Aspects of Land-Use Control" *National Cooperative Highway Research Program Report 31,* 1966.

Maslov, A.H. and Mintz, N.L., "Effects of Aesthetic Surroundings". *Journal of Psychology,* 1956, 41, p. 247-254.

Meadauis, R. Roadside Advertising and Identification. *Traffic Quarterly* 1968, 22.

Myra, R. *Some Theoretical Aspects of Attitudes and Perception.* Working Paper 15, University of Toronto, 1970.

McMonagle, J. Carl, "Accident Analysis—Telegraph Road, 1947-48" *Highway Research Board Bulletin No. 30.* Progress in Roadside Protection, 1951.

McMonagle, J. Carl, "How Roadside Affects Traffic Accident Experience" *American Association of State Highway Officials.* Convention group meetings, papers, and discussions, 1949.

McMonagle, J. Carl, Traffic Accidents and Roadside Features. *Highway Research Board,* Land Acquisition and Control of Adjacent Areas Bulletin No. 55, 1952.

McMonagle, J. Carl. "The Relation of Traffic Signals to Intersection Accidents" *H.R.B. Bulletin No. 74,* Washington, p. 45-53.

Michigan Highway Department. "How Roadside Features Affect Traffic Accident Experience" *(Lansing,* 1949-1952).

Minnesota Department of Highways. "Minnesota Rural Trunk Highway Accident, Access Point and Advertising Sign Study". (St. Paul, 1952).

Moore, R.L. and A.W. Christie. "Research on Traffic Signs," *Engineering for Traffic Conference.* London: Printer Hall, 1963.

MacGillvray, C.I. and Michael, H.I. "An Evaluation of Aesthetics of Junkyard Screening and Billboard Densities" *Proceedings of the 54th Annual Roadside School, Purdue University,* 1968, p. 175-185.

Michaels, Richard M., "Driver Tension Responses Generated on Urban Streets". *Public Roads,* Vol. 31, No. 3, p. 53.

Martin, W.J., Jr., and Nelson, E.D. "Land Use Control

and the Billboard" *California Law Review,* 1958, 46, 809-823.

Nairne, Ian. *The American Landscape.* New York: Random House, 1965.

Netherton, Ross, Markham, Marion. *Roadside Development and Beautification, Legal Authority and Aims Part II.* H.R.B., Washington, 1966.

Nairne, Ian. *Outrage.* Architectural Review. June, 1955.

New York State. Natural Beauty Commission. *Sample Provision of a Local Law to Regulate Signs.* 1965.

Neary, J., Blight Blossoms on the American Highway, *Life,* New York, July 24, 1970.

Neu, R.J. "Internally-Illuminated Traffic Signs". *Traffic Quarterly* 10, 1956, 247-259.

"Olympics: Art, Buildings, Graphics". *Architectural Forum,* New York, Urban America, Inc., October, 1968, Vol. 124, No. 3, p. 66-72.

Olson, R.M., Neilson, J.B. and Edward, T.C. "Break-Away Components Produce Safer Roadside Signs". *Highway Research Board* No. 174, 1967.

Oberlander, P. *Furnishing the Street.* Community Planning Review, 1951, 1 (4), 118-128.

"Public Hearings on Highway Beautification Act". *American Society of Planning Officials.* Chicago, Illinois, Aspo Planning Advisory Service, February 23, 1966.

Probability Study of Highway Accident Locations in Kansas City. *Traffic Engineering,* 1970, 40, No. 7.

Petty, Donald F. "The Triangular No Passing Zone Sign —An Evaluation". *Traffic Engineering,* 1969, p. 40.

Powers, L.D. "Evaluation of Advance-Route Turn Markers on City Streets". *Highway Research Board Proceedings,* 1962, 41, p. 483.

Petersen, S.G. & Schoppert, D.W. "Motorists Reaction to Signing on a Beltway" *Highway Research Record.* Washington, D.C., 1967, No. 170.

Pollack, Leslie, O. "Driver Distraction as Related to Physical Level Abutting Urban Streets". Illinois: Council of Planning Libraries, 1968.

Pritchard, Roy, "Stabilized Images on the Retina". *Scientific American Reprint No. 466.* San Francisco, June, 1961.

Pennsylvania Turnpike Commission. *Joint Safety Research Group Report.* 1959.

Pushkarev, B., "The Esthetics of Freeway Design". *Landscape,* 1960-61 10, No. 2, p. 6-15.

Plumb, W.L. "Telling People Where to Go: Subway Graphics". *Print 19* 1965, September/October, 13-23.

Rockwell, T.H. et al. *Development of a Methodology For Evaluating Road Signs.* Columbus, Ohio, Clearinghouse, 1970.

Reilly, W.R. & Woods, D.L. The driver and traffic control devices. *Traffic Engineering,* 1967, 27 (9), 49-52.

Robinson, C.C. Color in traffic control. *Traffic Engineering,* 1967, 37 (3), 25-29.

Rowan, N.J. & Olson, R.M. The development of safer highway sign supports. *Traffic Engineering,* 1967, 38 (2), 46-50.

Rural Traffic Signals Can Be Hazardous. *Rural and Urban Roads,* 1971, 9, No. 4.

Rice, Paul W. "The Yield Right of Way Sign". *Traffic Quarterly,* 1952, 6, p. 51.

Rusch, W.A. "Highway Accident Rates as Related to Roadside Business and Advertising". *Highway Research Board Bulletin 30,* 1949, p. 46.

"Relationship Between Traffic Signs and Accidents". *Traffic Safety Research Review,* 1967, 11, p. 9.

Rigolo, Arthur, Model Sign Control Ordinance: A Weapon for the "War on Community Ugliness", Committee on Aesthetics, AIA, November 4, 1965.

Rook, Al. No Advertising, 57 Reasons for Not Advertising. Denver, Colorado: Golden Bill Press, 1963.

Robinson, L. Thruway Review Anti-Sign Battle. *New York Times,* April 2, 1963.

Ray, J.C. "How to Make Traffic Signals Safe". *American City.* Sacramento County, California, October, 1966.

Research on Road Traffic, Department of Scientific and Industrial Road Research Laboratory. London: Her Majesty's Stationary Office.

Rose, Paul L., L.A.M.T.P.I., Solicitor, *Journal of Planning and Property Law,* Sweet and Maxwell Ltd. and Contributor London, 1970.

"San Francisco Cracks Down: Blight Becomes the Handmaiden of a Sign Explosion—Is Control Anti-Business?" *Vancouver Sun,* Vancouver, B.C., Pacific Press, Thursday, May 10, 1966.

Service of Municipal Planning. B.C. Lower Mainland Regional Planning Board. *Signs and Signboards—British Columbia.* Vancouver, B.C. Lower Mainland Regional Planning Board, September, 1967.

Schoppert, D.W., and Hoyt, D.W. Factors influencing safety at highway rail grade crossings. Highway Research Board. *National Cooperative Highway Research Program Report* 50, 1968.

Schoppert, D.W., Moskowitz, K. Hulbert, S.F. and Burg,

A. Some principles of freeway directional signing based on motorists experiences. Proceedings of the 38th Annual Meeting, January 5-9, 1959, Washington, D.C., *Highway Research Bulletin 244,* 1960.

Schultz, Duane P. *Sensory Restriction.* Effects on Behavior. New York Academic Press, 1965.

Silye, Hans. *The Stress of Life,* New York, McGraw-Hill, 1956.

Summerfield, Kenneth. Focus on Road Signs. Traffic Engineering and Control, 1970, 11, No. 10.

Secrest, Bill. "Upgraded Signs Give Positive Identity". *American City (Ed.)* Foster, 1970, 85, No. 4.

Shoaf, R.T. "Are Advertising Signs Near Freeways Traffic Hazards?" *Traffic Engineering,* 1955, Vol. 26.

Solomon, David. "Traffic Signals and Accidents in Michigan". *Public Road.* U.S. Bureau of Public Roads. 1958-1960, 30, No. 1.

Straub, A.L. "Causes and Costs of Highway Sign Replacement". *Highway Research Board,* (Ed) Burggrof, Ward & Miller, Washington, D.C. 1955.

Signs of the Times, *Recreation,* October, 1964, 380-381.

Solomon, David. "The Effect of Letter Width and Spacing on Night Legibility of Highway Signs". *Public Roads,* 1956, 29, No. 1.

Sielski, Matthew C., "How Road Users Appraise Roads", *Traffic Quarterly,* 1958, 12, 102-112.

Sample Provision for a Local Law to Regulate Signs. New York State Natural Beauty Commission, 1968.

Staffeld, Paul R. Accidents Related to Access Points and Advertising Signs in Study. *Traffic Quarterly,* 1953, January.

Szabo, Albert. *Man and the Visual Environment.*

Starks, H.J. and Miller, M.M. "Roadside Equipment and Accidents". *Roadside Research Laboratory Report No. 22,* Hammondsworth, 1966.

Stephen R., Rosen, D.A. et al., "Route Guidance: Third Generation Signing. An Electronic Route Guidance System," *H.R. Record, No. 265,* 1968.

Stephens, W., Michael R. Timesaving Between Two Driving Tasks: Simulated Steering and Recognition of Roadsigns. *Public Roads.* 35, No. 5, p. 81-89.

Stephens, B.W., Rosen, D.A. et al. "Third Generation Destination Signing: An Electronic Route Guidance System." *H.R. Record No. 265,* 1968.

Stipe, Robert E. *Perception and Environment: Foundations of Vohan Design.* The University of North Carolina at Chapel Hill, 1966.

Senders, J.W., et al. "The Attentional Demand of Automobile Driving", *Highway Research Board Record 195,* 1967, 15-33.

Southworth, M. "The Sonic Environment of Cities", *Environment and Behaviour,* 1969, Fall.

Sutton, James. *Signs in Action.* London: Studio Vista Ltd., 1965.

Terry, Deane S., and Willy, Donald S., Correlation of Painted Traffic Signal Poles and Intersection Accident Rates. *Traffic Engineering* 1970, 40, No. 11.

Thompson, A.H. "Billboards and Zoning". *Traffic Quarterly.* New York Columbia U. Press, Act. 1948.

The Vancouver Sun. *Blight Becomes the Handmaiden of a Sign Explosion.* Tuesday, May 10, 1966.

Traffic Quarterly. ENO Foundation for Transportation. An Independent Journal for Better Traffic. New York, Columbia University Press, 1947, Vol. 1.

Ibid., 1952, Vol. 6.

Traffic Quarterly. ENO Foundation for Transportation. An Independent Journal for Better Traffic. New York, Columbia University Press, 1955, Vol. 9.

Ibid., 1957, Vol. 11.
Ibid., 1959, Vol. 13.
Ibid., 1960, Vol. 14.
Ibid., 1963, Vol. 17.
Ibid., 1965, Vol. 19.
Ibid., 1966, Vol. 20.
Ibid., 1967, Vol. 21.
Ibid., 1968, Vol. 22.
Ibid., 1969, Vol. 23.
Ibid., 1970, Vol. 24.

Thompson, A.H., "The Sign Busters". *Newsweek.* New York: June 7, 1971, No. 23.

Thompson, A.H., "Sign Control Bulletin". *Downtown Idea Exchange,* August 15, 1967.

Usborne, T.G. "International Standardization of Road Traffic Signs" *Traffic Engineering,* 1967, 37, No. 14.

The Vancouver Sun. "Control of Outdoor Planning". *Town and Country Planning,* England: 1962, 20, No. 1.

The Vancouver Sun. "Signs of Life—Barbara Strauffacher's Outdoor Signs". *Progressive Architecture.* 1966, June, Vol. 47.

United States Department of Commerce, A Proposal for Scenic Roads and Parkways. Washington, D.C., June, 1966.

United States, *Federal Register,* January 28, 1966, 31 (9) 1063-1065.

United States, Department of City and Regional Planning. Signs in the City. Cambridge, Massachusetts Institute of Technology Press, 1963.

Urban and Institute. *The Community Builder's Handbook,* Washington Urban Land Institute, 1960.

Visibility and Safety in Positioning Road Signs. *Traffic Engineering and Control,* 1969, 11, No. 8.

"Visual Pollution: Sometimes it Hides the Scars," *Popular Gardening and Living Outdoors,* December, 1967, 24-25.

Visual Environment, R.J. Claus, K.E. Claus. Toronto: Collier-McMillan, 1971.

Vancouver By-Law on Sign Regulation, By-Law No. 2341.

Vancouver By-Law on Zoning and Development, By-Law 3575.

Vancouver By-Law 4495, amending By-Law 3575.

Walker, Richard. "Clash of Symbols" *Design,* London, Council of Industrial Design, April, 1969, Vol. 30, No. 244.

Weckesser, P.M. "Remote Controlled Signs Cut Turnpike Accidents, New Jersey Turnpike", *American City,* June, 1965.

Weckesser, P.M. "Candy-Cane Posts Cut Accidents: Stop Sign Poles", *American City,* 1968, Vol. 83.

Warner, E. "The Visibility of Highway Markings in the Atlantic Seaboard States". *Traffic Quarterly,* 1958, 188-207.

Wilson, Ruth I. "Billboards and the Right to be Seen from the Highway", Georgetown Law Journal 30, 1942, 723-750.

APPENDIX TABLE OF CONTENTS

APPENDIX A 165
Guidelines for Ordinance Development

APPENDIX B 213
Maximum Projection Formula

APPENDIX C 216
Synopsized Ordinance Specification

APPENDIX D 226
"Clutter-Itis"

APPENDIX E 230
Guidelines for Design Review

APPENDIX A

Part I—Definitions

For the purpose of this ordinance, the words and phrases listed below shall be construed as specified in this section. Words used in the singular indicate the plural, and the plural the singular.

1. *Approved plastics:* refers to those materials specified in Standard No. 52-1-61 of the Uniform Building Code which have a flame-spread ratio of 225 or less and a smoke density not greater than that obtained from the burning of untreated wood under similar conditions when tested in accordance to UBC Standard No. 31-1-61 in the way intended for use. The products of combustion shall be no more toxic than the burning of untreated wood under similar conditions.

2. *Administrator:* refers to the officer or other person charged with the administration and enforcement of this ordinance or his duly authorized deputy.

3. *Alteration:* refers to any major alteration to a sign, but shall not include routine maintenance, painting or change of copy of an existing sign.

4. *Architectural Projection:* shall mean any projection which is not intended for occupancy and which extends beyond the face of an exterior wall of a bulletin, but shall not include signs.

5. *Awning:* refers to a temporary hood or cover which projects from the wall of a building, and of a type which can be retracted, folded, or collapsed against the face of a supporting building.

6. *Building Facade:* refers to that portion of any exterior elevation of a building extending from grade to the top of the parapet wall or eaves and the entire width of the building elevation.

7. *Building Facade Facing:* refers to a resurfacing of an existing facade with approved material, illuminated or non-illuminated.

8. *Building Line:* is a line established by ordinance beyond which no building may extend. A building line may coincide with a property line. A building line may be referred to as "required setback." (See Curb Line).

9. *Business Frontage:* refers to the property lines or lease lines at the front of the building in which the business is located or the location of the main public entrance of said building.

10. *Canopy or Marquee:* refers to a permanent roof structure attached to and supported by the building and

Fig. 22: A canopy or marquee sign.

projecting over public property but does not include a projecting roof.

11. *Color:* refers to any hue or combination of values of these. Black and white shall not be considered as colors.

12. *Copy Area:* refers to the actual area of the sign copy applied to any background. Copy area should not be confused with coverage which includes frame background or support for a sign.

13. *Council:* refers to the Municipal Council of the Corporation.

14. *Curb Line:* refers to the line at the face of the curb nearest the street or roadway. In the absence of a curb, the curb line shall be established by the City Engineer (see Building Line).

15. *District:* refers to the zoning districts as designated on the Official Zoning Map of the Corporation and described in the District Regulations.

16. *Grade:* refers to the elevation or level of the street closest to the sign to which reference is made, measured at the street's centerline.

17. *Incombustible Material:* refers to any material which will not ignite at, or below, a temperature of 1200 degrees F. during an exposure of five minutes, and which will not continue to glow at that temperature. Tests shall be made as specified in UBC standard No. 4-1-61.

18. *Marquee:* (See Canopy).

19. *Lane:* refers to a public thoroughfare or way which affords a purely secondary means of access to a lot at the side or rear.

20. *Nonstructural Trim:* refers to any any molding, battens, caps, nailing strips, latticing, cut-outs or letters, and walk-ways which are attached to the sign structure.

21. *Person:* may include a firm, association, organization, partnership, trust, company, or corporation as well as an individual.

22. *Principal Use:* refers to the main purpose for which land, buildings or structures are ordinarily used.

23. *Residential Use Building:* refers to any dwelling, boarding, lodging, or rooming house, dormitory unit: fraternity or sorority house.

24. *Roof Line:* refers to the uppermost line of the roof of a building or, in the case of an extended facade, the uppermost height of said facade.

25. *Sign:* refers to any structure, device, advertisement, advertising device, or visual representation intended to advertise, identify, or communicate information to attract the attention of the public for any purpose and without prejudice to the generality of the foregoing includes any symbols, letters, figures, illustration, or forms painted or otherwise affixed to a building or structure and any beacon or searchlight intended to attract the attention of the public for any purpose and also any structure or device the prime purpose of which is to border, illuminate, animate, or project a visual representation, provided, however, that this definition shall not be held to include official notices issued by any Court or public office or officer in the performance of a public or official duty, and traffic control signs as defined in the "Motor Vehicle Act."

a. *Sign Area:* refers to the entire area within a single continuous perimeter of not more than eight straight lines enclosing the extreme limits of writing, representative emblem, or any figure of similar character, together with any material or color forming an integral part of the display or used to differentiate such sign from the background against which it is placed, provided that in the case of a sign designed with more than one exterior surface the area shall be computed as including only the maximum single display surface which is visible from any ground position at one time. The supports, uprights, or structures on which any sign is supported shall not be included in determining the sign area.

b. *Sign, maximum height of:* refers to the vertical distance measured from the grade to the top of such a sign. In the case of a roof sign, the maximum height shall be measured from the roof line or the parapet level, if applicable, at the location of such sign.

c. *Sign, minimum height of:* shall refer to the vertical distance measured from the nearest finished grade to the lower limit of such sign.

d. *Sign Structure:* refers to any structure which supports or is capable of supporting any sign. Said definition shall not include a building to which the sign is attached.

Types of Sign by Structure:

e. *Awning Sign:* refers to a non-illuminated identification sign affixed flat to the surface of an awning and which does not extend vertically or horizontally beyond the limits of such awning.

f. *Banners:* refers to a temporary sign such as used to announce open houses, g r a n d openings or s p e c i a l announcements.

g. *Billboard:* refers to a non-accessory s i g n erected for the purpose of advertising a product, event, person, or subject not entirely related to the premises on which said sign is located.

h. *Canopy Sign:* refers to a sign suspended from or forming part of a canopy or marquee and which does not e x t e n d horizontally beyond the limits of such canopy or marquee.

Fig. 23: An awning sign.

i. *Changeable C o p y Sign:* r e f e r s to any sign which is characterized by changeable copy, letters, or symbols, regardless of method of attachment.

j. *Facia Sign:* is a flat sign which does not project more than one foot from the face or wall of the building upon which it is affixed, painted, or attached, running parallel for its whole length to the face or wall of the building, and which does not extend beyond the horizontal width of such building. A facia sign is always a first-party business or identification sign and should not be confused with a non-accessory sign, which is included under "wall signs."

Fig. 24: A 24-sheet poster on a poster panel or billboard.

Fig. 25: A painted bulletin is larger than a poster panel and is generally painted as opposed to being "posted" with printed art.

k. *Flags:* refers to devices generally made of flexible materials, such as cloth, paper, or plastic, and displayed on strings. They may or may not include copy. This definition does not include the flag of any country or state.

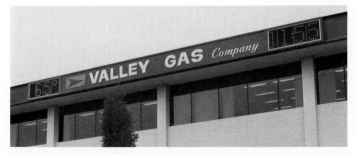

Fig. 26: A fascia building sign, which also may incorporate additional elements as time and temp. units in this case.

Signs. Legal Rights And Aesthetic Considerations/169

Fig. 27: The integration of architecture and sign is a requirement in sign identity design today.

l. *Freestanding Sign:* refers to a sign not attached to or forming part of a building which is a first-party business or identification sign.

m. *Ground Sign:* refers to a sign attached to the ground, within an architecturally planned wall or structure.

n. *Marquee Sign:* (See Canopy Sign).

o. *Projecting Sign:* shall mean a sign projecting more than 12 inches from the face of a building.

p. *Roof Sign:* refers to a sign erected upon the roof or parapet of a building, the entire face of which is situated above the roof level of the building to which it is attached, and which is wholly or partially supported by said building.

q. *Window Sign:* refers to a sign affixed to or within 3 feet of the inside of a window in view of the general public. This does not include merchandise on display.

Fig. 28: A projecting sign.

Fig. 29: Roof sign presents time and temperature public service value to largest possible area.

Fig. 30: A window sign, which generally refers to lettering applied directly to the glass.

Types of Signs by Function:

r. *Business Sign:* refers to a sign used for identification purposes, which directs attention to a business or profession conducted upon the premises at which the sign is located, and which may also refer to goods or services produced, offered for sale or obtained at such premises.

Fig. 31: A business sign identifying and advertising a commercial activity.

Fig. 32· A non-accessory or third party sign. This example is a painted bulletin.

s. *Non-Accessory Sign:* refers to a sign which directs attention to a business, commodity, service, or entertainment, not exclusively related to the premises at which the sign is located, or to a business, commodity service or entertainment which is conducted, sold or offered elsewhere than on the premises at which the sign is located.

172

t. *Identification Sign:* refers to a sign which contains no advertising but is limited to the name, address and number of a building, institution, or person and to the activity carried on in the building or institution or the occupation of the person.

u. *Incidental Sign:* refers to small signs less than 2 square feet in area of a non-commercial nature, intended primarily for the convenience of the public.

v. *Directional Sign:* refers to an on-premise sign designed to guide or direct pedestrian or vehicular traffic.

w. *Political Sign:* refers to any sign which states the name and/or picture of an individual seeking election or appointment to a public office, or pertaining to a forthcoming public election or referendum, or pertaining to or advocating political views or policies.

x. *Portable Sign:* refers to any sign not permanently attached to the ground or building.

y. *Public Service Sign:* refers to any sign primarily to promote items of general interest to the community.

z. *Real Estate Sign:* refers to a sign pertaining to the sale, lease, or rental of the property upon which it is located.

aa. *Special Purpose Sign:* refers to any sign other than a business, non-accessory, or identification sign.

Fig. 33: A time and temperature sign which alternates the information automatically on lamp banks.

Signs. Legal Rights And Aesthetic Considerations/173

This may include, but is not limited to, traffic signs, government signs, historical or memorial plaques, and temporary signs.

bb. *Temporary Sign:* refers to any sign, banner, pennant, valance, or advertising display constructed of cloth, canvas, light fabric, or cardboard, wallboard, or other light materials, with or without frames; intended to be displayed for a limited period of time only.

cc. *Time and Temperature Sign:* refers to a sign giving the time and temperature. (Figure 33).

dd. *Tract Development Sign:* refers to a sign indicating the location of a housing tract.

ee. *Tract Directional Sign:* refers to a sign indicating the location of a housing tract.

Types of Signs by Degree of Illumination:

ff. *Electric Sign:* refers to any sign containing electrical wiring but not including signs illuminated by an exterior light source.

gg. *Illuminated Sign:* refers to a sign designed to give forth any artificial or reflect light, either directly from a source of light incorporated in or connected

Fig. 34a: Installation of specialty signing.

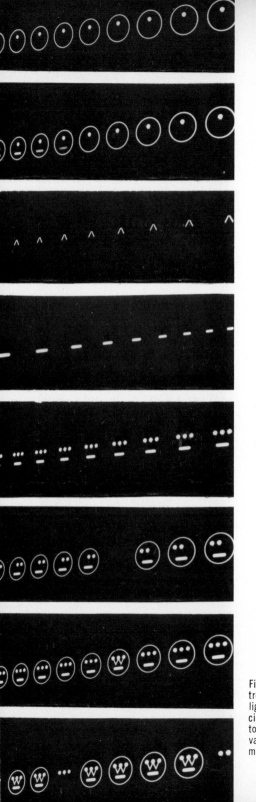

Fig. 34b: Computer controlled flashing introduces lighting excitement in specialty signing applications today and offers an infinite variety of visual entertainment as well as advertising.

with such sign, or indirectly from an artificial source, so shielded that no direct illumination from it is visible elsewhere than on the sign and in the immediate proximity thereof.

hh. *Animated Sign:* refers to a sign with action or motion, flashing, or color changes requiring electrical energy, electronic or manufactured sources of supply, but not including wind actuated elements such as flags, or banners. (Said definition shall not include public service signs, such as time and temperature displays and changeable copy signs).

ii. *Flashing Sign:* refers to an illumiated sign which contains flashing ights or exhibits noticeable changes in light intensity.

jj. *Revolving Sign:* refers to any sign, any part of which revolves.

26. *Street:* refers to a public highway, road, or thoroughfare which affords the principal means of access to adjacent lots.

27. *Street Frontage:* refers to the linear frontage of a parcel of property abutting a public street.

28. *Uniform Building Code (UBC):* refers to the current edition of the Uniform Building Code.

29. *Wall Surface of Building:* refers to the total horizontal surface area of the building face to which the sign is attached, including windows and door areas, measured to the extreme outer limits of such wall surface.

30. *Zoning or Land Use:* refers to the land use district or zone established by the authorized legislative body.

Part II—Application

1. Within the municipality, no sign shall hereafter be erected, placed, altered, or moved unless in conformity with this ordinance and the contrary shall be unlawful.

2. Signs which are lawfully in existence and in use prior to and at the time of the legal adoption of the proposed ordinance, may remain in use even though they do not conform with the provisions of the ordinance. Where a new ordinance permits advertising of equal value, an advertiser may be required to change or replace his non-conforming signs subject to Part IV of this ordinance.

3. Any sign lawfully in existence at the time of the adoption of this ordinance shall not be rebuilt, reconstructed, or altered with the exception of copy change unless in conformity with the provisions of this ordinance, and the contrary shall be unlawful.

4. Nothing in this ordinance shall be taken to relieve any person from complying with the provisions of any other ordinances or bylaws of the municipality.

Part III—Administration and Enforcement

1. *Administration:*

This ordinance shall be administered by a Sign Code Administrator appointed by the Council.

2. *Permits:*

Every person shall, before erecting, placing, rebuilding, reconstructing, altering, or moving any sign, other than an incidental sign, obtain from the Administrator a permit to do so as provided in this ordinance.

3. *Preliminary Plan Approval:*

a. With the exception of the special purpose and temporary signs listed in Clauses 1 to 12 inclusive of Schedule 1 of this ordinance, and those changes listed in Section 3.C. of Part III of this ordinance, any person wishing to erect, place, rebuild, reconstruct, alter, or move any sign shall apply for and receive preliminary plan approval.

b. Every application for preliminary plan approval shall be accompanied by a plan or plans drawn to scale and including:

(1) the dimensions and weight of the sign and, where applicable, the dimensions of the wall surface of the building to which it is to be attached.

(2) the dimensions and weight of the sign's supporting members.

(3) the maximum and minimum height of the sign.

(4) the proposed location of the sign in relation to the face of the building, in front of which or above which it is to be erected.

(5) the proposed location of the sign in relation to the boundaries of the lot upon which it is to be situated.

(6) if the sign is to be illuminated or animated, the colors to be used and the technical means by which this is to be accomplished.

(7) where the sign is to be attached to an existing building, a diagram or photograph of the face of the building to which the sign is to be attached.

(8) the name and address of the user of the sign and the location of the sign.

c. The following changes shall not require a sign permit. These exceptions shall not be construed as relieving the owner of the sign from the responsibility of its erection and maintenance, and its compliance with the provisions of this ordinance or any other law or ordinance regulating the same.

(1) The changing of the advertising copy or message of a painted or printed sign. Except for theatre marquees and changeable copy signs specifically designed for the use of replaceable copy, electric signs shall not be included in this exception.

(2) Painting, repainting, or cleaning of an advertising structure or the changing of the advertising copy or message thereon shall not be considered an erection or alteration which requires a sign permit unless a major structural change is made.

d. Copies of applications shall be available to the public on request.

e. A sign permit shall become null and void if the work for which the permit was issued has not been completed within one year of its issuance.

4. *Comprehensive Sign Plan:*

A comprehensive sign plan may be provided for business premises which occupy the entire frontage in one or more block fronts or for the whole of a shopping center development. Such a plan, which shall include the location, size, height, color, lighting, and orientation of all signs, shall be submitted for preliminary plan approval regulations of the municipality. Provided that such a comprehensive plan is presented, exceptions to the Sign Schedule regulations of this ordinance may be permitted, if the sign areas and densities for the plan as a whole are in conformity with the intent of this ordinance and if such exception results in an improved relationship between the various parts of the plan.

5. *Maintenance:*

All signs, together with all of their supports, braces, guys, and anchors, shall be kept in repair and in proper state of preservation. The display surfaces of all signs shall be kept neatly painted or posted at all times. Every sign and the immediate surrounding premises shall be maintained by the owner or person in charge thereof in a clean, sanitary, and inoffensive condition and free and clear of all obnoxious substances, rubbish, and weeds. Notice shall be given to the Administrator of any change in sign user, sign owner or owner of the property on which the sign is located.

6. *Inspection:*

All signs for which a permit is required shall be subject to inspection by the Administrator. The Administrator, or any other official of the municipality who may be appointed by him is hereby authorized to enter upon any property or premises to ascertain whether the provisions of this ordinance are being obeyed. Such entrance shall be made during business hours unless an emergency exists. The Administrator may order the removal of any sign that is not maintained in accordance with the maintenance provisions of this ordinance.

7. *Enforcement:*

a. It shall be unlawful for any person to erect, place, rebuild, construct, alter, or move any sign or to do any act contrary to or in a manner contrary to any direction, instruction, specification, or provision contained in or adopted by this ordinance or any notice lawfully given or posted pursuant to the provisions of this ordinance or without any permit hereby required or contrary to the conditions upon which any permit has been issued pursuant to this ordinance; or to refrain from doing or taking or to fail to do or take any act or precaution required to be done or taken prior to or in doing anything permitted, as in this ordinance or in any regulation or specification adopted by this ordinance provided or by any notice lawfully given or posted pursuant to the provisions of this ordinance; and whether or not in any such case it is expressly stated that the doing of or the failure to do the thing mentioned, shall be lawful.

b. Every person who violates any of the provisions of the ordinance, or who causes, suffers, or permits any act or thing to be done in contravention or in violation of any of the provisions of this ordinance, or who neglects or refrains from doing anything required to be done by any of the provisions of this ordinance, or who carries out or who suffers, causes, or permits to be carried out any development in a manner prohibited by or contrary to any of the provisions of this ordinance or who fails to comply with any order, direction, or notice given under this ordinance shall be deemed to be guilty of an infraction of this ordinance and shall be liable to the penalties hereby imposed. For each day that a violation is permitted to exist, it shall constitute a separate offense.

c. Where any sign or part thereof contravenes this ordinance or where any sign is in such a condition as to be in danger of falling or is a menace to the safety of persons or property the Administrator shall give to the owner or person in charge of the sign written notice specifying the danger of the violation, ordering the cessation thereof and requiring either the removal of the sign or the carrying out of remedial work in the time and in the manner that the notice shall specify. Such notice shall be posted by registered mail, return receipt requested. In the event of failure to comply after 30 days from receipt of said notice, the administrator may remove the sign or cause such remedial work to be done and cost thereof shall be recoverable by the municipality by summary process at law in any court of competent jurisdiction. In the event of default of payment of such assessed costs, then a charge shall be placed upon the property and the said costs, when certified by the Treasurer, shall be entered in the Collector's Roll and collected in the same manner as the taxes shown thereon. If a sign which has been removed is not reclaimed and fines paid within 30 days of its removal, said sign may be sold or otherwise disposed of by the city. If a sign is found to be an immediate and serious danger to the public because of its unsafe condition, it may be removed without notice and written notice of removal and reasons for such shall be served as soon as possible under the terms of 7.c. of Part III of this ordinance.

8. *Penalties:*

Every person who commits an offense against this ordinance is liable to a civil fine and penalty not exceeding Three Hundred ($300.00) Dollars and costs, or in default of payment thereof, to imprisonment for any period not exceeding 90 days.

b. Where an offense against this ordinance is of a continuing nature, it shall be lawful for the convicting magistrate, in his discretion, to impose a fine against the offender, not exceeding Fifty ($50.00) Dollars for each day such offense is continued by him.

9. *Appeals:*

a. When a permit is denied, the Administrator shall give notice in writing to the applicant of denial, together with a brief resume of the reasons for such denial.

In order to provide for reasonable interpretation of the provisions of this ordinance, there is hereby established a Board of Appeals to hear appeals from the decision of the Administrator unless such denial is based on violations of the Uniform Building Code, the Uniform Sign Code, or the National Electrical Code. Denial for these reasons must be appealed to the Building Code Board of Appeals.

b. The failure of the Administrator to either formally grant or deny in writing a proposed sign within 30 days of submittal of the application shall be grounds for appeal to the Board of Appeals.

c. *Procedure Upon Appeals*

(1) Delivery of Sign Application to Board. Upon the filing of a notice of appeal with the City Clerk, the Administrator shall promptly submit to the Board of Appeals the appropriate permit application for the

sign in question, the written notice of denial with reasons for such denial, and all plans, specifications, and other papers pertaining to the application. If the appeal is from failure of the Administrator to grant a permit within 30 days, the Administrator shall, in addition to the foregoing, furnish the Board with a brief written statement of the reasons for such failure. If Board of Appeals fails to act within 30 days after the appeal is filed the permit is to be granted without a hearing.

(2) Upon any appeal, the Administrator may, at his discretion, furnish the Board with a written statement of his position on the appeal and may therein reply to the position of the applicant. Such statements must be filed with the Board of Appeals at least 10 days in advance of the hearing on the appeal.

(3) If upon hearing by Board of Appeals the permit applicant is found to be conforming in all aspects to the sign ordinance, reasonable damages are to be assessed against the governmental body in question at a rate of not less than $50.00 a day. Said compensation is not to exceed $1,500.00 plus all legal fees. This is to be full liquidation damages to sign user, property owner, and sign company-designer.

d. *Membership of Board*

The Board shall consist of seven voting members and two non-voting members, all of whom shall be appointed and removable by the City Manager. Each member shall serve without compensation and for a term of three years, or until his successor is appointed after the expiration of his term. First appointees to the Board shall, however, serve staggered terms of: three for one year; three for two years; and three for three years, respectively. Vacancies on the Board shall be filled by appointment of the City Manager for the unexpired term of the vacating member.

(1) *Identity of Voting Members.* The seven voting members of the Board shall represent the interests of the City as a whole. No voting member shall be a City employee or have any financial interest in the sign industry.

(2) *Identity of Non-Voting Members.* Of the three non-voting members of the Board, one shall be or have been actively employed in or by the sign industry, one shall be a city employee, and one shall be an architect or a member of the academic community connected with urban planning or design.

e. *Board Jurisdiction and Power*

The Board shall have the power and duty to (1) hear

and decide appeals by the sign permit applicant from the decision of the Administrator of this ordinance, or failure to grant a sign permit within 30 days of application: (2) grant variances from the requirements of this ordinance as part of disposition of an appeal from action of the Administrator denying or failing to grant a sign permit; (3) hear and decide appeals by a sign owner, user, or owner of the property on which a sign is located from characterization of a sign as legal non-conforming or illegal non-conforming under Part IV, and the Administrator's fixing the replacement value of a non-conforming sign or expenditure to bring a non-conforming sign into conformity under Part IV; (4) make recommendations to the City Council for changes to this ordinance, and (5) advise the Sign Code Administrator when requested by him.

The Board shall not have jurisdiction to hear appeals from the denial of a sign permit on grounds of non-compliance with requirements of the Uniform Sign Code, Uniform Building Code, or National Electrical Code. Such appeals shall be heard and determined by the Building Code Board of Appeals.

f. *Criteria for Board Decision*

(1) *Appeals Without Petition for Variance.* In appeals to the Board from decision of the Administrator denying a sign permit in connection with which no petition for variance has been filed, the Board's scope of review shall be limited to determining whether or not the Administrator's decision is in accordance with the requirements of this ordinance and, accordingly, to affirm or reverse his decision. No variance from the requirements of this ordinance shall be granted or allowed. If the Administrator's decision is reversed, the Board shall direct the Administrator to issue the permit in accordance with its decision. If the Administrator fails to do so for five days from receipt of the direction from the Board, the Board may issue the permit.

In appeals from failure of the Administrator to grant a permit within 30 days of application, the Board shall determine whether the sign and the application meet the requirements of this ordinance. If so, the Board shall grant the permit; if not, the Board shall deny the permit. No variance from the requirements of the ordinance shall be granted or allowed.

(2) *Appeals with Petition for Variance.* In appeals from decision of the Administrator denying or refusing to grant a sign permit in connection with which the appealing party or any other interested party has filed a Petition for Variance, the Board shall have the power and duty described

in III 9.f.(1) hereinabove, and, in addition, shall have the power to hear, decide, and grant or deny the requested variance from the provisions or requirements of this ordinance.

The Board may grant a variance from the provisions or requirements of this ordinance only where:

(a) The literal interpretation and strict application of the provisions and requirements of this ordinance would cause undue and unnecessary hardship to the sign user because of unique or unusual conditions pertaining to the specific building or parcel of property in question; and

(b) The granting of the requested variance would not be materially detrimental to property owners in the vicinity; and

(c) The unusual conditions applying to the specific property do not apply generally to other properties in the municipality; and

(d) The granting of the variance will not be contrary to the general objective of this ordinance enforcing quality standards and district homogeneity.

Where there is insufficient evidence, in the opinion of the Board, to support a finding of "undue and unnecessary hardship" under (a) above, but some hardship does exist, the Board may consider the requirement fulfilled if: (i) the proposed signing will be of particular benefit to the community; and (ii) the entire site has been or will be particularly well-landscaped.

g. *Perfection of Appeal and Stay of Proceedings*

(1) An appeal with or without petition for variance may be considered by the Board only if:

(a) Written notice of appeal, with or without petition for variance, is filed with the municipality: (i) within 10 days of the decision of the Administrator denying a sign permit; (ii) within 40 days of the submission of a sign permit application which the Administrator has neither granted or denied within 30 days; (iii) within 60 days of the Administrator's characterization of a sign as "non-conforming" or fixing the sign's replacement value or expenditure to bring into compliance under IV 5, which period shall begin to run with the mailing or delivery or notice of such characterization to the sign user or sign owner, or owner of the property on which the sign is located; or the posting of the notice on the sign or the associated business premises;

(b) The notice of appeal is accompanied by a fee of $25.00;

(c) The appellant serves upon the Board of the City a written statement of the reasons in support of his position five days before the hearing on the appeal.

(2) The Board shall, on its own motion, or on the motion of any interested party, dismiss an appeal for failure of the appellant to meet any of the requirements of III 9. g (1) or for failure of the appellant to otherwise diligently prosecute the appeal, or if the Board finds the appellant has made any knowingly false or misleading statement or representation in his sign application or appeal.

h. *Board Procedure*

(1) *General.* The voting members of the Board shall choose a chairman from among their number who shall serve a term of one year, and shall adopt rules and regulations for its own government. The presence of at least four of the seven voting members of the Board and an affirmative vote of a majority of those present at any meeting shall be required for any Board decision or action.

(2) *Notice of Hearing.* The Board shall hear and decide appeals within 30 days of the filing of the notice of appeal. Notice of the hearing on an appeal shall be given by the Board not less than 10 days prior to the hearing to: (a) the appellant, in writing, at the address given on the notice of appeal; (b) the Code Administrator, in writing; (c) to any person filing a written statement in opposition to the appellant's position taken in the appeal; (d) any person filing a written request with the City for special notice of Board hearings in the six months following giving of the request; (e) to the public by posting a copy of the notice of hearing in a conspicuous place within the City Hall; (f) to the property owners in the vicinity of the property which is concerned in the appeal by posting three placards in conspicuous places on or within 50 feet of the property concerned. Such notices and placards shall be in a form prescribed by the Board and shall set forth the time, place, and purpose of the hearing.

(3) *Hearing.* All hearings of the Board shall be open to the public, and those in attendance shall be afforded an opportunity, the length and conditions of which shall be prescribed by the Board, to address the Board on the issues to be determined. The appellant and Code Administrator or his representative shall be afforded an opportunity to address the Board on any matter at issue. Any party or interested person may be represented by another at the hearing.

(4) *Hearing Minutes and Decision.* The Board shall keep minutes of its proceedings, shall cause to be kept a verbatim record of the hearing on any appeal or petition for variance, and shall prepare a notice of its decision on any appeal together with its findings of fact in support of that decision, all of which shall be open to public inspection. Copies of the Board's decisions on appeals and petitions for variances shall be mailed or delivered to the applicant, to the Code Administrator, and to persons filing requests for special notice of hearings pursuant to III.9.h.(2)(d).

i. *Superior Court Review of Board Decisions.*

Review or appeal of any Board decision may be taken by any interested person to a Superior Court.

j. *Clerical Assistance for Board.*

The office of the City Clerk shall furnish the Board with the clerical and administrative assistance that it requires.

Part IV—Amortization of Non-Conforming Signs

1. *General*

To ease the economic impact of an ordinance on those who are using non-conforming signs on or before the date of adoption of this ordinance, the ordinance provides for up to seven years of continued use of a non-conforming sign in its existing state, assuming the ordinance allows an equal but not similar sign to be constructed. During this period, it is expected that the sign may be amortized on federal income taxes; however, whether it may be so amortized shall not affect the application of this section. Such an amortization period shall also be allowed signs in areas annexed to the municipality after the enactment of this ordinance.

2. *Legal Non-Conforming Signs*

a. *Definition of Legal Non-conforming Signs:* Any on-premise business sign located within the municipality on the date of adoption of this ordinance, or located in areas annexed to the municipality thereafter, which does not conform with the provisions of this Code, is eligible for characterization as a "legal non-conforming" sign, provided it also meets the following requirements:

(1) The sign has a replacement value of more than $250 as estimated by the procedures set out in IV 5 of this ordinance;

(2) The sign cannot be brought into compliance with the ordinance for an expenditure of $250 or less, as estimated by the procedures set out in IV 5 of this ordinance;

(3) The sign was covered by a sign permit on the date of adoption of this ordinance if one was required under applicable law; or,

(4) If no sign permit was required under applicable law for the sign in question, the sign was in all respects in compliance with applicable law on the date of adoption of this ordinance.

Provided, however, no temporary or incidental signs, as defined by Part I of this Code shall be eligible.

b. *Notification of Non-Conformity.* After the enactment of this ordinance, the Administrator shall, as soon as practicable, survey the municipality for signs which do not conform to the requirements of this ordinance. Upon determination that a sign is non-conforming, the Administrator shall use reasonable efforts to so notify either personally or in writing the user or owner of the signs or the owner of the property on which the sign is located of (a) the sign's non-conformity; (b) whether the sign is eligible for characterization as legal non-conforming; (c) the Administrator's estimate of whether the sign's replacement cost is less than or greater than $250; and (d) if the sign's replacement cost is greater than $250, the Administrator's estimate of whether the expenditure required to bring the sign into conformity is less than or greater than $250. Failing determination of the sign owner, user, or owner of the property on which the sign is located, the notice may be affixed in a conspicuous place to the sign or to the business premises with which the sign is associated.

c. *Characterization as "Legal Non-Conforming."* Each sign user within the municipality having existing non-conforming signs meeting the requirements of IV 2.a shall be permitted to designate one such sign for characterization as "legally non-conforming," for each street upon which the business premises front. Such designation shall be made in the application for a legal non-conforming sign permit.

d. *Permit for Legal Non-Conforming Signs.* A legal non-conforming sign permit is required for each legal non-conforming sign designated under IV 2.c. The permit shall be obtained by the sign user or the sign owner, or the owner of the property on which the sign is located within 60 days of notification by the municipality as specified in IV 2.b that the sign is non-conforming. The permit shall be issued without fee and shall expire at the end of the amortization period prescribed in IV 4.

Applications for the non-conforming sign permit shall contain the name and address of the sign user, the sign owner, and, if available, the owner of the property on which the sign is located and such other pertinent information as the Administrator may require to ensure compliance with the ordinance, including proof of the date of installation of the sign.

A non-conforming sign for which no permit has been issued within the 60-day period shall be immediately brought into compliance with the ordinance or removed. Failure to comply shall subject the sign user, owner, or owner of the property on which the sign is located to the remedies and penalities of Part III.8 of this ordinance.

e. *Loss of Legal Non-Conforming Status.* A legal non-conforming sign shall immediately lose its legal non-conforming designation if:

(a) The sign is altered in any way in structure (except normal maintenance) which tends to or makes the

188

sign less in compliance with the requirements of this ordinance than it was before the alteration; or

(b) The sign is relocated to a position making it less in compliance with the requirements of this ordinance,

(c) The sign is replaced, or

(d) Any new primary sign is erected or placed in connection with the enterprise using the legal non-conforming sign. Should any of the actions described in (a), (b), c), or (d) be undertaken, the permit for legal non-conforming sign status shall be automatically cancelled and the sign shall be immediately brought into compliance with this ordinance with a new permit secured therefor or shall be removed.

3. *Illegal Non-Conforming Signs*

An illegal non-conforming sign is any sign which does not comply with the requirements of this ordinance within the limits of the municipality as they now or hereafter exist, and (a) which has a replacement value of $250 or less; or (b) which has a replacement value of more than $250 but which may be brought into conformity with an expenditure of $250 or less; or (c) which has a replacement value of more than $250 but is not eligible for characterization as legal non-conforming under IV 2.a. As provided in IV 4.a, such signs must be brought into compliance or removed within three months of the date of notification of their non-conformity.

4. *Amortization Period for Non-Conforming Signs.*

a. *Illegal Non-Conforming Signs.* Illegal non-conforming signs as defined in IV 3 above, may remain in a non-conforming state for three months after the date of notification of non-conformity by the City (IV 2.b). Thereafter such signs shall be brought into conformity with this ordinance with a permit issued therefor or be removed.

b. *Legal Non-Conforming Signs.* Legal non-conforming signs, as defined in IV 2 above, for which a legal non-conforming sign permit has been issued, may remain in a non-conforming state for seven years after the date of installation of the sign, or four years after notification by the municipality of the sign's non-conformity, whichever is longer. Thereafter the sign shall be brought into conformity with this ordinance with a permit issued therefor or be removed. Provided, however, that the amortization period established herein may be used only so long as the sign retains its legal non-conforming status (see IV 2.e).

5. *Fixing of "Replacement Value" and "Expenditure to Bring Into Conformity."*

Replacement value of a sign as used herein is the expenditure required for replacement of the sign in question by a reputable sign maker, as estimated by the Administrator. The Administrator may use the valuation fixed by the County Assessor as a basis of his valuation.

Expenditure to bring a sign into conformity is that expenditure required for a reputable sign maker to bring the sign in question into conformity with the provisions of this ordinance, as estimated by the Administrator.

The Administrator's estimate may be appealed to the Board of Appeals by the sign owner, user, or owner of the property on which the sign is located if notice of appeal is given within 60 days of the date on which written notice of the estimate is given under IV 2.b.

6. *Non-Conforming Sign Maintenance and Repair.*

Nothing in this chapter shall be construed as relieving the owner or user of a legal non-conforming sign or owner of the property on which the legal non-conforming sign is located from the provisions of this ordinance regarding safety, maintenance, and repair of signs contained in III 5 of this ordinance. Provided, however, that any repainting, cleaning, and other normal maintenance or repair of the sign or sign structure shall not modify the sign structure or copy in any way which makes it more non-conforming or the sign may lose its legal non-conforming status (see IV 2.e).

Fig. 35: Enclosed sign structure.   Fig. 36: Enclosed sign structure.

Part V—General Requirements

1. No sign permitted by this ordinance shall, by reason of its location, color, or intensity, create a hazard to the safe, efficient movement of vehicular or pedestrian traffic. No private sign shall contain words which might be construed as traffic controls, such as "Stop," "Caution," "Warning, " etc., unless such sign is intended to direct traffic on the premises.

2. Every sign shall have its weight and the maker's name permanently attached to or painted on the exterior or structural supports of the sign.

3. No sign shall be attached to or hung from any building until all necessary wall and roof attachments have been approved by the Administrator.

4. Wherever possible, signs shall be of such a design that all framework for the lateral support of the sign shall be contained within the sign's body or within the structure of building to which it is attached in such a manner as not to be visible to any person, as shown in Figures 34 thru 36. On older buildings, where such support is not possible, guys shall be allowed at the top and bottom of a sign.

5. Where necessary, the projecting cantilever system shall be used to support signs, and in no case shall the "A" frame system be used.

6. No sign, nor any guy, stay, or attachment thereto shall be erected, placed or maintained by any person on rocks, fences, or trees, nor in such a manner as to interfere with any electric light, power, telephone, or telegraph wires, or the supports thereof.

7. Signs that are not specifically permitted in this ordinance are hereby prohibited. Without restricting or limiting the generality of the provisions of the foregoing, the following signs are specifically prohibited:

   a. Balcony signs and signs mounted or supported on balcony.

   b. Any sign that obstructs any part of a doorway or fire escape.

8. All signs containing electrical wiring shall be subject to the provisions of the governing electrical code and the electrical components used shall bear the label of an approved testing agency.

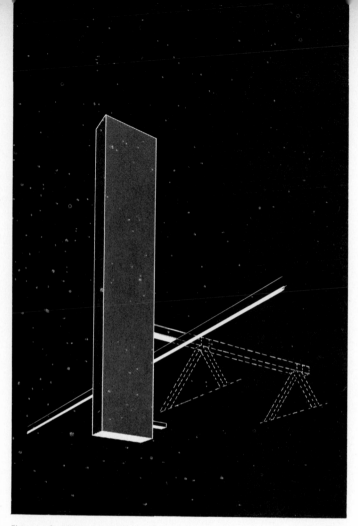

Fig. **37** : Cantilever supports.

1. *General:*

This section provides minimum standards of quality and performance for the basic materials used in the construction of "on premise" electrical signs. Just as proper proportions are necessary to good design, quality, and durability of the materials that make up electrical signs ensure long term appearance and reliability.

2. *Design and Construction:*

a. Only materials as permitted in the current edition of the *Uniform Building Code, Vol. V: Signs,* governing structural requirements, shall be used in the manufacture and erection of on-premise signs.

b. The design and construction of on-premise electrical signs shall be in accordance with the requirements set forth by *UBC V: Signs,* Chapter 4.

3. *Aluminum:*

a. Structural:
Structural requirements and allowable stresses shall conform to the requirements of the Uniform Building Code.

b. Finishes:
Anodized finishes shall conform to the "Aluminum Association Standards for Anodically Coated Aluminum Alloys for Architectural Applications."

4. *Electrical:*

a. General:
All electrically illuminated signs shall have electrical components, connections, and installations that conform to the following specifications:
(1) National Electrical Code
(2) Underwriters' Laboratories
(3) Any and all federal, state, and local codes, ordinances and regulations.

b. Inside Box Assemblies:
All components shall be Underwriters' Laboratories approved and the completed sign shall bear the Underwriters' Laboratories label.

5. *Paint:*

a. Plastic Decorations:
(1) Non-crazing paint used shall be formulated specifically for use on plastic substrates recommended by the manufacturer for exterior use. Incorrectly formu-

lated paints can cause crazing and subsequent break-
age of sign faces.

(2) Non-fading paint shall be type formulated for
maximum ultra-violet resistance and applied at correct film thickness to achieve long-term durability and
satisfactory appearance.

(3) Loss of adhesion: The recommendations of manufacturers of sign paints should be followed to prevent
peeling and flaking of paint.

b. Metal Decorations:

(1) Aluminum:

If not alodized or anodized, raw extrusions should be
coated with a satisfactory priming system prior to top
coating with recommended exterior coatings for aluminum substrates.

(2) Steel:

All grades of steel should be properly primed and
top coated for maximum corrosion resistance.

6. *Plastic:*

a. Approved Plastic Materials:

Approved plastic materials shall be those meeting the
requirements of *UBC V: Signs.* The mechanical and
thermal properties of plastics vary between manufacturers as well as types of plastics. This fact must
be considered when designing sign faces. Manufacturer's recommendations will be utilized when available and applicable.

b. Construction:

(1) Wind Load Requirements:

The sign face shall be designed to withstand the wind
pressure specified in the building code adopted by
the locality where the sign is to be erected.

(2) Flat Sign Faces:

Flat sign faces shall be designed to limit deflection of
the face from damaging internal lighting components
or disengagement under positive wind loads, and
from disengagement or suck-out under negative wind
loads without creating stress build-up in the face
which will cause fracture or crazing of the plastic.
The design must also ensure against buckling and sagging of the face under the weight of the face and the
design temperatures and otherwise provide for a
visually acceptable appearance of the sign face.

(3) Forming Sign Faces:

Formed faces shall be in accordance with the same
criteria specified for flat sign faces. In addition, the

plastic manufacturer's recommendations for minimum inside edge and corner radii must be followed.

(4) Sign Face Deflection:

The maximum deflection of the sign face under the design wind load will be limited to 3 inches or 5 per cent of the short dimension of the face, whichever is greater, except where excessive stress is developed in the plastic.

(5) Edge Engagement:

The retainer system shall be designed to provide a depth of engagement considering expansion and contraction due to thermal and humidity conditions, foreshortening due to the maximum face deflection, shifting of the face and fabricating tolerances. The retainer must be of sufficient rigidity to withstand the design wind loads.

(6) Hanging Sign Faces:

When the sign face is of sufficient size to cause bowing or sagging of the face due to the weight of the plastic, the face must be supported or hung from the top edge.

(7) Corrugated Faces:

When faces are to be fabricated from corrugated plastic, the corrugations must be parallel to the short dimension of the sign face.

(8) Channel Faces:

Channels will be positioned vertically in the sign cabinet. Overlays shall not be cemented to more than one channel, with any overlap of adjacent channels being loosely supported by mechanical fasteners.

(9) Tie Backs:

Tie Backs must be positioned in order that each individual tie back is subjected to approximately the same load. The tie back system must be capable of resisting both the positive and negative design wind loads. In no case will the faces of a double-faced sign be interconnected.

(10) Reinforcing Ribs:

Ribs shall be a minimum of .250 inch thick and 3 inches deep. The ribs will run parallel to the short dimension and extend to the edges of the face.

(1) Bumpers:

Bumpers will be designed to resist buckling under the positive design wind load and with a resilient tip. The tip of the bumper shall be positioned at least one inch from the face. Each bumper shall be positioned for equal design loading.

(12) Positive Edge Retainers:

Formed faces may employ positive edge retainers to limit deflection from negative wind loads. For square faces, retainers will be provided on all sides with the retainers being stopped 12 inches short of the corners. Retainers can be provided only along the long side of rectangular faces.

(13) Cement Joints:

In braced multiple panel faces, the cement joint shall be located approximately a quarter distance between supports. All cemented joints and members shall be in accordance with the plastic manufacturer's recommendations.

(14) Testing:

Physical testing of sign faces under simulated design wind loads shall be by vacuum or uniform loading with pre-weighed sand bags, in accordance with the plastic manufacturer's recommendations.

(15) Qualifications:

If, in the opinion of the building official, the sign design does not meet the above standards, a certified record of a physical test of the sign face under design conditions will be submitted by the sign manufacturer to the official for approval.

c. Color:

All integral plastic colors shall provide maximum ultra-violet resistance to achieve long term durability and satisfactory appearance.

7. *Structural Steel:*

Structural steel used in the construction of on-premise electrical signs must meet the requirements of *UBC V: Signs.* Exposed steel shall conform to AISC specifications for architecturally exposed steel.

8. *Miscellaneous:*

All exposed metal, unless galvanized or non-corroding, shall be painted in accordance with the requirements of the paint specifications for metal decorations (VI 5.b).

Part VII—Freestanding Signs

1. Freestanding signs shall be constructed of incombustible material except as provided in V 7.c(2) of this ordinance.

2. All supports of signs shall be placed upon private property and shall be securely built, constructed, and erected to conform with requirements specified in Part V.

3. A freestanding sign may be located in a required yard, provided that such sign is not closer than 10 feet to:

    a. The point of intersection of the intersecting street lines on a corner lot;

    b. Any adjoining lot.

4. The area of the display surface of a freestanding sign which projects over public property shall not exceed one hundred and fifty square feet per face.

5. The minimum height of a freestanding sign shall be 9 feet, except where a smaller sign does not interfere with pedestrian or vehicular traffic.

6. In no case shall the height of a freestanding sign, as otherwise permitted by this ordinance, exceed a height equal to one and one-half feet for each foot of distance from the center line of the adjacent street to the nearest column or columns of the sign. The height shall be measured vertically from the average grade nearest the supporting column(s) to the highest point of said sign, not including superficial ornamentation, trim, column or column covers, or symbol tape appendages of a non-message bearing character, but in no case will this height exceed 70 feet to the top of the sign.

Part VIII—Roof Signs

1. Roof signs shall be constructed of incombustible materials except as specified in V 7.c(2) of this ordinance.

2. Roof signs shall be thoroughly secured and anchored to the frame of the building over which they are constructed and erected, and shall be designed in accordance with the requirement specified in Part V.

3. No portion of a roof sign shall extend beyond the periphery of the roof on which it is erected.

4. There shall be one passage or access opening as follows:

    a. For each roof sign upon a building.

    b. An access opening for every 50 lineal feet of horizontal roof sign extension.

    c. Within 20 feet of walls and parapets when roof signs are at right angles to a face of the building.

5. The allowable height of a roof sign shall in no case exceed a height above the roof equal to the height of the elevation of the building upon which the sign is located. The height above the roof may be equal to the height from the grade to the top of a parapet wall or the highest point of the roof. Regardless of the height of building, no roof sign installed on a C-class (open joist) construction will exceed the height of 20 feet from the roof, nor if installed on an A-class (reinforced concrete) or B-class (laminated timber type of roof) exceed 40 feet in height.

Part IX—Facia Signs

1. Facia signs should be constructed of incombustible material except as provided in V 7.c (2) of this ordinance.

2. Facia signs shall be designed in accordance with the requirements specified in Part V.

3. No facia sign shall have a projection over public property or beyond a building line greater than one foot. No sign or sign structure shall project into any public alley whatsoever, below a height of 14 feet above grade nor more than six inches when over 14 feet above grade.

4. Copy area of a facia sign shall not exceed 30 per cent of the building facing to which it is applied.

Part X—Projecting Signs

1. Projecting signs shall be constructed of incombustible materials, except as specified in V 7.c(2) of this ordinance.

2. Projecting signs shall be designed in accordance with the requirements specified in Part V.

3. Signs may project over public property or a building line a distance determined by the formula set out in Appendix B to this ordinance.

4. No sign shall project within two feet of the curb line.

5. No sign or sign structure shall project into any public alley whatsoever below a height of 14 feet above grade, nor more than six inches when over 14 feet above grade.

6. No sign or sign structure should be erected in such a manner that any portion of its surface or supports will interfere in any way with the free use of any fire escape, exit, or stand-pipe. No sign shall obstruct any window to such an extent that any light or ventilation is reduced to a point below that required by any law or ordinance. Signs shall be so located as to maintain all required clearances from overhead power and service lines.

7. The minimum height of a projecting sign above grade shall be nine feet.

8. The minimum height of a projecting sign above the roof line shall be five feet.

Part XI—Canopy or Marquee Signs

1. Signs may be placed on, attached to, or constructed in a marquee.

2. The minimum height of a canopy or marquee sign shall be nine feet.

3. No canopy or marquee sign shall extend or project above the upper edge of a canopy or marquee more than three feet, six inches.

Part XII—Electric Signs

1. Electric signs shall be constructed of incombustible materials, except as provided by V 7.c (2) of this ordinance.

2. Electrical equipment used in connection with display signs shall be installed in accordance with VI 4 of this ordinance.

3. Every electric sign projecting over any street or alley or public place shall have painted on the surface of the sign or sign structure the name of the sign erector and date of erection. Such name and date shall be of sufficient size and contrast to be readable from a reasonable distance. Failure to provide such name and date shall be grounds for rejection of the sign by the Building Inspector.

4. *Animated Signs:*

    a. No animated signs shall be erected or maintained in any residential land use district.

    b. No animated signs shall be erected or maintained closer than 75 feet from any residential land use district on which there exists structures used for residential purposes.

    c. No animated sign may be erected in any location which would obstruct the vision of or be confused with a traffic signal or stop sign.

5. *Revolving Signs:*

    a. No revolving unit may revolve more than eight revolutions per minute.

6. Searchlights may be used for the grand opening of a new enterprise or an enterprise under new management for a period not to exceed seven days. Other enterprises may use such a device once yearly for a maximum of seven consecutive days. The beam of such searchlight shall not flash against any building.

Part XIII—Non-Accessory Signs

1. *Location of Poster Panels or Bulletins (Billboards)*
   a. Poster panels or bulletins may be located in commercial and industrial areas, subject to restrictions set out in this ordinance.

Part XIV—Temporary Signs

1. No temporary sign shall exceed 100 square feet in area. Temporary signs of rigid material shall not exceed 24 square feet in area, or six feet in height, nor shall any such sign be fastened to the ground. Temporary signs may remain in place for a period not exceeding 60 days.

2. Every temporary cloth sign shall be supported and attached with wire rope of ⅜-inch minimum diameter. No strings, fiber ropes, or wood slats shall be permitted for support or anchorage purposes. Cloth signs and panels shall be perforated over at least 10 per cent of their area to reduce wind resistance, with the following exceptions:

   a. Temporary cloth signs over private property not exceeding 60 square feet shall be supported and attached with wire rope which will meet the requirements of Part V of this ordinance.

3. Cloth signs may extend over public property. Cloth signs may extend across the public street only by permission of the governing body and shall be subject to all related laws and ordinances. Such signs, when extended over a public street, shall maintain a minimum clearance of 20 feet.

4. Temporary signs, other than cloth, when eight feet or more above the ground, may project not more than six inches over public property or beyond the building line.

Part XV—Distance from Power Lines

1. Signs shall not be located with less than six feet horizontal or twelve feet vertical clearance from overhead electric conductors which are energized in excess of 750 volts.

2. The term "overhead electric conductors" as used in this section, means any electric conductor (either bare or insulated) installed above the ground, except such conductors as are enclosed in iron pipe or other metal covering of equal strength.

Signs shall be permitted as set forth in Sign Schedules I to VI inclusive, which are hereby made and declared to be an integral part of this ordinance.

Schedule No. I: All Districts

The following special purpose and temporary signs shall be permitted in all districts, subject to the limitations set forth below:

1. Traffic control signs as defined in the "Motor Vehicle Act" subject to the provisions of said Act.

2. Signs required to be maintained or posted by law or governmental order, rule, or regulation.

3. Memorial plaques, cornerstones, historical tablets, and the like.

4. On-site directional signs, not exceeding two square feet in area, intended to facilitate the movement of pedestrians and vehicles within the site upon which such signs are located.

5. Directional signs not more than two in number identifying the location and nature of a building, structure, or use which is not readily visible from the street, serving such buildings, structure, or use on lands forming part of the site of such buildings, structure, or uses, provided that each such sign is not more than ten square feet in area.

6. Signs not exceeding two square feet in area located upon private property and directed toward the prevention of trespassing.

7. Window signs which do not exceed 20 per cent of the window area.

8. Awning signs.

9. Temporary political signs promoting any candidate, party, or cause which may be displayed for 30 days prior to an election or referendum, provided that such signs are removed within seven days following said election or referendum.

10. Temporary signs pertaining to campaigns, drives, or events of political, civic, philanthropic, educational, or religious organizations, provided that permission of the Council must be obtained to erect such signs upon or over public property and provided further that such signs shall not be erected or posted for a period of more than 14 days prior to the date of the event and shall be removed within three days thereafter.

11. Flags or emblems of political, civic, philanthropic, educational, or religious organizations.

12. Temporary on-site signs advertising the sale, lease, or rental of the lot or premises upon which such signs are situated, provided that the combined area of such signs fronting upon each street which bounds such lot or premises shall not exceed a ratio of one square foot of sign area for each 1,000 square feet of lot area, but need not be less than six square feet. In no case shall the combined area of such signs fronting upon each street exceed 35 square feet.

13. One on-site temporary sign advertising a group of lots for sale within a subdivision or a group of houses for sale within a housing project along each street frontage which bounds such subdivision or project, provided that the total area of such sign shall not exceed 60 square feet with no single dimension in excess of 12 feet. The display of such sign shall be limited to a six-month period. At the expiration of such period the applicant may request a further extension of time, otherwise the sign shall be removed.

14. Temporary on-site signs indicating the name and nature of a construction or demolition project, plus the names of the contractors, sub-contractors, and professional advisors, provided that the combined area of such signs fronting upon each street which bounds such project shall not exceed a ratio of two square feet of sign area for each 1,000 square feet of lot area. In no case shall the combined area of such signs fronting upon each street exceed 60 square feet with no single dimension in excess of 12 feet. The display of such signs shall be limited to a period not to exceed the duration of the said construction or demolition project, at which time such signs shall be removed.

Schedule II: Single and Multi-Family Residential Districts.

1. *Permitted Signs:*

a. Signs permitted in Schedule I of this ordinance, as regulated therein.

b. One facia sign of not more than two square feet in areas giving the name and occupation of the occupant of a building carrying on a home occupation as defined in the municipal zoning ordinance.

c. One business or identification facia or freestanding sign of not more than eight square feet in area, fronting on each street which bounds a lot in an Apartment District.

d. One facia or freestanding identification sign of not more than eight square feet in area for an apartment building, dormitory unit, fraternity, or sorority house in a residential district.

2. *Requirements:*

a. The maximum height of a freestanding sign shall be eight feet.

b. Projecting signs shall be limited by the formula set out in Appendix B.

c. All illuminated signs shall be shielded in such a way as to protect the rights of adjacent property owners from nuisance.

d. No animated signs shall be permitted.

e. No billboards shall be permitted.

3. *Maximum Number of Signs:*

In no case shall the number of signs per building exceed one.

Schedule No. III: Office Districts

1. *Permitted Signs:*

a. Signs permitted in Schedule I of this ordinance, as regulated therein.

b. One business or identification canopy or facia or freestanding sign fronting each street bounding the property on which the sign is located.

2. *Requirements:*

a. The total copy area of a canopy sign or a facia sign shall not exceed a ratio of one square foot of sign copy for each lineal foot of street frontage of the building to which the sign is attached. In the case of multiple occupancy, the wall surface for each tenant or user shall include only the surface area of the exterior facade of the premises occupied by such tenant or user.

b. The projection of a projecting sign shall be limited by the formula set out in Appendix B.

c. The total area of a freestanding sign shall not exceed 40 square feet.

d. In no case shall the height of a freestanding sign as otherwise permitted by this section exceed the distance in feet and inches measured from the center line of the street fronting upon its location to the structural member located nearest the street front. Said height shall be measured vertically from the street to the uppermost point of the said sign, but in no case will this height exceed 40 feet to the top of the sign. Superficial ornamentation, trim, column, or column covers or symbol type appendages of non-message bearing character shall not be included in determining height.

e. Roof signs shall in no case exceed a height above the roof equal to a distance of the height of the elevation of the building upon which sign is located. The height above the roof may be equal to the height from grade to the top of a parapet wall, ridge line, or the highest point of a roof, but in no case will the height of the sign exceed 20 feet from this point to the top of the sign. Superficial ornamentation, trim, column or column covers, or symbol type appendages of non-message bearing character shall not be included in determining height.

f. No animated signs shall be permitted.

3. *Maximum Number of Signs:*

In no case shall more than one sign per tenant or one freestanding sign per building be permitted.

Schedule No. IV: Industrial and Manufacturing Districts

1. *Permitted Signs:*

a. Signs permitted in Schedule I of this ordinance and regulated therein.

b. Two business signs and one non-accessory canopy or facia or freestanding sign fronting each street bounding the property on which the sign is located, provided, however, that non-accessory signs shall not be permitted within 50 feet of any property in a single or multiple family residential district.

2. *Requirements:*

a. The total copy area of canopy signs or facia signs shall not exceed a ratio of two square feet of sign copy for each lineal foot of street frontage of the building to which the signs are attached. In the case of multiple occupancy, the wall surface for each tenant or user shall include only the surface area of the exterior facade of the premises occupied by such tenant or user.

b. The projection of projecting signs shall be limited by the formula set out in Appendix B.

c. The total area of a freestanding sign shall not exceed 100 square feet.

d. In no case shall the height of a freestanding sign as otherwise permitted by this section, exceed a height equal to one and one-half feet for each foot of setback said measurements shall be computed from the center line of the street upon which the sign is located and measured to the column or columns nearest the street front. The height shall be measured vertically from the average street grade nearest the supporting columns to the highest point of said sign, but in no case will this height exceed 50 feet to the top of the sign. Superficial ornamentation, trim, column or column covers, or symbol type appendages of a non-message bearing character shall not be included in determining height.

e. Roof signs shall in no case exceed a height above the roof equal to a distance of the height of the elevation of the building upon which such sign is located. The height above the roof may be equal to the height from grade to the top of a parapet wall, ridge line, or the highest point of a roof, but in no case will this height exceed 30 feet from this point to the top of the sign. Superficial ornamentation, trim, column or column covers, or symbol type appendages of non-message bearing character shall not be included in determining height.

3. *Maximum Number of Signs:*

a. The permissible number of signs for each user is dependent upon the surface area of the largest face of his building. The permitted number of signs is as follows (not including incidental signs):

Surface Area of Largest Facade	Maximum No. of Signs
Less than 500 square feet	2
500-1,499 square feet	3
1,500-2,999 square feet	4
Over 3,000 square feet	5

Building or enterprises with more than 3,000 square feet on any face are permitted one sign for each clearly differentiated department with a separate exterior entrance, in addition to the five allotted above.

b. Buildings on Intersecting Streets, or Buildings Facing Two Parallel Streets: Single occupancy buildings or tenants in multiple occupancy buildings facing two intersecting streets with customer entrances on both streets or buildings which extend through a block to face two parallel streets with customer entrances on both streets shall be permitted 150 per cent of the total sign area. Two freestanding signs are permitted if they are located on two different streets and are separated more than 100 feet, measured in a straight line between signs. If two are used, they shall together comprise no more than 150 per cent of the total area stipulated in Section 2.c of Schedule No. IV.

The maximum number of signs stipulated in Section 3.a. of Schedule IV may be increased by one if a building is located at an intersection.

Schedule No. V: Commercial and Retailing Districts

1. *Permitted Signs:*

a. Signs permitted in Schedule I of this ordinance, as regulated therein.

b. For each occupant of a building, two business or one business and one non-accessory canopy or facia or freestanding or projecting or roof sign fronting each street bounding the property on which the sign is located shall be allowed, provided, however, that non-accessory signs shall not be permitted within 50 feet of any property in a single or multiple family residential district, and further that no more than one freestanding sign shall be permitted per building.

2. *Requirements:*

a. The total area of canopy signs shall not exceed a ratio of four square feet of sign copy for each lineal foot of street frontage of the building to which the signs are attached.

b. The maximum projection of projecting signs shall be determined by the formula set out in Appendix B.

c. The total copy area of facia signs shall not exceed 20 per cent of the wall surface to which the signs are attached. In the case of multiple occupancy, the wall surface for each tenant or user shall include only the surface area of the exterior facade of the premises occupied by such tenant or user.

d. The maximum area of a freestanding business sign shall be as follows:

Lot Area	*Total Sign Copy Area*
6,000 sq. ft. or less	100 sq. ft.
6,000 sq. ft. to 1 acre	150 sq. ft.
More than 1 acre	200 sq. ft.

e. In no case shall the height of a freestanding business sign as otherwise permitted by this section exceed a height equal to one and one-half feet for each foot of setback. Said measurements shall be computed from the center line of the street upon which the sign is located and measured to the column or columns nearest the street front. The height shall be measured vertically from the average street grade nearest the supporting column(s) to the highest point of said sign, but in no case will this height exceed 70 feet to the top of the sign. Superficial ornamentation, trim, column or column covers, or symbol type appendages of a non-message bearing character shall not be included in determining height.

f. Non-accessory signs shall not exceed 1200 square feet in area and shall be constructed of the vertical cantilever type if freestanding or roof signs.

g. Roof signs shall in no case exceed a height above the roof equal to a distance of the height of the elevation of the building upon which such sign is located. The height above the roof may be equal to the height from grade to the top of a parapet wall, ridge line, or the highest point of a roof, but in no case will this height exceed 40 feet from this point to the top of the sign. Superficial ornamentation, trim, column or column covers, or symbol type appendages of non-message bearing character shall not be included in determining height.

3. *Maximum Number of Signs:*

The maximum permissible number of signs shall be as stipulated in Section III a of Schedule IV.

Buildings on Intersecting Streets or Buildings Facing Two Parallel Streets: Single occupancy buildings or tenants in multiple occupancy buildings facing two intersecting streets with customer entrances on both streets or buildings which extend through a block to face two parallel streets with customer entrances on both streets shall be permitted 150 per cent of the total allowable sign area. Two freestanding signs are permitted if they are located on two different streets and are separated by more than 100 feet, measured in a straight line between signs. If two such signs are used, they shall together comprise no more than 150 per cent of the total stimulated in Section 2.d. of Schedule V. The maximum number of signs stipulated in Section 3.a. may be increased by one if a building is located at an intersection.

Schedule No. VI: Special Areas

1. Shopping centers and other comprehensive developments shall be subject to the submittal of a Comprehensive Sign Plan, as regulated by Section 4 of Part III of this ordinance.

APPENDIX B
Formula for Determining Maximum Projection Over Public Property of Projecting Signs

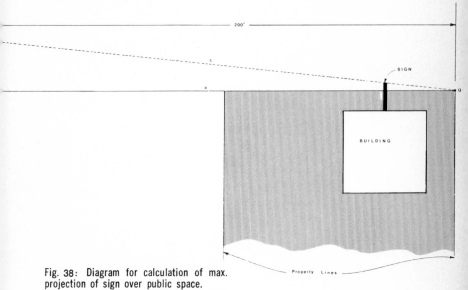

Fig. 38: Diagram for calculation of max. projection of sign over public space.

In Figure 39:

Line a = 200 feet from the property limit closest to the sign and parallel to the face of the building on which the sign will be located.

Line b = 20 feet from the end of line a, farthest from the building and perpendicular to that line.

p = maximum viewing angle.

The values for a and b may be re-assigned depending on the type of street or area.

Line c = line from the furthest extension of the property (Q) to point P.

The tangent of the angle between sides c and a gives the number of feet of allowable projection past the property front per running foot of frontage to the nearest property line. This angle as described by the values for a (200 feet) and b (20 feet) is 5:75°. Thus, where W = calculated allowable extension past the property front and $n =$ number of feet to the nearest property, then:

$$(a) \; W = TAN \; (5.75) \; x \; n$$

In order to limit the maximum extension (independent of frontage) and provide a lower limit on W for very small frontages, a second criterion must be met. A proposed extension (W_1) past the property front must pass the following test:

$$(b) \; W_1 = MAX(MIN(WM_2)M_1)$$

where $W =$ the value calculated in (a)

$M_1 =$ a lower limit assigned for very small frontage (should be zero unless sign is at the proper center)

$M_2 =$ The greatest extension allowed for any size frontage

The following values for W are based on:

$$a = 200 \; feet$$
$$b = 20 \; feet$$

NUMBER OF FEET TO NEAREST PROPERTY LINE W

feet	inches		feet	inches
1	1	20	2	2
2	2.5	30	3	2.5
3	3.5	40	4	3
4	5	50	5	3.5
5	6	60	6	4
6	7	70	7	5
7	8.5	80	8	5.5
8	9.5	90	9	6
9	11	100	10	6.5
10	1			

These values are additive. For example, if the distance to the nearest property line is 13 feet, then:

$$W = 13'' + 3.5'' = 16.5''$$
(13'' is the value given for 10 feet,
3.5'' is the value given for 3 feet).

An Alternate Projection Formula

There is an alternate formula which is just as applicable. A simpler approach, it also permits projections based on the lineal frontage of a commercial property and also takes into consideration the need for projection for a corner building.

It permits so many inches of projection ("x") for each lineal foot of building frontage from the sign to the **nearest** property line. As an example, if x were to equal 3 inches and a store tenant was to install a projecting display at the center point on a 50-foot long storefront, he would be permitted a 75-inch projection (3 x 25=75 inches).

In this same illustration, however, if the tenant desired the sign to be erected in an off-center position, let's say 10 feet from one of the building, then the allowable projection would be correspondingly reduced to 3 x 10 or 30 inches.

Regarding corner properties, the factor "x" is increased by 20 per cent providing that the sign is erected at a 45-degree angle to the corner. The increase is justified due to the angular projection to gain the required visibility to traffic approaching from either thoroughfare.

Each of the above formulae has been developed to control the extent of projection in relation to the building frontage and to restrict the potential of one display visually blocking out the identity of an abutting property.

In the latter formula, of course, the value of "x" can be varied dependent upon the business district, the width of the sidewalk and other pertinent considerations. The value of 3 inches appears to be an advantageous ratio factor for application in most business areas.

APPENDIX C
Synopsized Ordinance Specifications
for Five Municipalities in the
Greater Vancouver
Metropolitan Area

CITY OF NORTH VANCOUVER

ZONE	DETAIL	FACIA	FREESTANDIN
COMMERCIAL	MAX. AREA	SEE "FACIA" BELOW	100 SQ. FT.
ALL	MAX. PROJECTION	12 INCHES	10' OR 2' TO C
AND	MAX. HEIGHT	1 FT. ABOVE ROOF	NO LIMIT
INDUSTRIAL	MIN. CLEARANCE	9 FT. ABOVE GRADE	9 FT. ABOVE GF

ROOF SIGNS: Allowed for 1st party only. Area—Max. 100 Sq. Ft. No height or w
restrictions.

PROJECTING	CANOPY SIGN	UNDER CANOPY
100 SQ. FT.	100 SQ. FT.	100 SQ. FT.
10′ OR 2′ TO CURB	10′ OR 2′ TO CURB	TO FRONT EDGE OF CANOPY
NO LIMIT	NO LIMIT	CEILING OF CANOPY
9 FT. ABOVE GRADE	9 FT. ABOVE GRADE	9 FT. ABOVE GRADE

ACIA SIGNS: Max. Area—3 Sq. Ft. per lineal foot of wall length. No limit on number f signs, but total area not to exceed maximum allowable and no one sign can exceed 00 sq. ft .

NORTH VANCOUVER DISTRICT

ZONE	DETAIL	FACIA
ALL	MAX. AREA	30% of Wall Area
COMMERCIAL	MAX. PROJECTION	12 inches
&	MAX. HEIGHT	2′ above roof line
INDUSTRIAL	MIN. CLEARANCE	8′ above sidewalk
	LOCATION	Confined to Premises
	SPECIAL	See "Facia & D.F." bel(

GENERAL: No Flashing: No rotating beacons. Rotating O.K. (one visible moving pa
For Directional and Identification signs, in any zone, see pages 8 and 9 in sign by-la

FACIA & D.F. SIGNS: "30% of Wall Area" includes total area of Facia and D.F. signs
facade. "Premises" means that part of building occupied by the business to which
facia of D.F. refers. "Projection"—2″ per front foot of premises to 10′ maximum or
within 2′ of curb.

FREESTANDING	D. F. PROJECTING	CANOPY SIGN	UNDER CANOPY
% of site to 300 ft.	50 sq. ft.	15% of Wall Area	4 ft. x 1 ft.
n allowed	2" per lin. ft. to 10'	To 2' from curb	To front of canopy
' to top of pole	2' above roof line	2' above roof line	—
above grade	8' above sidewalk	8' above sidewalk	8' above sidewalk
' from building n.	Middle ⅓ of front	On faces or top	—
e "Freestanding" low	See "Facia & D.F. Signs" below	—	—

REESTANDING SIGNS: Total area of all freestanding signs on property cannot exceed ■0 sq. ft. (This area refers to area visible from any one side). No part of pole, or pporting members, to project above or to the sides of sign area more than twelve (12) ches.

RICHMOND AND DELTA

ZONE	DETAIL	FACIA SIGN	FREESTANDING
	MAX. AREA	3 to 1 RATIO*	3 to 1 RATIO*
GENERAL	MAX. PROJECTION	12 INCHES	NONE ALLOWED
COMMERCIAL	MAX. HEIGHT	25' OR TOP OF WALL	SEE BELOW
(OTHER—SEE	MIN. CLEARANCE	8' ABOVE GRADE	8' ABOVE GRADE
BELOW)	LOCATION	CONFINE TO PREMISES	ANYWHERE ON SITE
	SPECIAL		BLDG. MUST BE 25' FROM PROPERTY LIN

LOCAL COMMERCIAL—As above and below **but** areas subject to ½ to 1 Ratio.

GAS STATION: Freestanding signs in this zone allowed 70 Sq. Ft. (Counting All Face Min. Clearance 10'. Max. Height 25'.

*3 to 1 RATIO—means the sign area is limited to 3 sq. ft. per lineal foot of frontage the premises, and includes total area of all faces of sign. Maximum area for a Fre standing sign—including all faces is 500 sq. ft.

Where a **COMBINATION** of facia, canopy, projecting and freestanding signs is involved, total area not in excess of 4½ sq. ft. per lineal foot of frontage is allowed **but no o sign** can exceed the "3 to 1 Ratio". For example, freestanding can be 3 to 1 ratio a the remaining 1½ to 1 can be used for facia, canopy, etc.

D.F. PROJECTING	CANOPY	UNDER CANOPY SIGN
to 1 RATIO*	3 to 1 RATIO*	8 SQ. FT. INC. BOTH SIDES
6" (DELTA—6'2")	12" FROM CANOPY FACE	5'6" OVER PROP. LINE
' OR TOP OF WALL	25' OR TOP OF WALL	8" DEEP SIGN. 6" LETTER 12' ABOVE GRADE
ABOVE GRADE	8' ABOVE GRADE	8' ABOVE GRADE
ONFINE TO PREMISES	FRONT AND SIDES	OPP. MAIN ENTRANCE
) "A" FRAMES	SEE BELOW	

REESTANDING SIGNS—2 allowed per site if 100 ft. apart. One extra freestanding sign lowed (that is, a total of 3) if site is 5 acres or more and all signs are 100' apart. tal area of all faces of all signs can not exceed "3 to 1 ratio" or a maximum of 500 . ft. counting all faces.

AX. HEIGHT—up to 250 sq. ft., counting all faces, 25 feet: 250 to 300 sq. ft., 30 feet; 0 to 350 sq. ft., 35 feet; 350 to 500 sq. ft., 40 feet.

IN. CLEARANCE—if not over parking lot or roadway, clearance can be less than 8'.

ANOPY SIGNS—Can be in height 4' above lower edge of canopy. Can not extend below wer edge. Can not be higher than top of wall.

WEST VANCOUVER

ZONE	DETAIL	FACIA	FREESTANDING
General	Max. Area	25% of facade or wall	35 sq. ft. (see below)
Commercial	Max. Projection	24 inches	Non allowed
	Max. Height	Top of wall	10 ft. (see below)
	Min. Clearance	9 ft. above sidewalk	Non (if protected)
	Location		
Gas Station	Max. Area	As above	25 sq. ft. (see below)
Zone 1	Max. Projection	As above	Non allowed
(Residential	Max. Height	As above	12 ft. (see below)
Commercial)	Min. Clearance	As above	Non (if protected)
	Location	As above	Entirely behind P.L.

FREESTANDING GENERAL COMMERCIAL AREA: Add 1 sq. ft. for each 3 ft. of frontage over 105 ft. to max. of 250 sq. ft.

HEIGHT: (a) Add 1 ft. for each ft. of set-back from front property line to Max. Height of 35 ft.
  (b) Add 1 ft. for each ft. of frontage over 50 ft. to max. height of 35 ft.
  (c) Use combination of (a) or (b) to max. height of 35 ft.

FREESTANDING—GAS STATION ZONE 1 AREA & HEIGHT: If sign is 15 ft. or more from front property line, regulations for "General Commercial" apply.

GENERAL RESTRICTIONS

1. No roof signs in any area
2. No 3rd party signs in any area
3. Not over ⅓ sign area to product advertising unless product represents 25% or more of gross revenue

222

PROJECTING	CANOPY	UNDER CANOPY
to 1 ratio to 20 sq. ft.	25% of area of facade 30 sq. ft. on ea. side max.	4 sq. ft. (any dimension) to 2 ft. from front edge
1 ft. from curb	1 ft. from curb line	
ft. above wall top	2 ft. above top canopy (not higher than roof line)	
ft. above sidewalk	9 ft. (can't go below apron)	9′ above sidewalk
ddle ⅓ of wall	On canopy face only (See No. 7 below)	Center ⅓ of premises
above	As above	As above
above	As above	As above
above	As above	As above
above	As above	As above
above	As above	As above

No revolving, flashing or animation other than time and temperature indicators

Two (2) signs per business only in combination as follows:

(a) 1 facia and 1 projecting

(b) 1 facia and 1 freestanding

(c) 1 projecting and 1 freestanding

(d) Under canopy sign allowed with any above combination. Above allowed on each frontage EXCEPT 1 only freestanding sign

. If 3 sides of canopy used for signs no other signs allowed other than under canopy sign

. Canopy signs must be "integrated" with canopy and cannot be mounted on top of canopy—only on faces

. Signs viewed from within property boundaries only not restricted in number

VANCOUVER

ZONE	DETAIL	FACIA	FREE STANDING	D.F. PROJECTIN
C-1	MAX. AREA	No limit	35 sq. ft.	No limit
	MAX. PROJECTION	12″	12′ or 1′ from curb	12′ or 1′ fr curb
	MAX. HEIGHT	30′ from grade	25′	30′ from gra
	MIN. CLEARANCE	8′	10′6″	10′6″
	FLASHING	No	No	No
	ROTATING	—	Yes	Yes
	SPECIAL			
C-2	MAX. AREA	No limit	No limit	No limit
	MAX. PROJECTION	12″	12′ or 1′ from curb	12′ or 1′ fr curb
	MAX. HEIGHT	40′-5′ above roof	40′ from grade	40′ (12″ abc parapet)
	MIN. CLEARANCE	8′	10′6″	10′6″
	FLASHING	Yes	Yes	Yes
	ROTATING	—	Yes	Yes
C-3	MAX. AREA	No limit	No limit	No limit
	MAX. PROJECTION	12″	12′ or 1′ from curb	12′ or 1′ fr curb
	MAX. HEIGHT	100′-5′ above roof	100′ from grade	100′ (12″ above parapet)
	MIN. CLEARANCE	8′	10′6″	10′6″
	FLASHING	Yes	Yes	Yes
	ROTATING	—	Yes	Yes
	SPECIAL			

C-5 and CD-1—Special Commercial—restricted—require Planning Department approval–No 3rd Party.

CM-1, CM-2—Downtown Commercial areas—Same as C-3 but Roof Signs Allowed. Ref to Schedule "G 1 to 7" By-Law Around Bridges. See zone map in sales area.

CANOPY (SIGN)	UNDER CANOPY	ROOF	3rd PARTY
No limit	4 sq. ft.	No limit	
1' from curb	To canopy edge	1'	Not
4'6"—sign height	12"—sign height	2'6" roof to top 30' from grade	Allowed
Bottom of apron	9'	Non required	
No	No	No	
Yes	Yes	Yes	
50% min. of front and sides must be lit			
Same as	Same as		Allowed
C-1	C-1	Not	
except	above	Allowed	
flashing	except		
allowed	flashing		
	allowed		
Same as	Same as		Allowed
C-1	C-1	Not	
except	except	Allowed	
flashing	flashing		
allowed	allowed		

M-1, M-2—Industrial—same as CM-1, except in Schedule "G" area around 401 Freeway.
Refer to Schedule "G1 to 7" By-Law Around Bridges.

APPENDIX D
"Clutter-Itis"—Disease that Plagues Bellevue
By Mike Buckley from *The Bellevue American*, Thursday, Oct. 10, 1968*

A disease is ravaging America. And it is spreading from city to city, town to town with unprecedented speed. The disease has conquered Seattle and threatens to do much the same to the communities of the East Side. The disease is called in common terms, "clutter-itis."

It is not with levity that one refers to clutter-itis as a disease. For like many other epidemics, clutter-itis chokes and decays. It causes a gap in the relationship between man and his environment which fosters even worse problems. Clutter-itis can and does breed slums, it lowers property values and promotes slovenliness.

What is clutter-itis? For years, especially the two and a half decades since the Second World War, a growing concern has been felt for the decline of American cities. Ugliness and unsightliness have become the rule rather than the exception in the older cities of the East such as New York, Chicago and Pittsburgh. Even our nation's capital suffers from the problem.

Time and time again groups of men and women, some private, some representing municipalities, and even the Federal government, have sought to discover what creates the ugly conditions which haunt our cities. And without excep-

---

*(Editor's Note—Early in the summer of this year, the City of Bellevue formed a committee to review the problem of "clutter-itis" in the community. Believing that signs were an integral part of this cluttering of our commercial area, the committee was called the Sign Ordinance Review Committee. After researching the problems which faced the city to some lengths a process which has not yet ended, the committee found that signs were only a small part of the cluttering and unsightliness being felt in Bellevue. Though they still retain the same name, the committee received permission to broaden its study's scope. With that permission granted, the group went on to make more and more discoveries about the city in which it lives and the many problems of aesthetics which are faced. This is the first of a series of articles dealing with the problem of clutter-itis and the progress of that committee).

tion, the blame for most of the problem has been placed on signs. Signs of varying types from the billboards of our highways to the banners which fly in fabulous numbers over the used car lots of the nation. And in some of the older cities of the nation, signs were a great part of the problem of clutter-itis.

But early this year, the city council of Bellevue through the city manager's office, formed a committee to review the existing sign ordinance and make recommendations on a new law which would prevent Bellevue from following along the path of some of the other cities of the Northwest and the nation.

The committee, composed of businessmen, lawyers, engineers, civic leaders, and others has and is still working on the problem. But one thing became apparent after a short while of studying Bellevue and its signs. That if all the signs were removed from the streets and buildings of our community, not only would the problem of clutter-itis still be present, it might even be worse than it is now.

In finding out how the committee reached such a conclusion, one of its members, Dave Senescu, was asked to discuss their study. Senescu, himself an official of one of the largest custom sign companies in the nation, made these comments:

"We in the sign industry have long resented being taken to task for a problem which we have spent millions to eradicate," stated Senescu. "Although there are hundreds, even thousands of signs which are unsightly, we have made many studies and each one has shown that the removal of these signs would improve the situation which exists in our cities only a small amount.

"The technology with which the larger sign companies design and manufacture their product has developed to such an extent over the years that it is no longer difficult for any business to have a sign which conveys quality in both design and construction.

"Granted, in years past, signs were manufactured out of many materials, some which would not withstand the rigors of weather, sun, and the like. Some companies even today still use these materials. But these are a minority and it is only the blindness of immediate monetary savings which makes a business deal with this element of the industry.

"Therefore, when I joined the committee here in Bellevue, I expected the problems to arise in which signs would immediately be blamed for all the problems of "clutter-itis" which we are beginning to face.

"Much to my amazement, the committee immediately

saw the far-reaching scope of the problem and agreed that although signs must be regulated, it would be a qualitative rather than quantitative matter. And that other factors contributing to the problem should be removed.

"Almost immediately after beginning the study," he went on, "we discovered the first problem which exists in Bellevue. Most of the commercial district, except for areas such as old main street, are oriented to the vehicle rather than the pedestrian. We actually have in this city, acres and acres of asphalt separated by more asphalt. Unbroken, except for occasional white lines and curbing, these areas present an immediately ugly picture when compared to the multitude of trees and green belts which abound on this side of the Lake.

"These areas of asphalt are necessary—or so we believe. We must have a place to park our automobiles while shopping in the stores. But these parking lots and the asphalt streets in between need not be unbroken gray areas. Well-planned tree plantings, shrubbery, and boulevard treatment of streets could make our commercial areas not only more beautiful, but more pleasant to shop in and therefore make them more economically stable.

Senescu went on to comment on some of the other discoveries made by his group.

"We found too," stated the sign executive, "That many problems were caused by poorly maintained buildings. Some of these were intentionally left to grow shoddy because of the psychological atmosphere which was created and because of the type of business which the owner conducted.

"In other cases, temporary construction or simply haphazard construction, barely within the limits of the law, played a great role in detracting from the communities appearance.

"Temporary signs, some of a commercial nature, but the majority political, added their undesirable impact to the whole picture.

"On the whole," Senescu went on, "we discovered that although the laws of the community were being followed in many respects, they were being followed to the letter rather than the spirit.

"The result of all of these facets has been an unfortunate decline in the community's visual appearance. And it is a decline that must be stopped now, and effectively, before the trend becomes irreversible.

"The problem, then, of clutter-itis as we see it is one that is as critical to our cities as those of water and air pollution.

If left unhampered, clutter-itis will drive us from this city as it has done in many others."

What success Senescu and the other members of the committee will have in solving Bellevue's problems will be known only after the passage of some time. But it is important that they receive the support of others in the community in attempting to halt a disease that may well mean the end of the City of Bellevue as we know it.

The authors feel that the following Appendix, *Guidelines for Design Review*, by the CCAIA has much to offer any community concerned about social amenity in particular areas, such as a historical area or a civic center district. However, certain cautionary notes must be added. First, the areas for design review must be carefully laid out. Such control should not be applied to the entire city. Zoning and building codes are adequate for most areas, and if they are not, they should be rewritten to fulfill this function.

The concept of a design review committee for certain areas of a municipality is basically a good idea. It could help a builder or a sign company concerned with components within the visual environment to establish the mood and trends within an area without placing undue or unnecessary restrictions upon him. The success of a design review committee in influencing land use phenomena depends upon three factors: (1) the attitudes towards control under which the committee operates, the makeup of the committee, and the knowledge of the individuals about the task they are performing.

The attitude of a committee is a critical factor to the committee's functioning. If the committee is made up of individuals who realize the need for creativity in design and have some background in planning, the products of the committee will be recommendations to foster moods or trends and help establish the social amenity desired in an area. These will suggest some of the things that might be done by a builder or an architect in order to ensure that his project will fit into the social makeup of an area. But the attitude of the committee must revolve around the fact that they are not a "design control committee". Direct negative criticism of architectural form just because it is different should not be permitted.

This, of course, brings up the whole problem of semantics. In our society, we are apparently given to using phrases and words that carry with them vague meanings. (The word *planner* is probably the greatest misnomer in the whole municipal vocabulary. He is a land use coordinator or director. Whether he should do any planning is an open question.) If a design review committee sees itself as a "quality recommendation committee," rather than a "design control committee", design creativity in a community can be encouraged rather than hindered.

The makeup of these committees is also critical. The committee definitely should not be made up of only one or two groups of individuals, such as salaried city officials and architects. The members of the committee should come from varied backgrounds with specialties in the areas to which their recommendations are directed. To put an overwhelmingly large number of architects on a committee, on the assumption that they know a lot about signs, would be a mistake. The average architect knows little if anything about signs that any other informed citizen doesn't know. He is not a marketing expert, and the primary function of signs is communication for marketing. This point cannot be overstressed. If the makeup of a committee falls to people who do not know what they are doing, it is going to be met with hostility by the industry, and there will probably be little long-range input from the industry. The question of makeup of a committee is primarily one of informaton.

If a design review committee drifts into the hands of planners who understand little about signs and marketing, it is very apt to become merely a stumbling block to development and will put a greater burden on the city council. Too often, salaried municipal officials, under the guise of being "planning experts", do not understand that they are only to make recommendations about possible layout features and perhaps some design accoutrements without formally handing down dictates. If such discretionary authority is placed in the hands of the salaried city officials, the format set out in the following *Guidelines for Design Review* will not be even partially adhered to in decisions concerning individual developments. In one author's contact with a design control committee in northern California, all of the criteria for a decision were given *post hoc*. In fact, when asked for specification of the reasons for the refusal of the permit, one reason was given at the meeting and later another was given in a letter to council justifying the refusal.

Guidelines for Design Review*

Design Review is the means by which a community can assure itself of development which is reasonably in harmony with the character and quality of environment which it finds desirable to foster. The method is to guide what is built in the community in ways not now covered by building codes

*CCAIA DOCUMENT NO. 503-69 (C)1969. by California Council. The American Institute of Architects.

and zoning ordinances, and to do so within the framework of the community's government.

It consists of the review by qualified persons of demonstrated ability of all proposed developments, public and private, to assure conformance with certain considerations of design which the city itself sets up and administers.

Through this process the public accepts the responsibility for attaining and preserving the desirable character of the community's physical environment and is bound to actions in the public interest. Through it, too, the growth and change of the community can be reflected harmoniously in the physical environment.

Those communities which have decided for Design Review have achieved direct benefits in the form of pleasant environments for living and working, preservation and maintenance of land and property values and, thus, increased tax revenues to the city from improved property conditions, and retardation or prevention of development of slum or blighted areas. They have also found indirect results in the beneficial influence of pleasant environments on behavioral patterns and increased dollar volume of commercial activity.

Not every community decides for Design Review, however. It is for the community itself to determine whether it finds that the attainment of a particular quality of environment is its goal and whether a process of government is the means by which it wishes to accomplish such a goal.

There is ample precedent for establishment of the Design Review process, both in the United States, and in European countries where it has been used for many decades. Increasingly communities throughout the United States are turning to this process as a means of assuring that their communities shall not suffer from the ills which have beset so many cities, large and small.

Design Review of public works, wholly or in part financed with public moneys, is a natural and accepted procedure in the public interest, and is established practice in many cities throughout the United States.

Design Review of privately financed and owned projects requires a different approach, but such review is no less an act in the public interest than is the review of publicly financed and owned projects. It is the sum of many private projects which, in the main, makes up the physical character of a community. If that character—the physical appearance of the city—is unpleasant or below the standard set by the community for its development, the public interest is not being served. Early instances of Design Review of private projects encountered difficulties in the lack of clear and precise criteria for review. In the proposed methods of Design Review presented here this problem has been given careful consideration and we believe that criteria of a precise and clear type have been provided. In addition, the Design Review Board is recommended as an Advisory Board, not a Legislative Board.

There may be opposition to Design Review from individuals affected or by segments of the community which will carry through to a challenge of the validity of the Design Review ordinance. This has been the experience in the past in related fields of zoning and other limitations on the use of property such as sign display, setbacks, and height limitations. Nevertheless, it is our belief that a proper Design Review ordinance can be prepared by the city's attorney which will comply with constitutional and statutory requirements.

The essentials of Design Review, which will be workable as well as fair, for a specific area, are: (1) Clear criteria; (2) Competent reviewers; and (3) Adequate procedures.

Enforcement is the implementation of the Design Review process. In regard to public work, it is by authority of the city's government. In regard to private work it is by persuasion, and where so legislated, by authority of the city's government. Cooperation as a result of agreement to stated principles and aims is the finest form of enforcement. It calls for the best efforts of the design professionals whose work is to be reviewed, and for acceptance by the community itself of the Design Review process as the means to obtain what it has determined the quality of its environment should be.

Merchants and citizens' organizations are important elements in the community. If these groups can recognize the benefits, direct and indirect, material and spiritual, which will result from improvement—gradual though it may be— in the community appearance, they can greatly ease the enforcement of a Design Review ordinance.

Nevertheless certain requirements and restraints must be built into an ordinance to assure conformance to its provisions. A community can withhold building and occupancy permits until it is satisfied that the ordinance has been complied with. There is little difference between requiring this kind of conformance in the public interest and requiring conformance to the stipulations of zoning codes which are now indispensable, if occasionally controversial, parts of the city's regulatory powers.

Design Review in Use

Design Review Boards or Commissions exist in many

California cities and counties. Some have particular design districts where control is in effect, others have Design Review ordinances which are city-wide in effect. It is for the community itself to decide the extent of application of such an ordinance.

The following California cities are among those which now use a Design Review process in some form:

Carmel	Palm Springs
Laguna Beach	Santa Clara
Mill Valley	Redwood City
Mountain View	Santa Barbara

Los Angeles

In Berkeley, the Design Review Committee of the Civic Art Commission reviews all public and quasi public projects and is available for recommendation on private projects.

In San Francisco, the Civic Design Committee of the Art Commission reviews all civic projects and private projects on public land.

Other cities have Planning Commission which act as a Design Review agency. Among such are:

Claremont	Pleasant Hill
Palos Verdes	San Gabriel

San Marino

Counties also have found the process valuable and have instituted review boards. Among the California counties which are using a Design Review process are:

Marin	San Mateo
Monterey	Solano
Kern	Santa Clara

In other states, cities and counties are also finding that a review process is essential to improving the quality of their communities. Such procedures are in existence in:

Anchorage, Alaska	Oak Ridge, Tenn.
Seattle, Wash.	Rye, N.Y.
Binghamton, N.Y.	Shaker Heights, Ohio
Fox Point, Wis.	St. Clair, Mich.
Stockbridge, Mass.	Dade County, Fla.
King County, Wash.	Numerous other places
Warwick County, Va.	throughout the country

Establishing the Process

The need for Design Review must be determined by the community itself. A group of citizens, agreed upon the need for such a review process, may make recommendations to the city's governing board for the establishment of such a process, setting forth its reasons and the particular characteristics it finds desirable for the community environment.

234

Such considerations of character should incorporate the fact that a community is never static but grows and changes. The potential for growth and change, and for maintenance and enhancement of the community, must be inherent in the goal set for the review board.

A community may wish to make Design Review applicable to its entire area, or only to certain areas of special concern. Such special areas are termed "Zones of Protection," "Design Zones," "Design Districts." These may include vistas, special residential or commercial zones, or entry districts, scenic districts, government center districts, city-core districts, etc.

Santa Barbara	New Orleans
Santa Fe	Portland
Charleston	

In some cities, certain districts (other than historical) are designated for review for special reasons (civic center area, park districts, etc.). Among the cities which have special design districts (in addition to general review of public projects) are:

Berkeley	Philadelphia
St. Louis	San Diego
Niagara Falls	Stratford, Conn.
Palm Springs	

Whether the review process is applicable to the entire area or to a special district, clearly design review considerations which will be legal as well as workable must be set up.

There must be adequate procedures and enforcement methods. (Suggestions for a sample ordinance which give some detail appear further on in this document.)

The essentials of the procedure are:

1. Establishment of Design Review by Ordinance.
2. Description of area where Design Review shall apply.
3. Description of goal and criteria.
4. Description of required submittals (schematic and construction documents).
5. Provision for Review in schematic design and construction document stages.
6. Provision for statement of reasons in case of required modification or of rejection.
7. Provision for re-review and time limits.
8. Provision for appeal.
9. Provision for review of completed building and, if it does not comply with approved submittals, provision for remedies.
10. Enforcement: building permits not to be issued if application before construction of project does not pass

Design Review. Occupancy permit not to be issued if completed building does not comply.

Selection of Board Members

Members of a Design Review Board should be persons who by experience, training, education, or occupation have demonstrated talent and interest in developing the aesthetics of environmental design within the framework of practical considerations. The capability of each proposed member should be analyzed as to his:

1. Civic responsibility.
2. Ability to give objective, effective and constructive, and unprejudiced criticism.
3. Ability to give direction and suggestion to his criticism.
4. Diplomacy in exercising judgment.

Qualifications of professional members:

1. Licensed architects or educators at, or graduates of, accredited schools of architecture.
2. Licensed landscape architects or educators at, or graduates of, accredited schools of landscape architecture.

Qualifications of non-professional members:

1. Demonstrated creative ability in the visual arts or,
2. Educators at, or graduates of, accredited art schools.

When asked to do so by a city, the local (or nearest) chapter of the American Institute of Architects will propose the names of qualified architects as possible professional members of the review board.

When asked to do so, the local (or nearest) chapter of the American Society of Landscape Architects will provide the names of three qualified landscape architects as possible members of the review board. Where no architects are resident within the jurisdictional boundaries of the community the American Institute of Architects (local or nearest chapter) will provide the names of three architects from nearby communities who will be agreeable to serve, at appropriate compensation for the expenses incurred, as consultants to the community.

No city employee should serve on a Design Review Board.

It is desirable that one member of the board should be a member of the business community, preferably of the Chamber of Commerce.

The Design Review Board should consist of a majority of professional members to assure the quality of review which will lead to the desired result. A recommended ratio

236

of professionals to non-professionals is: two (2) architects, one (1) landscape architect, two (2) specially-qualified representatives of the community.

Community members should be persons of demonstrated ability in some field of visual art to assure that the work of the Design Review Board can be accomplished expeditiously as well as competently.

The community members are an important element in the review process, bringing to the process, when they are visually aware, a breadth of judgment that is of great value to the community. (Community members who are not so qualified, however, require instruction and experience in the act of visual awareness and the time involved in such instruction is a delay to the work of the Board. For this reason, specially-qualified persons who also are representative of the community, are required.)

The role of the professional, on the other hand, is indispensable since it is from his knowledge and experience, and his unbiased judgment, that the community can derive the continuity in design character, the harmony in environment and the practical considerations essential to implementation, which can assure attainment of its stated goal.

Administrative Standards

In an area or district in which it is decided to establish Design Review, considerations for conformance cover only those aspects of such an ordinance as should be applicable to all work done after the effective date of the ordinance including new work, modification, repainting and site improvement, signs, and exterior lighting.

To be legal as well as workable, the criteria which any Design must meet and the geographic area within which the criteria apply must be defined.

Specific aspects of design should be examined to determine whether the proposed development will provide desirable environment for its occupants as well as for its neighbors, and whether, aesthetically, it is of good composition, materials, textures, and colors. To the list of the aspects which will be examined should be appended a gauge of how conformance will be evaluated. This gauge should be described as "administrative standards" and should comprise the following:

1. Maximum height, area, and setbacks (if not covered in zoning ordinance).
2. Over-all mass as well as parts of any structure (buildings, walls, screens, towers, or signs) and effective concealment of exposed mechanical and electrical equipment.

3. A limited palette of colors.
4. A limited number of materials on the exterior face of the building or structure.
5. Avoidance of repetition of identical entities, wherever possible.
6. Harmonious relationship with existing and proposed adjoining developments, avoiding both excessive variety and monotonous repetition, but allowing similarity of style, if warranted.
7. Site layout, orientation, and location of structures and relationship to one another and to open spaces and topography, definition of pedestrian and vehicular areas, i.e., sidewalks as distinct from parking lot areas.
8. Location and type of planting, with due regard to preservation of specimen and landmark trees, and to maintenance of all planting.
9. Design and appropriateness of signs as well as of exterior lighting and, where subject to control of overhead utility lines.
10. Harmony of material, colors, and composition of those sides of a structure which are visible simultaneously.
11. Consistency of composition and treatment.

Suggestions for an Ordinance

The following suggestions for inclusion in an ordinance creating an Architectural Review Board would require assistance from design professionals to assure the workability of the ordinance. It is assumed that city attorneys would draft their community's ordinance, cross-referencing provisions on architectural review board ordinance with other city ordinances.

Legislative Findings

The City Council finds that there exist in this city conditions which promote disharmony and reduce land and property values; and that the lack of appropriate guidelines for the design of new buildings and design of structures on the city's streets contributes to these conditions; and it further finds desirable the provision of such guidelines for the protection and enhancement of land and property values, for the promotion of health, safety, and general welfare in the community.

Purpose

The purpose of this Ordinance is to: recognize the interpedendence of land values and aesthetics and to provide a method by which the City may implement this interdependence to its benefit;

Encourage development of private property in harmony with the desired character of the City and in conformance with the guidelines herein provided with due regard to the public and private interests involved;

Foster attainment of those sections of the City's Master Plan which specifically refer to preservation and enhancement of the particular character of this city and its harmonious development, through encouraging private interests to assist in their implementation;

Assure that the public benefits derived from expenditures of public funds for improvement and beautification of streets and other public structures and spaces shall be protected by the exercise of reasonable controls over the character and design of private buildings and open spaces.

Design Review

The City Council creates by this Ordinance a Design Review Board.

Duties

The duties of the Design Review Board shall be to make recommendations on any matter requiring qualified aesthetic and architectural judgment to the end that the general appearance of any improvement shall preserve or enhance the physical environment and character of the community.

Membership

The Design Review Board shall consist of five (5) members, of whom two shall be licensed architects, one shall be a licensed landscape architect and two shall be representatives of the community who have demonstrated a knowledge of, or experience in, the visual arts. Alternates of similar qualification should be appointed to serve in the absence of regular members.

Procedures

The Design Review Board shall meet...................times a month. Its members shall be compensated for each meeting at the rate of $...................per meeting.

The Design Review Board shall review applications for permits to build in the................... (The city must designate the extent of application of the ordinance: in certain districts, on specified streets, or throughout the city.) The Project Designer or his representative shall be present and shall participate in the review process.

Applicants shall submit, both at the design development phase of the project and when construction documents are completed, information describing the proposed work. Before building permit is issued, the project for which application is made shall conform to the recommendations of the Design Review Board as approved by the Planning Commission (or other designated city agency).

Before an occupancy permit is issued, the completed building must be inspected by the Director of Inspection Services for compliance with the recommendations of the Design Revew Board as approved by the Planning Commission (or other designated agency of city government).

No occupancy permit shall be issued unless landscaping also complies with the approved plans. If for any reason this cannot be completed at the same time as the building, a performance bond shall be posted by the owner.

If modification is required or if the proposed design is rejected, the Board shall prepare a statement of the reasons for its action.

Evaluation

The Design Review Board shall examine the material submitted with the application by considering the following aspects for conformance with the purpose of this ordinance:

General Site Utilization Considerations
General Architectural Considerations
a. Height, bulk, and area of buildings.
b. Colors and types of building and installation.
c. Physical and architectural relation with existing and proposed structures.
d. Site layout, orientation, and location of buildings and relationship with open areas and topography
e. Height, materials, colors, and variations in boundary walls, fences, or screen planting.
f. Location and type of landscaping including, but not limited to, all street parking areas.
g. Appropriateness of sign design and exterior lighting.
General Landscape Considerations
Graphics

Conformance will be evaluated by Administrative Standards to be determined by the Design Review Board and adopted by the City Council (or other legislative authority) and periodically updated. For the guidance of applicants, a copy of these standards is attached as Appendix A of this ordinance.

Enforcement

The Design Review Board shall make its recommendations on each application to the City Council, Board of Adjustments, or Planning Commission, under whichever authority it functions, which shall either approve or overrule the recommendations of the Design Review Board.

The recommendations of the Design Review Board as approved will carry for no longer than one year, at the end of which time, if the building (or buildings) is (are) not completed or under construction, applicant must apply for a new permit and repeat the review process.

Materials For Applications

Prior to application for a permit to erect, construct, alter, move, remodel, reface or repaint, or otherwise change a building or structure (in whatever districts or on whatever streets, or throughout the city), the applicant must file with the Director of Planning (or other designated city officer) for review by the Design Review Board the following drawings:

1. In the design development phase of the project:
a. Site plan showing:
   Roof plan of building.
   Location of existing trees and structures if any.
   Location and dimensions of streets and highway desigtions.
   Locations of off-street parking and loading facilities.
   Location of points of entry and exit for vehicles and internal circulation patterns.
   Location of walls and fences and indication of their height and material of construction.
   Exterior lighting standards and devices.
   Grading and slopes, where these affect the relationship of the buildings.
b. Architectural drawings
   Plan to scale.
   Four elevations to include all sides of development.
   (Optional) perspective, model, or other suitable graphic materials.
c. Preliminary landscape plan, including the plant names.
d. Site photographs (snapshots)—site itself and adjacent properties to intersections.
e. Color and texture chips of actual material samples.
2. With final application for building permit, the same information, developed into completed construction documents shall be submitted.